1-2-3 Macro Library

David Paul Ewing

Que Corporation
Indianapolis

Library of Congress Catalog No.: LC 84-62755
ISBN 0-88022-147-X

Editor
Virginia Noble, M.L.S.

Editorial Director
David F. Noble, Ph.D.

88 87 86 85   8 7 6 5 4

Interpretation of the printing code: the rightmost double-digit number is the year of the book's printing; the rightmost single-digit number, the number of the book's printing. For example, a printing code of 83-4 shows that the fourth printing of the book occurred in 1983.

Dedication

To Bob and Pat Clancy

In appreciation of their love and support

About the Author

David Paul Ewing is Training Products Director for Que Corporation. He is coauthor of Que's *Using Symphony* and author of Que's *Using 1-2-3 Workbook and Disk*. Mr. Ewing received his B.A. from Duquesne University and his M.A. from North Carolina State University. He is presently completing his Ph.D. at Purdue University. Prior to his position at Que, he was the Assistant Director of the Business Writing Program at Purdue University, where he developed course materials and trained instructors. For eight years, Mr. Ewing taught college-level writing and business communications courses. He has published articles in leading business communications books and journals and given numerous presentations at national conferences on writing and business communications.

Table of Contents

4

Macros for Data Base Management

5

Macros for File Operations

6

Macros for Printing

7
Macros for Graphics

8
Macros for Special Applications

Index

Acknowledgments

Que Corporation would like to thank the following individuals whose macros, originally submitted for publication to *Absolute Reference: the Journal for 1-2-3 and Symphony Users* or *IBM PC UPDATE: New Techniques for Professionals*, are included in this book.

James Barnes, Lake Success, NY, macro for converting decimals to fractions

John Clements, Weymouth, MA, graphics slide show macro

Melanie Cullen, Oakland, CA, macro for creating multiple graphs

James Decker, Muncie, IN, macro for comparing data

Jay DeNovo, Madison, WI, macro for managing client files

R. William Geary, Alma, GA, self-modifying print macro

Kevin Gilman, Avon, CO, macro for printing multiple copies of worksheets

David Hamilton, Santa Clara, CA, macro for printing range names

James P. Harris, Troy, MI, macro for using subdirectories

Doug Hill, Corpus Christi, TX, /Data Find macro

Roger Jenan, Visalia, CA, macro for moving the cursor to {HOME}

David Jordan, Broomall, PA, macro for saving files to one or two disks

Ron Kurtz, Woodland Hills, CA, macro for changing zeros to dashes

Steve Levitas, McLean, VA, macro for comparing character strings

Patrick Magee, Bellevue, WA, macros for use with an integrated financial planning model and macros for use with a 1-2-3 ledger

Sam Moeller, Philipp Brothers, New York, NY, macro for printing worksheets from different files

Mark Moritz, Phoenix, AZ, macros for building amortization tables and macro for transposing rows and columns

James Opperman, Fairfax, VA, simple validation macro

Michael Rubenstein, San Francisco, CA, macro for printing form letters

G. Bradley Schlossman, Fargo, ND, macro for converting values to dollars and cents (used with numeric keypad macro)

Stan Scott, New York, NY, an enhancement on the numeric keypad
    macro and macro for saving worksheet files
William Spangler, Freeport, IL, accumulator macro
Robert Sproule, Reading, PA, macro for creating windows
Charles Timmerman, Indianapolis, IN, macro for creating
    logarithmic plots and macro for projecting water consumption
Mark Winkelhake, Minneapolis, MN, macro for printing amortization
    schedules

Trademark Acknowledgments

COMPAQ is a trademark of COMPAQ Computer Corporation.

IBM is a registered trademark of International Business Machines Corporation.

ProKey and RoseSoft are trademarks of RoseSoft, Inc.

SuperCalc is a registered trademark of Sorcim Corporation.

Symphony, 1-2-3, and Lotus are trademarks of Lotus Development Corporation.

VisiCalc is a registered trademark of VisiCorp.

Que Corporation has made every attempt to supply trademark information about company names, products, and services mentioned in this book. Trademarks indicated were derived from various sources. Que Corporation cannot attest to the accuracy of this information.

Composed in ITC Garamond by
Que Corporation

Printed and bound by
George Banta Company, Inc.

Cover designed by
Listenberger Design Associates

Conventions Used in This Book

A number of conventions are used in the *1-2-3 Macro Library* to help you understand the macros. So that you will be able to distinguish among the different elements in 1-2-3 macros, the following conventions are used:

1. Macro names appear with the backslash (\ ) and single character name. Whenever the character is a letter, it appears in lowercase, as in \c. The \ indicates that you press simultaneously the Alt key and the *c*. Note that here and throughout this book, *simultaneously* means pressing and holding down the first key while you also press the second key.

2. Range names used in macros and for naming macro subroutines appear in uppercase letters.

3. All 1-2-3 functions appear in uppercase letters.

4. 1-2-3 commands (/rnc) appear in macros in lowercase letters.

5. In macros, representations of cursor keys, such as {DOWN}; function keys, such as {CALC}; and editing keys, such as {DEL}, appear in uppercase letters.

6. Macro commands (/xi, /xq, /xg, /xc, /xr, /xn, /xl, and /xm) appear in lowercase letters.

The following sample shows each of these conventions used in a macro.

Macro name, cursor key, range name -->	\z {GOTO}RANGE~
1-2-3 function -->	@DATE({?})~
1-2-3 commands -->	/rfd~~/wcs12~~
Cursor key -->	{DOWN}
Macro command -->	/xg\z~

Like macros that appear in the 1-2-3 screen display, macros appearing throughout the book do not show a label prefix (') at the beginning of each macro line. Remember, therefore, that you will need to enter the prefix (') for those lines that begin with a 1-2-3 function, number, operator, backslash (\), and slash (/). See Chapters 1 and 2 for more information on creating 1-2-3 macros.

In addition to the special conventions used in the macros, the *1-2-3 Macro Library* contains the following conventions:

1. Whenever reference to a 1-2-3 command indicates the sequence of keystrokes for selecting the command(s), the slash (/) and first letter of each command appear in boldface. /**R**ange **F**ormat **C**urrency, for example, indicates that you type /rfc to select this command if you were entering it manually.

2. Because a 1-2-3 macro is invoked by pressing the keys for the macro's name (the Alt key and the single character key), this keystroke combination is indicated in the text as the following:

Alta
Altb
Altc
Altd
Alt...(other letters or 0)

Remember also that Alta is the same as \a—the macro name.

3. Although represented differently on some keyboards, ENTER is used in the text instead of RETURN or ↵. In a macro, however, ENTER is represented by the tilde (~).

4. 1-2-3 modes (READY, VALUE, LABEL, EDIT, POINT, MENU, HELP, ERROR, WAIT, FIND, CMD, and SST) appear in uppercase letters.

5. Ctrl Break means that you should press the Ctrl key and Break key simultaneously.

Introduction

Imagine decreasing significantly the time you spend in creating, changing, and printing 1-2-3 spreadsheets, data bases, and graphs. If you've used 1-2-3 for a while, you may have developed some sophisticated models and techniques that already simplify your worksheet tasks. But you can simplify these tasks even more—once you begin to make full use of 1-2-3's macro capabilities. The *1-2-3 Macro Library* will help you learn how to make and use a wide variety of 1-2-3 macros. And you'll be able to apply right away many of the macros presented in the following chapters.

To the novice 1-2-3 user, the term "1-2-3 macro" may sound like a topic for experienced users, maybe even a topic for those who know a bit about computer programming. Lotus 1-2-3 documentation, in fact, leads you to think that 1-2-3 macros are for the advanced microcomputer user. Lotus' treatment of macros makes them a well-kept secret. Consider the title of one section of the 1-2-3 manual—"Advanced Topic: Do You Sincerely Want to Become a Programmer?" Only ten pages are devoted to the subject of keyboard macros in the Lotus 1-2-3 manual.

Yes, 1-2-3 macros can be complex, and some may involve sophisticated programming techniques. But you don't have to be a programmer to use 1-2-3 macros. Even a beginning 1-2-3 user can make and use many of the macros in this book. These macros can expand program capabilities and decrease the amount of time spent keying in commands and data. Because 1-2-3 macros tremendously increase the power of 1-2-3, they're not for the experienced, program-minded user only—they're for anyone who uses 1-2-3. The *1-2-3 Macro Library* will help both new and advanced users get the most out of 1-2-3's macro capability.

1-2-3 Macro Library

As the title indicates, this book is a collection of macros. Over 100 macros are included in eight chapters. Experienced 1-2-3 macro users will be able to apply right away many of these macros to the use of 1-2-3. Those who are new to 1-2-3 macros will first learn the fundamental concepts important for understanding, making, and using macros.

Basic concepts are introduced early in the book, and each macro is presented with an explanation of how to create and use it. Some macros are presented with worksheet models. Sections describing these macros tell you about not only the macros but also the models, particularly how to create such models for your own use.

The examples of macros throughout the book were collected from many sources. Included, for example, are macros originally published in *Absolute Reference: The Journal for 1-2-3 and Symphony Users* and submitted by Lotus 1-2-3 users throughout the country. These macros represent many different applications, from macros for updating loan amortization schedules to macros for printing range names. Other macros—some previously published in the books *Using 1-2-3* and *1-2-3 Tips, Tricks, and Traps*—include the simple but "golden" macros, which make some of the most commonly used 1-2-3 operations as easy as pressing two keys (a two-keystroke combination). In addition, many new macros appear for the first time. All these make up a complete collection of macros for general worksheet operations, data management, file operations, printing, graphics, and special applications. Organized into chapters by macro application, the *1-2-3 Macro Library* provides macros ready for use as soon as you enter them into your own 1-2-3 worksheets.

The library of macros contained in this book will allow you to create your own library file on disk. You can select those macros that will help you the most with your everyday use of 1-2-3. With a 1-2-3 macro library file, you'll be able to copy these macros into any worksheet file whenever you want. Spending just a little time in creating your own macro library file will result in saving the time you spend in creating, changing, and printing 1-2-3 worksheets and graphs. To save you the trouble of keying in the macros yourself, a disk is also available containing many of the macros in this book. (See the information in the back of the book.)

Who Should Buy This Book?

Whether you're a beginning or an advanced macro user, this book is for you. You will find all the explanations you need to understand 1-2-3 macros. But *1-2-3 Macro Library* goes far beyond introducing you to keyboard macros. You'll also be able to apply macros immediately, create sophisticated models controlled by 1-2-3 macros, and modify macros for your own special needs.

- For beginning macro users, this book contains what you need to get started: a definition of 1-2-3 macros, an explanation of all macro commands, and guidelines on how to create, edit, and use 1-2-3 macros. This book shows you how to begin making simple macros that are "keyboard alternatives" and then moving toward more complex ones.

- For the experienced macro user, this book provides an extensive collection of macros to add to those you are now using. You'll also find many valuable hints for making and applying your own macros to 1-2-3 spreadsheets, data bases, and graphics. Also throughout the book are examples that show how to develop sophisticated self-modifying macros, linking macros, and menu macros.

About This Book

Chapter 1, "Macro Fundamentals," provides the background for getting started if you are just beginning to use macros. Divided into two sections, Chapter 1 explains what a 1-2-3 macro is and discusses the elements available for creating 1-2-3 macros. You will find detailed explanations of 1-2-3's special macro commands—/xi, /xq, /xg, /xc, /xr, /xn, /xl, and /xm—including examples of how to use them effectively in 1-2-3 macros.

Chapter 2, "Creating and Using 1-2-3 Macros," explains how to make macros on your own and how to modify the macros presented in the library. In addition, this chapter contains specific guidelines for macro format and length and for storing, documenting, naming, and executing macros. The last section of the chapter discusses common errors that can occur when users create 1-2-3 macros, and methods for debugging macros when problems arise.

Chapter 3, "Worksheet Macros," is the beginning of the book's collection of macros. This chapter presents macros that can make many worksheet operations easier and faster for you. You will find in this chapter, for example, macros for cursor movement, for entering data, for date entry, for changing the worksheet, for worksheet calculation, and for password protecting a worksheet. All these macros can be applied to many types of spreadsheets and data bases.

In Chapter 4, "Macros for Data Management," you will learn ways that macros can expand 1-2-3's data management commands and functions. Included are macros for data input forms, for storing data query settings, for performing a label lookup, for improving /Data Find capabilities, and for comparing character strings in a data base. These macros will help you get more out of 1-2-3's data management capability.

The macros in Chapter 5, "Macros for File Operations," are some of the most valuable macros in the book. Macros for file operations help you manage and save worksheet files. A macro for backing up worksheets automatically and a macro for managing disk space are just two of the file macros presented and described in Chapter 5.

Chapter 6, "Macros for Printing," contains macros that enable you to store print settings, print range names, or perform printing operations not part of 1-2-3's regular program capabilities. One macro, for example, will print form letters. Another macro prints labels. In addition, Chapter 6 offers macros for printing amortization tables and multiple copies of a worksheet. In this chapter, you will also learn how to use some special macro techniques. One macro, for instance, shows how to use self-modifying macro techniques for making a macro that prints multipage printouts.

The macros in Chapter 7, "Macros for Creating Graphs," automate the process of creating and printing graphs. With these macros, you can easily create any of the types of 1-2-3 graphs. This chapter also shows how to expand 1-2-3 graphics' capabilities by presenting and describing a macro for creating logarithmic plots. Finally, you will learn in this chapter how to create a ProKey macro for automating the whole process of creating and printing 1-2-3 graphs.

Chapter 8, "Macros for Special Applications," illustrates how macros can be customized for special applications or for 1-2-3 models. Macros for creating customized help screens, building amortization tables, managing client files, and using 1-2-3 as a word processor are among the special macro applications provided in this chapter. Some of the models and macros you'll be able to use directly for your own work. Others will help you find ways to apply macros to your special needs.

What Can This Book Do for You?

If you've used 1-2-3 macros, then you probably know the answer to the question: this book can save you valuable time. With the macros in the following chapters, you can turn operations requiring multiple key-strokes into operations requiring only a two-keystroke combination.

Beyond just being time-savers, though, the macros in this book can help you get the full benefits of applying 1-2-3 to your own particular needs. These 1-2-3 macros, for example, can manage sophisticated worksheet models enabling you to combine and print worksheets, or simply move about worksheets easily. And if you would like 1-2-3 to perform operations not part of regular program functions, macros can accomplish such tasks for you. A macro for printing form letters and labels, one for transposing rows and columns, and another for per-forming a label lookup in a data base are just three of the many macros that can expand 1-2-3's capabilities.

How to Use This Book

Chapters 1 and 2 discuss in detail the fundamentals of 1-2-3 macros—what they are and how you can make and use them. You'll find this information especially valuable when you begin creating your own 1-2-3 macro library file. To get you started, though, here are a few gen-eral tips for setting up a macro library file.

As you read through the following chapters, consider which macros will be particularly useful for you—those that automate operations you frequently perform with 1-2-3. Make a list of the macros you want to use, then begin to create your own macro library file, following the directions provided with each macro. And keep in mind the suggested conventions for making 1-2-3 macros and a macro library.

Suppose, for example, that you want to store the following macros in a library file:

```
\c    /rfc0~

\k    {?}
      {DOWN}
      /xg\k~

\d    /xnEnter the date: ~~
```

The first macro is a currency format macro (\c), the second is a numeric keypad macro (\k), and the third is a date entry macro

(\d). The first step in creating a macro library is to enter these macros into a blank worksheet, as shown in figure A.

When you set up your macro file, you'll need to follow a few important conventions. First, every macro should occupy three columns. The first column contains the macro name, entered as labels. For example, the name \d was entered by typing a single quotation mark (') followed by a backslash and a *d*. Naming macros this way is essential if the macros are to be stored in a macro library. In fact, you should get into the habit of always naming macros on the worksheet.

The second column contains the actual macro code. The third column holds internal documentation, consisting of notes that explain exactly what each part of the macro does. This internal documentation makes macros easier to understand.

Another important convention to follow when you create a macro library is to consider carefully the location for your macros. In the sample in figure A, macros are placed in columns AA, AB, and AC. This range was chosen for locating the macros because column AA is outside the area of the worksheet used by most models, yet not so far from cell A1 that the distance causes too much memory to be lost.

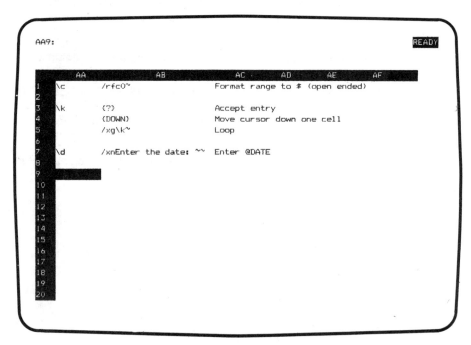

Fig. A

In most cases, you will want to store your macros outside the worksheet area occupied by the main model. (Some macros in this book are placed close to the models to make editing and modification of the macro easier.) You can store your macros in any part of the worksheet you want. But reserving a special area away from your spreadsheet and data base models can prevent you from overwriting a macro accidentally.

You should also consider carefully the location of your macro library in order to make the task of copying macros to other files easier. Suppose, for example, that you have created the macro in figure B, which saves a worksheet by reading the file name from a designated cell in the worksheet.

As the documentation indicates, this macro contains an open cell (AB5) that is reserved for copying the worksheet file name. If you store this macro in your macro library and then copy it into another worksheet, you need to copy the macro to range AA1..AC6. Otherwise, you must change the cell (AB5) in line 3 to reflect the new location. Planning the location of your macro library and planning your worksheets with the location of macros in mind can eliminate the need for later editing whenever you copy a macro or group of macros into a new worksheet.

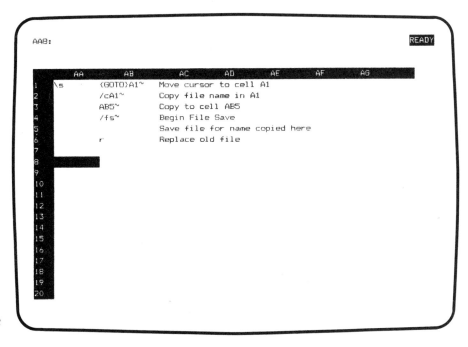

Fig. B

One other basic convention is essential when you create your macro library: naming the macros. Naming can be done easily by using the /Range Name Label Right command. The command assigns the names in column AA to the adjoining cells in column AB. For example, the name \c is assigned to cell AB1, and the name \k is given to cell AB4.

After you have entered the macros from this book into your library worksheet, you should save the worksheet, using the /File Save command. Give the macro library worksheet the name LIBRARY, which will then be ready to use whenever you need it.

The macro library file can be the beginning for every worksheet you create. Whenever you want to create a new worksheet, simply load your library file and start typing. Then when you are ready to save the worksheet you have created, choose a *new name* for the worksheet when you save it for the first time. Otherwise, you will overwrite your library with the new worksheet. Be sure to keep your LIBRARY file as the storage file for all macros.

If you discover in this book a macro that will help you with using 1-2-3, try out the macro. Most of the macros included here are easy to duplicate and use. Begin building your macro library by storing some of these simple macros, then testing them. As you become more experienced, you'll want to modify your growing collection of macros and create your own. *And you don't need to be a programmer!*

More 1-2-3 Knowledge

Que is the leading publisher of periodicals and books about Lotus 1-2-3. No matter what your interest in 1-2-3 may be, Que has relevant information for you.

Books

If you are new to 1-2-3 and need a comprehensive 1-2-3 tutorial, try *Using 1-2-3* by Douglas Cobb and Geoffrey T. LeBlond. Over 100,000 users have relied on this popular book to introduce them to 1-2-3. *Using 1-2-3* has a suggested price of $17.95. You can find the book in your bookstore or your computer store, or you can order directly from Que.

Also for 1-2-3 beginners, the *Using 1-2-3 Workbook and Disk*, by David Ewing, guides the user through building a 1-2-3 model, explaining how to use all the commands necessary to create a practical, comprehensive 1-2-3 application. For use at home or in 1-2-3 training programs, the *Using 1-2-3 Workbook and Disk*, with a suggested price of $29.95, will help any new user to learn the program quickly and easily.

To help users apply 1-2-3 to their business tasks, *1-2-3 for Business*, by Douglas Cobb and Leith Anderson, presents fourteen 1-2-3 worksheets. This book contains practical applications for many of 1-2-3's commands and functions. *1-2-3 for Business* sells for $16.95.

Another 1-2-3 title, *1-2-3 Tips, Tricks, and Traps*, by Dick Andersen and Douglas Cobb, presents over 100 suggestions for getting the most out of 1-2-3. Also included are discussions of some of 1-2-3's traps, or problem areas. *1-2-3 Tips, Tricks, and Traps* makes an excellent reference guide for the 1-2-3 user who wants to take full advantage of 1-2-3's capabilities.

Periodicals

Absolute Reference: The Journal for 1-2-3 and Symphony Users, published by Que, offers tips on how to use 1-2-3, columns that discuss 1-2-3's commands and functions, and features designed to help 1-2-3 users get the most from their software. A one-year subscription to *Absolute Reference* costs $60. You can use the convenient form at the back of this book for ordering a subscription to *Absolute Reference* or any of Que's 1-2-3 titles.

1

1-2-3 Macro Fundamentals

If you have ever created 1-2-3 macros, then you may be familiar with the specific procedures and rules for making and using these macros. But if you haven't had much experience, you will need to acquaint yourself with keyboard macros before you can discover how they can help you perform 1-2-3's spreadsheet, graphics, and data management tasks. This chapter illustrates how macros are created, offers general guidelines for using macros successfully, and prepares you for using the macros contained in the library in the following chapters.

The chapter is divided into two major sections. "What Is a 1-2-3 Macro?" contains explanations and examples of different kinds of 1-2-3 macros, from simple ones that duplicate a series of keystrokes to more complex macros that use 1-2-3's special macro commands. "The Elements of 1-2-3's Macro Language" describes the elements available in 1-2-3 for creating macros and discusses the functions of macro commands.

If you are unfamiliar with the various types of 1-2-3 macros and their range of complexity, this chapter provides the background for getting started. If you have used and created your own 1-2-3 macros, however, you may want to move on to the macro library itself. In either case, you will find the tables and guidelines in this chapter helpful for making and editing your macros.

What Is a 1-2-3 Macro?

A 1-2-3 macro, like other keyboard macros, is a set of special commands that can be executed with a two-keystroke combination: pressing and holding down the Alt key while at the same time pressing the key representing the macro's name. (On IBM PC and PC-compatible

11

equipment, the Alt key is located to the left of the space bar beneath the Shift key. See fig. 1.1.)

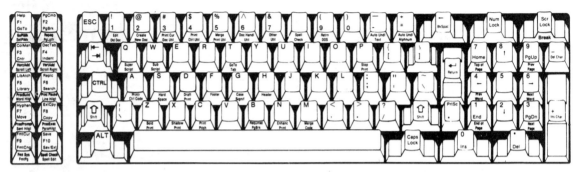

Fig. 1.1.

When Lotus first introduced 1-2-3's macro capability, the macros were referred to as "typing alternatives." Such macros reduce the number of keystrokes normally required for primary, frequently used 1-2-3 operations. Instead of pressing five or six different keys on your computer's keyboard to perform a worksheet operation, you can use a 1-2-3 macro and reduce the operation to a two-keystroke combination. But if you use 1-2-3's full macro capability, macros can be much more than just typing alternatives.

Many of the examples in this macro library go far beyond being typing alternatives and in fact use programming techniques to perform operations not available in Versions 1 and 1A of 1-2-3 (although some of the operations are included in Symphony). In the section "Macros for Data Management," for example, you will find a macro for simulating a "label lookup." You'll also find macros that allow you to store settings, such as data query settings and print settings. This capability is not available in Versions 1 and 1A of 1-2-3.

Other macros included in this book are more than just "keyboard alternatives," because the macros can perform extremely sophisticated applications to help you in your work. Macros in Chapter 8, "Special Applications," are tailored particularly to special 1-2-3 worksheet models and applications. For example, one macro in the chapter shows how to manage client files, and another macro shows how to compare worksheet files.

The Simple "Typing Alternative"

Probably the best way for you to learn how to use 1-2-3 macros is first to make ones that are actually typing alternatives. Such macros simply store the keystrokes you would enter if you were performing an operation within any of 1-2-3's applications.

If, for example, you frequently use the /Range Format Currency command to format worksheets, a 1-2-3 macro can simplify the process by entering the required keystrokes for formatting a range in Currency format. For such a task, you would normally enter the following keystrokes:

Keystroke 1: Press the / key to retrieve the 1-2-3 command menu.

Keystroke 2: Select the Range command from 1-2-3's menu.

Keystroke 3: Select the Format command from the Range menu.

Keystroke 4: Select the Currency format.

Keystroke 5: Enter the number of decimal places.

Keystroke 6: Indicate the range to be formatted (or press ENTER if you are formatting the cell where the cursor is presently located).

Keystroke 7: Press ENTER.

When you create a macro to perform these same operations (see fig. 1.2), you can reduce your keystrokes to a two-keystroke combination. You simply invoke the range currency format macro by typing Alt and *f* simultaneously.

Table 1.1 compares the keystrokes required for using the /Range Format Currency command with each element in the macro shown in figure 1.2. As the table indicates, the single line of the range format currency macro contains a command for each keystroke.

Because a keyboard macro follows the same process you use when entering commands and data one step at a time, you should begin creating macros by writing down each step as you work through the process at the keyboard. (Whether you are making simple or complex macros, begin by jotting down each step.) In some cases your macros will be the sum of the keystrokes necessary to complete an operation. As shown in table 1.1, the range format currency macro duplicates the keystrokes you would enter manually.

To create this macro, you enter it into the worksheet in exactly the same way that you would enter any other label: by typing a label prefix followed by the characters in the label. (The label prefix informs 1-2-3 that what follows the prefix should be treated as a label.) If a prefix were not used, 1-2-3 would automatically interpret the next

Keystrokes	Macro Elements
Keystroke 1: Press the / key to retrieve the 1-2-3 command menu.	/
Keystroke 2: Select the **Range** command from 1-2-3's menu.	r
Keystroke 3: Select the **Format** command from the Range menu.	f
Keystroke 4: Select the **Currency** format.	c
Keystroke 5: Enter the number of decimal places.	0
Keystroke 6: Indicate the range to be formatted. (Press ENTER for the current cell.)	~
Keystroke 7: Press ENTER.	~

Table 1.1

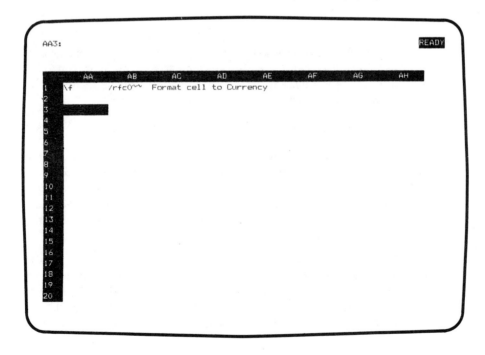

Fig. 1.2.

character (/) as a command to be executed immediately rather than stored in the cell. All three of the label prefixes (', ", or ^) will work equally well. The ' label prefix is commonly used for a label aligned at the left edge of a cell. Remember that all macro lines beginning with a nontext character (/, +, -, or any number) must first begin with a label prefix. Otherwise, 1-2-3 will interpret the characters in the line as numbers or commands.

The four characters following the ' in the '/rfc0 macro represent the command used to create the desired format. /rfc is simply shorthand for **/R**ange **F**ormat **C**urrency. The zero (0) tells 1-2-3 that no digits are to be displayed to the right of the decimal. If you are entering this command from the keyboard, you type the 0 in response to a prompt. In the macro the 0 is simply assumed by 1-2-3.

At the end of the macro are two tildes (~~). When used in a macro, a tilde represents the ENTER key. In this case the two tildes signal that the ENTER key should be pressed twice, which is how many times you would press ENTER after typing 0 if you were entering the command from the keyboard.

More Complex Macros

The range format currency macro performs one single operation on the worksheet: changing a range to Currency format. At the next level of complexity, however, are macros that combine a series of operations into one. When executed, each of these macros performs two or more operations before ending. The macro in figure 1.3, for instance, performs four different operations: (1) enters the @DATE, (2) formats the cell, (3) adjusts column width, and (4) moves the cursor down one cell. Notice that all these operations are part of the single macro, executed when you press Altz.

The Elements of 1-2-3's Macro Language

The macro in figure 1.3 consists of a series of linked operations, a command (/xg) that is special to 1-2-3's macro language, and the macro name itself—indicated by the \z in the last line of the macro. Even if you have never used 1-2-3 macros, you probably know that each macro must be named by using the 1-2-3 **/R**ange **N**ame command. When naming a 1-2-3 macro, you must follow certain requirements. The range name must be only one character (an alphabetical character or

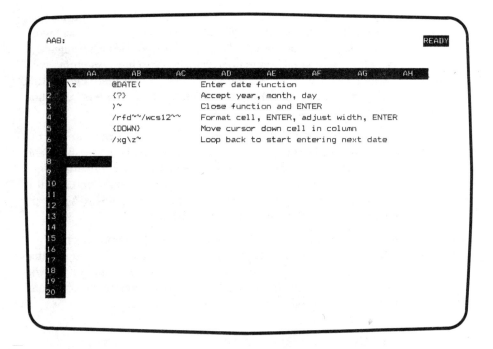

	AA	AB	AC	AD	AE	AF	AG	AH

```
        AA         AB         AC         AD         AE         AF         AG         AH
 1  \z         @DATE(              Enter date function
 2             {?}                 Accept year, month, day
 3             )~                  Close function and ENTER
 4             /rfd~~/wcs12~~      Format cell, ENTER, adjust width, ENTER
 5             {DOWN}              Move cursor down cell in column
 6             /xg\z~              Loop back to start entering next date
 7
 8
 9
10
11
12
13
14
15
16
17
18
19
20
```

Fig. 1.3.

a 0), and the name must be preceded by a backslash (\). (For more information see the section "Naming Macros.")

In 1-2-3 the elements available to you for making macros are the following:

1. The actual keystrokes you use when selecting a 1-2-3 command (for example, /rfc0)

2. Data that should be entered into the worksheet or entered in response to a command operation. (Examples of data include range names and cell addresses.)

3. Key representations for moving or anchoring the cursor. (See table 1.2.)

4. Key representations for the function keys. (See table 1.3.)

5. Key representations for editing. (See table 1.4.)

6. Key representation for ENTER: ~

7. Key representation for entering input within the macro: {?}

8. Special macro commands, such as a command to tell the macro to quit execution: /xq. (See table 1.5.) A discussion of special macro commands is provided later in this chapter.

Depending on which elements are used, 1-2-3 macros fall into two categories. First, a 1-2-3 macro can contain elements you normally use when selecting commands and entering data (items 1-5). Second, a 1-2-3 macro can contain special key representations or commands used exclusively for creating macros (items 6-8). The special key representation for ENTER (~) is the easiest of the macro elements to understand. The last two elements—the {?} and the special macro commands—require further explanation.

{UP}	Moves the cursor up 1 row
{DOWN}	Moves the cursor down 1 row
{LEFT}	Moves the cursor left 1 column
{RIGHT}	Moves the cursor right 1 column
{PGUP}	Moves the cursor up 20 rows
{PGDN}	Moves the cursor down 20 rows
{HOME}	Moves the cursor to cell A1
{END}	Used with {UP}, {DOWN}, {LEFT}, or {RIGHT} to move the cursor to the lower right corner of the defined worksheet

Table 1.2. Cursor-Movement Key Representations

{EDIT}	Edits contents of current cell. (Same as F2)
{NAME}	Displays list of range names in current worksheet. (Same as F3)
{ABS}	Converts relative reference to absolute. (Same as F4)
{GOTO}	Jumps the cursor to cell coordinates. (Same as F5)
{WINDOW}	Moves the cursor to the other side of a split screen. (Same as F6)
{QUERY}	Repeats the most recent query operation. (Same as F7)
{TABLE}	Repeats the most recent table operations. (Same as F8)
{CALC}	Recalculates the worksheet. (Same as F9)
{GRAPH}	Redraws the current graph. (Same as F10)

Table 1.3. Function Key Representations

{DEL}	Used with {EDIT} to delete a single character from a cell definition
{ESC}	Esc key
{BS}	Backspace key

Table 1.4. Editing Keys

/xi	If-then-else command
/xq	Command for quitting execution of a macro
/xg	Command instructing the macro to continue
/xc	Command for accessing a macro subroutine
/xr	Command to resume processing on next line
/xn	Input command accepting only numeric entries
/xl	Input command accepting only labels
/xm	Command for creating menus

Table 1.5. Special Macro Commands

Using {?} in Macros

As indicated in item 7 of the previous list, the {?} command allows a user to enter numbers or text at a specified point in the macro. But the {?} input command can do much more. Suppose you wrote the following portion of a macro:

```
\a     {?}
       /rncINPUT~~
       {GOTO}A1~
       +INPUT/12
```

The {?} in the first line not only causes the macro to stop and wait for you to enter a number or label, but also allows you to move the cursor before you make an entry. With such a macro, you can choose the input cell. After you enter the data, the macro uses the /**Range** Name Create command to assign the name INPUT to the selected cell. The fourth line then uses the range name INPUT to access the data you have entered.

The {?} command can also be used in the middle of a macro so that you can designate a range for print, copy, graph, or some other function. The macro

```
\c     /c{?}~{?}~
```

19

therefore lets you copy the contents of a range designated by the first {?} into the range designated by the second {?}. The {?} command can also be used from within the /xn command; this alternative can lead to some interesting results. For example, when the one-line macro

```
/xnEnter a number: ~{?}~
```

is run, 1-2-3 moves into the CMD POINT mode. In this mode, you can move the cursor around the worksheet and point to the cell where you want to store the number you'll be entering. After you have pointed to the correct cell and pressed ENTER, the prompt "Enter a number: " appears in the control panel. The number you enter is then stored in the cell to which you just pointed. Why the command works in reverse—first point to the destination, then enter the number—is not clear. The command would be more convenient if the /xn-{?} combination worked in reverse, prompting you to enter a number and then allowing you to place that number in any cell you choose.

The more complex the task you want the macro to perform, the more elements it will contain. You will particularly need to use the special macro commands to get the full power from 1-2-3's macro capability. Because these commands allow you to create a "program" for your own special needs, you have, in effect, a limited programming language available for your use.

If you have done any programming in a language such as BASIC, you will find that learning how to make and use 1-2-3 macros is relatively easy. You should nevertheless acquaint yourself with the macros included in this library before you begin to experiment in creating the complex macros you may need for particular tasks.

The macro library is organized and written so that you can readily apply the macros to your use of 1-2-3. Many of the macros contained in each of the library's sections are simple, generic macros that most 1-2-3 users will find helpful. You will discover, too, that you can string together some of the simple macros to make more complex ones.

The Macro Commands

As previously suggested, 1-2-3's macro capability allows you to do much more than just duplicate and thus reduce the keystrokes you enter. Once you begin making macros, you will find that you actually have a limited programming language available to you primarily through 1-2-3 macro commands.

Such commands are also called "invisible" commands because they cannot be issued from the keyboard but only from within a macro. This section describes each of the macro commands and shows how they can be used. The complete list of macro commands includes the following:

/xg	Command instructing the macro to continue
/xi	If-then-else command
/xn	Input command accepting only numeric entries
/xl	Input command accepting only labels
/xm	Command for creating menus
/xc	Command for accessing a macro subroutine
/xr	Command to resume processing on next line
/xq	Command for quitting execution of a macro

The /xg Command

This command, which is similar to BASIC's GOTO command, causes the macro to proceed to another line or set of commands. Often /xg is used with the /xi command, which is discussed in the next section.

Now let's see how the /xg command is used in a simple macro. In the macro in figure 1.4, /xg appears in the last line. This handy macro lets you use the numeric keypad to enter numbers into the worksheet, thus solving a common problem for many 1-2-3 users.

Most IBM PC owners frequently complain about having to use the numeric keypad for both entering numeric data and moving the cursor. Because only one of these tasks can be performed at a time, and because the keypad is typically used for moving the cursor, operators who want to use the keypad to enter numbers are out of luck. This is especially irritating to people who have been trained on a ten-key adding machine. In 1-2-3, however, you can make the macro shown in figure 1.4, which allows you to use the keypad for numeric entry without your having to move the cursor each time you enter a number.

This particular macro illustrates several interesting 1-2-3 techniques. First, the macro prompts the user to enter information in the worksheet. The {?} symbol in the first line is the simplest input command in the macro language. (Other input commands—/xn and /xl—are discussed later in the chapter.) The {?} command instructs the macro to stop processing and to wait for input from the keyboard. Either text or numbers can be entered. The macro will continue to wait until the user presses ENTER to signal the end of the input. While 1-2-3 is wait-

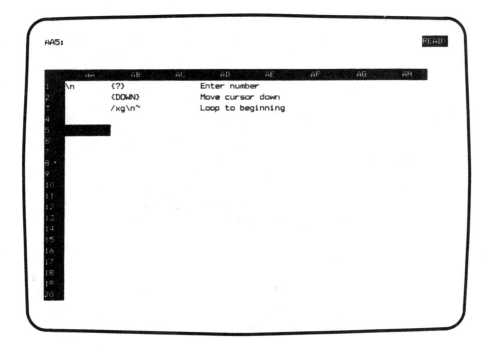

AA5:   READY

	AA	AB	AC	AD	AE	AF	AG	AH
1	\n	{?}		Enter number			
2		{DOWN}		Move cursor down			
3		/xg\n~		Loop to beginning			

Fig. 1.4.

ing for you to enter the data, the mode indicator in the upper right corner of the screen displays the prompt CMD READY. This prompt reminds you that a macro is under way and that 1-2-3 expects you to do something.

After you press ENTER, the macro proceeds to the second line, which moves the cursor down one row. The command {DOWN} in AB2 takes the place of the down-arrow key and eliminates the need to use the numeric keypad to position the cursor. This macro can also be designed to move the cursor one cell to the left or right or up one row simply by replacing the {DOWN} statement with another cursor movement instruction, such as {RIGHT} or {UP}.

The macro's last line, /xg\n, demonstrates 1-2-3's macro GOTO command. In effect, this command says, "Macro, go to the cell named \n and resume processing." Because cell AB1 is named \n, the macro simply loops back to the beginning and continues to process.

Many 1-2-3 users become confused about the difference between the macro GOTO command (/xg) and the more general {GOTO} command (F5). These two commands are not interchangeable in any way. {GOTO} is used to move the cell pointer from one location to another in the worksheet, whereas /xg is used to direct the flow of a keyboard macro. {GOTO} says, "Cell pointer, move to this location." /xg says, "Macro, your next instruction is located in this cell."

The \n macro in figure 1.4 is an example of an infinite loop. Once you execute such a macro, it cannot be stopped unless you press Ctrl Break—a key combination that will always stop a macro.

To use the \n macro, you move the cursor to the top of a column you want to fill with numbers, then type \n. The macro will wait for you to make an entry. Afterward, you press ENTER, and the macro will jump down one row and loop back to the beginning, pausing again for a new entry. Again, you type a number and press ENTER. This process is repeated until you have no more data to enter. Finally, you press Ctrl Break to stop the macro.

One limitation of the \n macro is that it can move the cursor in only one direction. You can, however, build more complex macros offering a choice of directions. An example of such a macro is included in Chapter 3. (See "Enhancements for the Numeric Keypad Macro.")

The /xi Command

Now let's look at a slightly more complex version of the numeric keypad macro. This version includes both the /xg and /xi commands. When these commands are used together, they provide a conditional statement in your macro. Suppose you want to use the numeric keypad macro to enter numbers in a worksheet. Furthermore, you want to test each number as it is entered to be certain that no error has been made. For example, you may want to make sure that every number in the list is less than 1,000,000. Figure 1.5 shows a macro that will perform this test.

The macros in figures 1.4 and 1.5 are similar. In fact, the first lines of both macros are the same, and the second and third lines of the macro in figure 1.4 are identical to the last two lines of the macro in figure 1.5. The test is performed by the second, third, and fourth lines. These lines create a range name for the current cell, test the value of that cell, and delete the range name. Line 2 begins the test with the formula

    /rncTEST~~

which translates as "Assign the name TEST to the current cell." To create the name, the macro issues the /Range Name Create command,

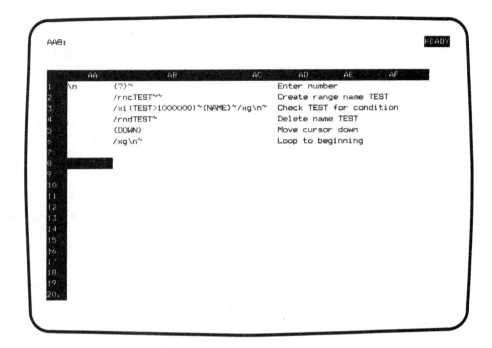

```
AA8:                                                          READY

        AA          AB              AC      AD      AE      AF
 1  \n      {?}~                             Enter number
 2          /rncTEST~~                       Create range name TEST
 3          /xi(TEST>1000000)~{NAME}~/xg\n~  Check TEST for condition
 4          /rndTEST~                        Delete name TEST
 5          {DOWN}                           Move cursor down
 6          /xg\n~                           Loop to beginning
 7
 8
 9
10
11
12
13
14
15
16
17
18
19
20
```

Fig. 1.5.

specifying the name TEST. This command then assigns the name to the current cell, the one into which you just made an entry. (Remember that in a macro the equivalent of ENTER is the tilde, ~.) After the macro assigns the name TEST, the next line contains the actual test for the number just entered.

Most programming languages offer some sort of IF statement, which usually takes the following form: if a condition is true, do one thing; otherwise, do something else. IF statements are used by the program to make decisions about what to do next, on the basis of the truth (or falsity) of a given condition. Like other languages, 1-2-3's macro language offers an IF command: /xi. This command is frequently used with /xg to set a condition for the macro to continue. Consider, for example, the following macro line:

```
/xi(TEST>1000000)~{NAME}~/xg\n~
```

The line says that if the value of the cell named TEST is greater than 1,000,000, issue the {NAME} command and return to the beginning of the macro. This statement accomplishes the test. If the value just entered in TEST is greater than 1,000,000 (the predefined limit), the macro will automatically loop back and pause for another entry. Because no instruction for cursor movement has been given, the new entry will be made in the current cell. When that entry is made, the test process will be repeated. The macro will not allow you to proceed until an entry that meets the predefined limit has been completed.

Why is the {NAME} command included in this line? {NAME} forces the computer to beep. The {NAME} key, F3, has meaning only when a 1-2-3 command such as /Copy or /Move has been issued. The use of the {NAME} command here does not make sense to 1-2-3, so the computer beeps. The beep alerts the user that an error has been made. Although {NAME} accomplishes the desired purpose, using this command is a rather inelegant way of solving the problem. Lotus designers have added to Symphony a {BEEP} command that can be used to alert users to errors.

Once an entry that passes the test is made, the macro continues to line 4. This line performs the housekeeping chore of erasing the range name TEST from the sheet, thereby freeing the name TEST for use in further tests.

The final two lines of the macro are identical to those in the simpler version. These lines move the cursor down one cell and loop the macro back to the beginning. As before, the entire process will be repeated until it is stopped with Ctrl Break.

The /xi macro is designed to test numbers for the specific condition >1000000. Suppose, however, that you want to make the testing limit more flexible. All you need to do is assign the name LIMIT to any cell in the worksheet and rewrite line 3 to read

```
/xi(TEST>LIMIT)~{NAME}~/xg\n~
```

When the macro is designed this way, the test will capture any entry that exceeds the value in cell LIMIT. You supply the testing limit by entering a value in cell LIMIT before you execute the macro. If you enter no new test limit and cell LIMIT has a value of 0, the test will reject all positive numbers.

Now let's assume that you want to perform a slightly different test. For instance, you may want to be sure that an entry is not equal to a specified amount. For this test, you rewrite line 3 as

```
/xi(TEST=0)~{NAME}~/xg\n~
```

This test will reject any entry that is equal to 0 and will pass all entries that are not equal to 0.

Finally, the /xi command can be used to break out of the loop. If the third line reads

```
/xi(TEST=0)~/rndTEST~/xq~
```

the macro will stop processing as soon as a 0 is entered in a cell. The line also deletes the range name TEST. Stopping the macro this way has its disadvantages: the macro will leave an unwanted zero in the column and will misinterpret the entry of a legitimate zero as a signal to stop processing. Nevertheless, the technique is a useful alternative to Ctrl Break, and ways are available to make the /xi approach even more elegant.

Using /xi with @COUNT

The /xi command can be followed by various kinds of conditions. You can use the @COUNT function, for example, when you have a continuous sequence of cells to loop through and you want to control the loop. In figure 1.6 the ninth line

```
/xi(@COUNT(T)=2)~/rndT~/xg\a~
```

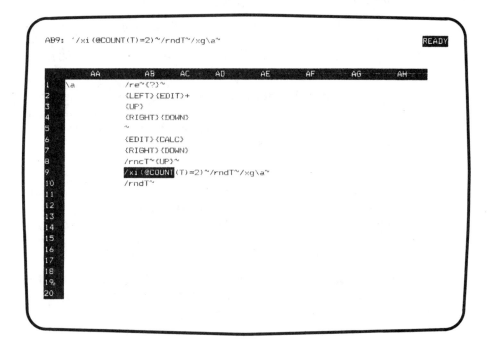

Fig. 1.6.

26

uses the @COUNT to set the condition for looping back to the beginning of the macro.

Line 9 says that if the count of the range named T equals 2, then delete the range name T and loop back to execute the macro again. The @COUNT counts the number of nonblank cells in a range. Therefore, as long as the range T contains two nonblank cells, the condition is met for looping back to the beginning of the macro. If, however, the macro reaches the bottom of the column of numbers, T will contain one blank and one nonblank cell. Failure to meet the condition for looping back causes the macro to proceed to the last line and stop.

Using /xi with @ISNA

Another function to use with the /xi command is @ISNA. Together they allow you to loop back until the macro finds the @NA. The macro in figure 1.7, for example, can be used when you have a column of labels you want to change into numbers.

This macro will continue to operate on cells until it reaches the @NA, at which time the macro ends. When using @ISNA with the /xi com-

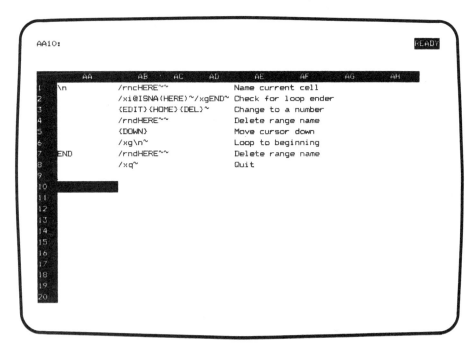

Fig. 1.7.

mand (as in line 2 of this macro), you must enter @NA in the work-sheet at the point where the macro should stop. If, for instance, you are converting a column from labels to numbers (see fig. 1.8), you enter @NA below the last number in the column.

Using /xi with Specific Conditions

Using @COUNT or @ISNA with the /xi command allows you to make the condition for /xi indeterminate. In the example of /xi with @COUNT, the condition is met when the cursor reaches a blank cell. In the example of /xi with @ISNA, the condition is met when the macro reads the @NA. In some cases, however, you will want to specify the exact condition. For instance, in the consolidation macro in figure 1.9, the /xi command tests a counter set up in the main body of the macro.

The counter, named DEPT_CT, has been set up with an initial value of 0 in cell B12, right after the macro itself. The first two lines of code use the /Data Fill command to increment DEPT_CT by 1 each time the loop is performed. The last statement in the macro checks to see

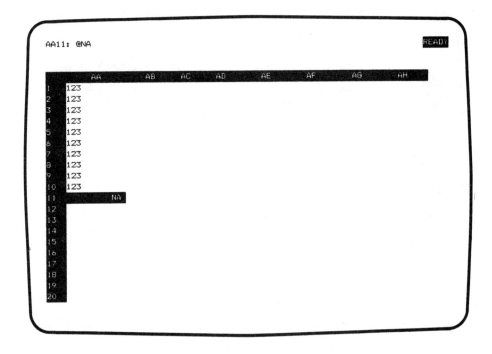

Fig. 1.8.

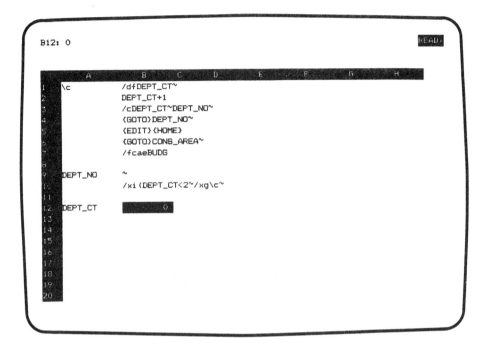

B12: 0   READY

```
          A              B         C         D       E       F       G       H
1    \c             /dfDEPT_CT~
2                   DEPT_CT+1
3                   /cDEPT_CT~DEPT_NO~
4                   {GOTO}DEPT_NO~
5                   {EDIT}{HOME}
6                   {GOTO}CONS_AREA~
7                   /fcaeBUDG
8
9    DEPT_NO        ~
10                  /xi(DEPT_CT<2~/xg\c~
11
12   DEPT_CT            0
13
14
15
16
17
18
19
20
```

Fig. 1.9.

whether DEPT_CT has reached 2. If the count has not reached 2, /xg\c~ causes the macro to loop back to the beginning. When the count reaches 2, the macro ends.

The /xn and /xl Commands

These commands were added to 1-2-3's macro language with 1-2-3 Release 1.1. They supplement the basic 1-2-3 macro input command, {?}. /xn and /xl are prompted input commands that supply a prompt, or message, giving the user instructions about what to enter. (As previously explained, the {?} command simply stops the macro and waits for the user to enter information; {?} does not provide any instructions.)

/xn and /xl are similar in most respects. The main difference between these commands is that /xn is used to enter only numbers, whereas /xl is used to enter only labels.

The form of the commands is identical. For example, the macro

```
/xnEnter a number: ~A1~
```

has three parts: (1) the command itself (/xn), (2) the prompt (Enter a number:), and (3) the destination, or location (A1). The prompt, which is a string of characters up to 39 characters long, is the message that is displayed to aid the user. A prompt can contain two or more words separated by spaces, or only one word, as in

/xnTotal: ~A1~

The colon (:) occurring after the prompt is a useful convention for separating the prompt from the input in the control panel. (See fig. 1.10.) The destination is the cell location where the input will be stored. If you do not provide a location, the number or label will be entered in the current cell.

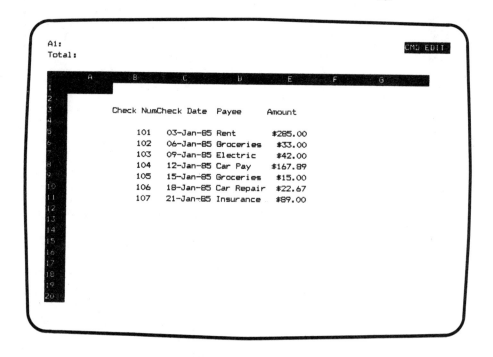

A1:
Total:

CMD EDIT

	A	B	C	D	E	F	G
3		Check Num	Check Date	Payee	Amount		
5		101	03-Jan-85	Rent	$285.00		
6		102	06-Jan-85	Groceries	$33.00		
7		103	09-Jan-85	Electric	$42.00		
8		104	12-Jan-85	Car Pay	$167.89		
9		105	15-Jan-85	Groceries	$15.00		
10		106	18-Jan-85	Car Repair	$22.67		
11		107	21-Jan-85	Insurance	$89.00		

Fig. 1.10.

When the macro is executed, the message

Enter a number:

will appear in the control panel. The macro will then pause for you to enter a number. Once you enter the number, the /xn command automatically enters that number in cell A1.

If you enter anything other than a number or a formula in response to a /xn command, 1-2-3 will beep and display the error message "Illegal number input." Simply press {ESC} or ENTER to remove the error message and try again. If you need to escape from the macro, press Ctrl Break.

When you enter a formula or function in response to a /xn command, 1-2-3 stores the absolute value of the formula in the destination cell. For example, suppose you enter the function

    @DATE(83, 11, 1)

in response to the command

    /xnEnter a number: ~A1~

1-2-3 stores the number 30621, which is the numeric value of the function, in the destination. When you enter the formula

    @SUM(C1. . D1)

in response to the same command, 1-2-3 stores in cell A1 the numeric value of the sum. If cell C1 contains the value 11 and D1 contains the value 100, the number 111 is entered in A1.

What happens when you enter a number in response to the /xl command? When you enter the number 10000 in response to

    /xlEnter a label: ~A1~

the number is entered as text in cell A1. If you move the cursor to cell A1, the cell legend in the control panel will read

    A1: '10000

If you do not enter any data but just press ENTER in response to the prompt, 1-2-3 assumes that you wish to enter a space in the indicated cell. Because a space is a label, pressing ENTER in response to the prompt causes no problem for /xl. But /xn responds to the ENTER key with the standard error message "Illegal number input." This difference between the commands is important to remember.

Using /xl to Post Messages

Because the /xl command does not require any response other than pressing the ENTER key, /xl can be used to display messages in the control panel. Suppose that at the end of the check writer macro (discussed in the next section) you want to remind yourself or another user to check for errors before printing. The macro line

```
Check for errors before printing!~C2~
```

will display in the command line the message

```
Check for errors before printing!
```

After reading the message, the user simply presses ENTER to remove the message, thus causing a space to be entered in cell C3. Because C3 is unused in the current worksheet, using this cell makes no difference.

You can also post messages to the screen by using menu macros. (See the later section on the /xm command.) But in some instances, like the one just cited, using the /xl command is simpler and just as functional.

The /xn and /xl commands can also be used for entering information in the current cell (the cell where the pointer is located). To enter information in this location, you eliminate the destination at the end of the macro line. For example, if the cell pointer is in cell A5, the line

```
/xnEnter a number: ~~
```

will cause the number you enter to be placed in cell A5.

Notice that a space is typically left between the colon (or other final character in the prompt) and the tilde (~) in the command. This space is left purely for stylistic purposes, to help separate the prompt from the input when the macro is run.

The /xl command always enters labels in left-justified format. If you want to display the label centered or right-justified, you need to include a /Range Labels command in the macro, immediately following the /xl command.

Using /xn and /xl to Enter Data

One of the nicest features of the /xn and /xl commands is that they allow data to be entered in the worksheet without requiring the cell pointer to move. Thus, you can enter data in cells A15, Z100, and AB5 without moving the cell pointer from cell A1.

Suppose, for example, that you want to build a 1-2-3 model for automating the process of writing checks. For each check you write, several pieces of information are required: the check number, the date, the payee, and the amount (in both dollars and text). The macro in figure 1.11 will simplify the entry of this data.

To enter data into the check form, you type Alti. The macro will prompt for the check number, date, payee, amount, and memo, one after another. No matter where the cursor lies, the macro will enter the information in the correct cells. In this macro the /xn command is used to enter a date.

After you press ENTER, 1-2-3 automatically changes the date function entered—for example, @DATE(83,11,15)—into its numeric value (30635). The /xn command always converts a formula into its numeric value before entering that formula in a cell.

The same combination of commands used in this check-writing macro can be used to insert data into almost any form. For example, the /xn and /xl commands can simplify the process of filling out your 1-2-3 Form 1040 template at tax time. These commands can also be used for entering data into templates for invoices, purchase orders, and bills of lading.

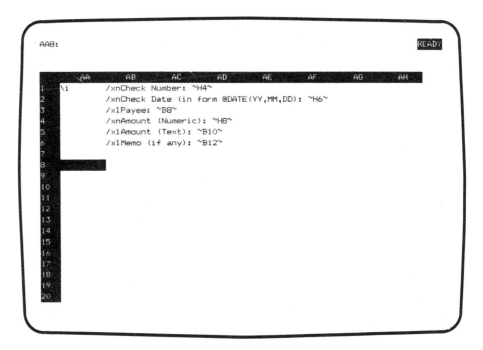

Fig. 1.11.

Using Range Names with /xn and /xl

Naturally, you can use range names instead of cell references in /xn and /xl commands. For example, if cell A5 is named INPUT, the macro

```
/xnEnter a number: ~INPUT~
```

causes the value entered to be stored in the cell INPUT (A5). What happens if the range A5..C7, instead of the single cell A5, is given the name INPUT? The effect of the macro is the same. Whenever the destination is a range instead of a single cell, the /xn and /xl commands store the entered data in the cell in the upper left corner of the indicated range.

Using range names instead of cell references also makes your macro more flexible. In the macro shown in figure 1.11, suppose you insert a row at row 4 in the worksheet. The cell named INPUT is now cell A6. If you use the name INPUT in the macro, it will run correctly. But if you use the cell reference version of the macro

```
/xnEnter a number: ~A5~
```

you will have a problem. Because the macro does not change when the row is inserted, the macro is now referring to the wrong cell. Instead of specifying cell A6 as the destination, the macro continues to specify A5. A quick edit will fix this simple problem, but in a larger macro with many /xn and /xl commands, the corrections may be overwhelming.

The /xm Command

The /xm command is one of the most powerful because it enables you to make your own menus. These menus, which appear while the macro is executing, operate exactly like the standard 1-2-3 menus. Displayed in the control panel, a menu created with the /xm command contains both the command and the explanation beneath the command. Such a menu not only allows the user to make choices, but also can be used during processing to give messages and warnings to the user.

The /xm command is probably the most useful but least understood macro command. /xm is really quite simple, however. It is a tool that can be used to create custom menus to handle a variety of tasks.

All 1-2-3 menus are accessed by the /xmLocations command. The location in the /xm command points to a menu range, which can be up to eight columns wide and two rows deep. Thus, you can create a menu containing eight separate choices, with explanations provided on the second line of each menu.

Let's consider a simple example of a macro using the /xm command. Suppose you want to make a macro that allows you to perform a /File Save Replace. For this operation, you can create the macro

\f   /fs~r~

Such a macro poses a problem for the user, however. Once the macro is executed, you have no chance to quit the macro before it actually replaces the file. But if you use /xm in the macro, as shown in figure 1.12, you'll have available a menu that provides the option of halting the /File Save operation before the macro replaces the existing file.

Divided into parts, the macro in figure 1.12 contains the following sections:

1. The /xm command, which displays the menu beginning in B2

    /xmB2~

2. The menu options and second-line explanations

    Yes   No

    Save Current   Remain in 1-2-3
    Worksheet

3. Command operations relating to each menu option

    fs~r~ /xq~
    /qy~

To run the macro, you begin by pressing Altq. Once the menu is displayed, you have the option of selecting Yes or No. If you select Yes, the macro will continue to process at cell B4. The statement in this cell instructs 1-2-3 to save the current file and quit from 1-2-3. (The program assumes that the file has already been saved once and therefore has a file name.) If you select No, the macro will continue processing at cell C4. This cell contains a simple /xq function that causes the macro to stop running.

When you create a macro that contains /xm, keep one point in mind. You can indicate the location of your menu in the /xm statement by referring to the cell where the menu begins (B2 in this example) or by assigning a range name to the menu and using that name after /xm. If you assign the name FSAVE to the menu beginning in B2, the first line of the macro appears as

/xmFSAVE~

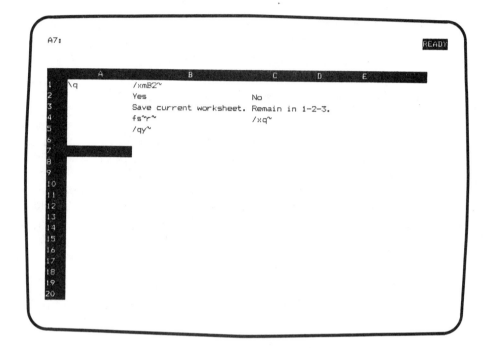

```
A7:                                                                READY

        A              B              C         D         E
1   \q          /xmB2~
2               Yes                   No
3               Save current worksheet. Remain in 1-2-3.
4               fs~r~                 /xq~
5               /qy~
6
7
8
9
10
11
12
13
14
15
16
17
18
19
20
```

Fig. 1.12.

Using range names for menus is especially helpful when you are creating macros with multiple menus. Range names help you immediately to identify different menus as you read through the macros.

When the /xm command is used, the only way to continue execution of the macro is to select one of the options presented in the menu. As in the example in figure 1.12, one of the simplest uses for a menu is to allow the user to answer a yes/no question from within a macro.

As with 1-2-3's standard menus, you can select an option from the macro menu in one of two ways. First, you can use the cursor to point to the option you want to select. In the example, pressing → will therefore move the menu cursor to the second option, which is No. Second, you can select an option by typing the first character in the option's name. To select the No option, you type N.

One major difference is evident when you use menus created with the /xm command rather than 1-2-3 standard menus. With menus created with /xm, you won't be able to use {ESC} to back up to a previous level unless you supply a special macro line at the end of each menu. With

1-2-3 standard menus, you can press {ESC} to move back up one menu level. To use {ESC} with your macro menus, you can expand the menus, as shown in figure 1.13.

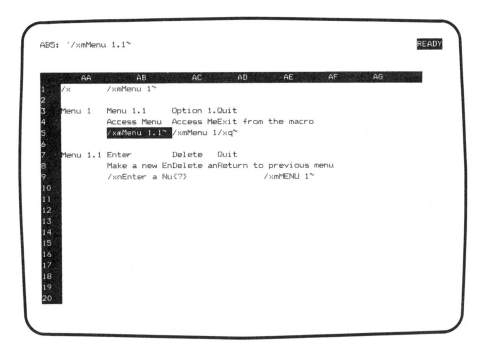

ABS: '/xmMenu 1.1~   READY

```
        AA        AB         AC        AD       AE       AF       AG
1   /x        /xmMenu 1~
2
3   Menu 1    Menu 1.1      Option 1.Quit
4             Access Menu   Access MeExit from the macro
5             /xmMenu 1.1~ /xmMenu 1/xq~
6
7   Menu 1.1 Enter          Delete    Quit
8            Make a new EnDelete anReturn to previous menu
9            /xnEnter a Nu{?}                 /xmMENU 1~
10
11
12
13
14
15
16
17
18
19
20
```

Fig. 1.13.

Two /xm commands are in cell AB5. The first /xm command, /xmMenu 1.1~, moves the macro to Menu 1.1. The second /xm command, /xmMenu 1~, causes the macro to "back up" one step to the main menu (Menu 1) if you press {ESC} after selecting this option.

Be certain to choose option names that begin with different letters. If you have in a menu two or more options with the same first letter, and you try to select one option by using the first-letter technique, 1-2-3 will automatically select the first option found that has the letter you specify.

In addition, you should include a **Quit** option in each menu. Whenever you have multiple levels of menus, you can use the **Quit** option for returning to the previous level. Using **Quit** allows you to move back through the menu tree.

If you create a menu that is too long to fit in the control panel, 1-2-3 will return the error message "Illegal menu." The same message is returned if the menu has more than eight options. Similarly, the secondary messages associated with each menu option can contain 80 characters each because the width of the IBM display is 80 characters.

The /xc and /xr Commands

The /xc and /xr commands are similar to BASIC's GOSUB and RETURN functions. /xc causes the macro to access a macro subroutine in a separate location. When the subroutine is finished, /xr causes processing to resume on the next line of the original macro. The /xc command is similar to the /xg command, but, unlike /xg, /xc provides a way to return the macro to the point of departure.

Let's assume that you want to make a macro that adds values from a column listing sales for the month to a column listing sales for the year to date, as shown in figure 1.14.

The accumulator macro in figure 1.15 will add the values from the month column to the year-to-date column, thus accumulating the totals.

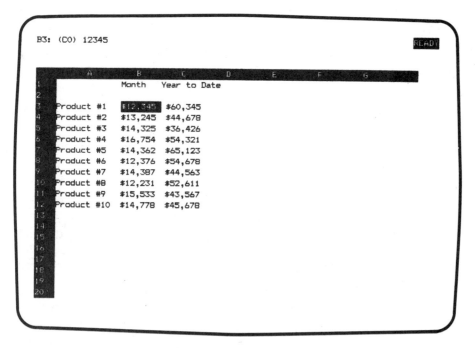

Fig. 1.14.

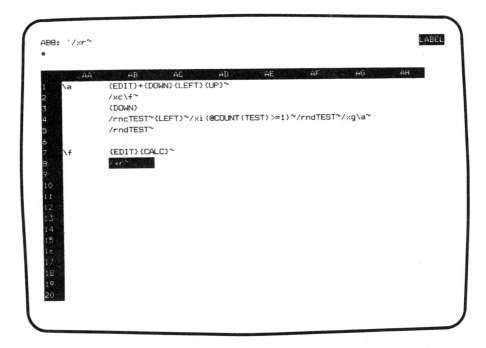

Fig. 1.15.

Notice particularly that the second and last lines of the macro contain the /xc and /xr commands. Here's how the commands function. First, the /xc command in line 2 lets the macro skip to another location and continue processing. In this macro the location is line 7. Second, the /xr command in line 8 sends the macro back to the point just below the /xc command to continue processing. In this case, /xr sends the macro back to line 3.

The /xq Command

The /xq command causes the macro to quit execution. This command is commonly used with /xi. For example, the two commands can be linked to form the statement

    /xiSALES>1000000~/xq~

which says, "If the contents of the cell named SALES are greater than 1,000,000, stop executing the macro." When /xq and /xi are buried in a macro, they will perform the test and either continue or stop the macro.

As you make your own macros, you should determine when such a conditional statement is appropriate. If you forget to add the /xq command, the macro may make changes that you don't want in your worksheet.

Another use for the /xq command is found within macro menus that provide the user with a **Quit** selection. In figure 1.16, for instance, /xq is used to quit execution of the macro whenever the user selects **Quit** from the DEL_MENU menu.

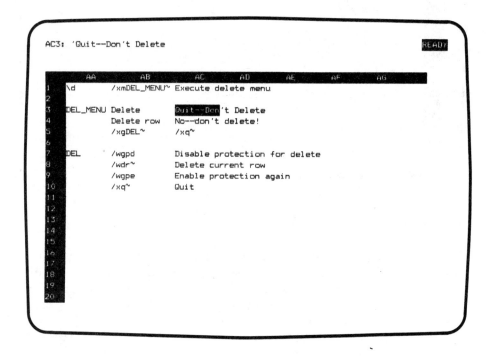

Fig. 1.16.

In the macros in this library, you will find various ways in which special macro commands are used. Such commands provide capabilities surpassing those of the simple "typing alternative." As you make your own 1-2-3 macros, you'll discover how powerful these special macro commands can be.

Conclusion

If you haven't had a chance to create and use 1-2-3 macros, this chapter has provided the basic information for getting started. The chapter has explained what 1-2-3 macros are, what differences exist between macros that are only "typing alternatives" and those that are more complex programming tools, what elements can be used in macros, and how special macro commands can be used.

2

Making and Using 1-2-3 Macros

Once you begin using the 1-2-3 macros in this book and making your own macros, you'll soon see how macros can simplify many of your 1-2-3 applications and reduce the time spent in creating worksheets, entering data, changing worksheet data, and printing reports and graphics. Making and using macros can be difficult tasks for the beginner; you may even find yourself spending as much time in debugging your macros as in creating them. If you keep in mind the guidelines in this chapter, however, your 1-2-3 macros will be much easier to make and use.

To help you modify the 1-2-3 macros in this book or those you make on your own, this chapter covers the whole process of creating macros, from making them to testing and using them. The following sections will help you become an experienced user:

1. Steps in making your own macros

2. Guidelines for creating and using 1-2-3 macros

3. Common macro errors

4. Debugging a macro

5. Editing a macro

Steps in Making Your Own Macros

If you approach the making of macros in a logical manner, by following certain steps, you should have greater success in getting your macros to perform as you want them to. To assure that your macros will run properly and with fewer bugs, you should follow three basic steps in making 1-2-3 macros.

Step 1: Specifying the General Macro Operations

When you create macros for your own special 1-2-3 applications, you should begin by making a general outline of the process to be performed by the macro. Let's examine a macro (found in Chapter 6) for printing amortization schedules. This particular macro enters print settings and prints loan amortization schedules for data entered into each schedule. (See fig. 2.1.)

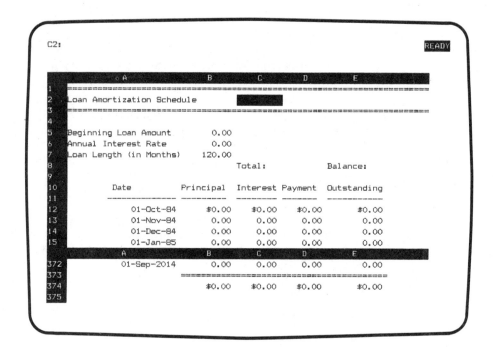

Fig. 2.1.

To make a macro that will print the amortization schedule shown in figure 2.1, begin by jotting down the general operations that the macro should perform:

1. Automatically update print settings every time the amortization schedule changes

2. Automatically print borders for all pages

3. Print totals for each amortization schedule

4. Clear borders before the macro quits

Step 2: Jotting Down Each Keystroke

After you have outlined what you want the macro to do, your next step is to proceed through the series of instructions you want to include in the macro to be entered from the keyboard. As you manually enter each keystroke, jot it down. That way, you won't forget to enter a keystroke when you actually type in the macro.

In the macro for printing amortization schedules, the jotted list of keystrokes consists of the following:

/	Retrieve the command menu
p	Retrieve the Print menu
p	Select printer
c	Clear any previous settings
b	Clear previous border settings
r	Set print range
	(Enter print range at this point)
o	Select options
b	Select borders
c	Set borders from column headings
	(Enter range for column headings)
g	Print body of amortization schedule
c	Clear previous borders
b	Set new borders (amortization schedule totals)
	(Enter range for amortization schedule totals)
g	Print totals
p	Advance page
q	Quit and return to READY mode

For printing a loan amortization schedule, this list includes only the basic selections from the Print menu. The list does not include any other special settings you may want, such as **Setup** for changing print size, **Header**, or **Footer**. A macro for printing amortization schedules must contain at least those keystrokes listed. But if you make a basic macro with only these keystrokes, it won't execute one of the most important operations: automatically determining and entering the range for printing every time the amortization schedule changes.

Step 3: Including Special Macro Lines

Before you continue to make the macro for printing amortization schedules, you must devise a way for the macro to determine automatically the new print range of the amortization schedule each time the schedule is changed. The macro in Chapter 6 is designed to determine the range of each new amortization schedule by reading the last row in the payment column. Before the actual print operations begin, the macro adjusts for the length of the amortization schedule and then enters that length into the macro cell which stores the end of the print range.

As you can see from the explanation of each macro line in figure 2.2, the macro includes the basic keystrokes for printing the amortization schedule plus macro lines for determining the correct range for each schedule.

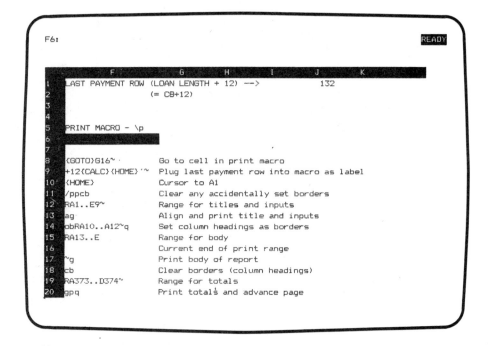

Fig. 2.2.

Much of this macro duplicates the order of selecting commands from the Print menu. Exceptions are the three lines at the beginning of the macro; these lines determine and enter the setting for the end of the print range. Although this macro doesn't include special macro commands, when you make other macros, you'll need to consider how such commands (/xi, /xq, /xg, /xc, /xr, /xn, /xl, and /xm) can be used to produce the operations you want performed.

Guidelines for Making and Using 1-2-3 Macros

In addition to the guidelines already listed, the following guidelines will help you whether you are making your own 1-2-3 macros or using and editing those created by someone else.

Guidelines for Macro Format

In 1-2-3 macros, certain formatting features are necessary for assuring successful operation. Other conventions make easier the tasks of reading and analyzing your macros. These tasks are particularly important when you need to debug or edit a macro by changing or adding an operation. The following guidelines will help assure that the macro runs properly:

1. The macro should contain empty cells when such cells are accounted for in the body of the macro. Suppose, for example, that you keep a list of file names on a separate worksheet. You can create a macro to retrieve any of the names on your list. This macro will contain one empty cell. (See fig. 2.3.) When the macro runs, the file name on which you have placed the cursor is copied into the blank cell in the macro. When the /**File Retrieve** operation begins, 1-2-3 then retrieves the file copied into the blank cell.

2. You should enter macro commands (/xg, /xi, /xq, etc.) and key representations as listed in tables 1.1 through 1.5 in Chapter 1. Be sure to use brackets or braces to enclose the representations for function, cursor-movement, editing, and special keys. Examples: {EDIT} and {DOWN}. And be careful not to mix types of brackets, or braces with parentheses. In other words, avoid a construction such as {DOWN).

3. Don't forget to include the tilde (~) when the ENTER operation is needed.

The following additional guidelines will simplify the task of editing macros:

1. Instead of running together many commands on one line, segment the different operations by providing a different line for each operation. (See fig. 2.4.) You will thus have a much easier time debugging or editing macro lines.

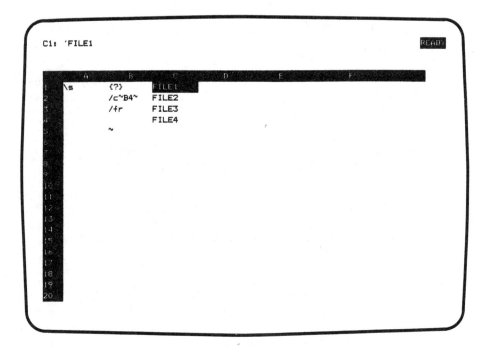

Fig. 2.3.

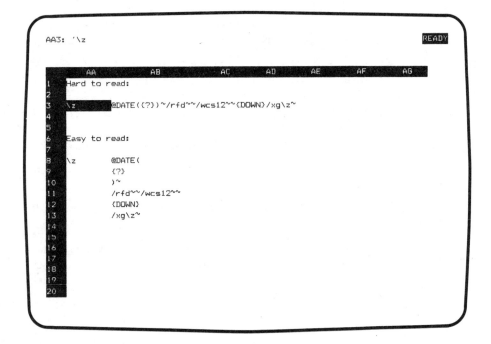

Fig. 2.4.

2. Use format conventions that will easily distinguish different elements in a macro line. For example, the line

    \a   /xi(@COUNT(T)=2)~/rndT~/xg\a~

contains the following elements:

    a.   The special macro commands /xi and /xg
    b.   The function @COUNT
    c.   The range name T
    d.   The value 2
    e.   The 1-2-3 command /rnd
    f.   The special key representation ~
    g.   The macro name \a

To distinguish among the different elements, follow these conventions:

    a.   Use all lowercase letters for special macro commands, 1-2-3 commands, and macro names.

    b.   Use all uppercase letters for range names, functions, and key representations.

Guidelines for Macro Length

You should keep your macros as short and simple as possible. Because the 1-2-3 macro language is versatile, you can create complex chains of macros that are menu-driven. But in some cases these chains are unnecessary. In fact, if your macro becomes too complex, you will find that 1-2-3's macro language does have its limitations. As a result, you may discover that a macro won't perform the desired operations. If the task you want performed is too complex, you should consider using a more traditional programming tool or an add-in macro program, such as ProKey, from RoseSoft. (See Chapter 7 for a discussion of ProKey.) You should also try to find the simplest combination of commands for the desired task. Consider the macros in figures 2.5 and 2.6.

Both macros can be used for the same application: to add the values from one column to another, as shown in figure 2.7. The first macro is much longer than the second one, however.

Although the two macros produce the same results, the macros differ in the following ways. The first macro (see fig. 2.5) operates by testing each cell value in the right column, adding the value to the cell directly to the left if that cell meets the test conditions, and looping back to begin again. The second macro (see fig. 2.6) uses the /**File X**tract and

Fig. 2.5.

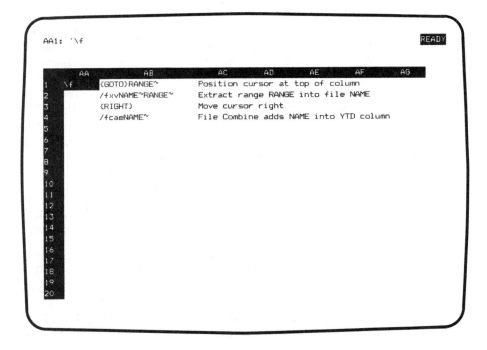

Fig. 2.6.

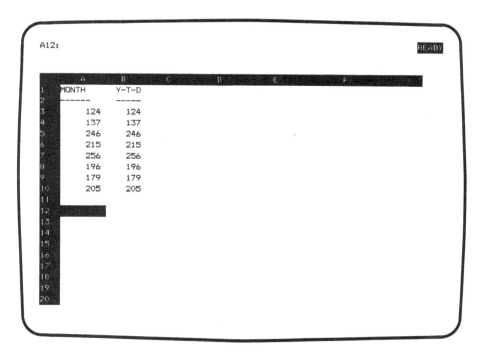

Fig. 2.7.

/File Combine commands to add values in column A to those in column B.

Creating the shortest macro right away may not always be easy. But if you get into the habit of searching for the shortest macro, you can save yourself some time in debugging the macro later. The macro in figure 2.5 may require much debugging because of its complexity. The macro in figure 2.6, however, should require little debugging because this macro contains fewer lines and commands.

Another method for simplifying macros is to use subroutines and menus whenever possible. Suppose, for example, that you want to make a macro for performing a series of complex operations. Instead of building one continuous macro for all the operations, you may want to separate each operation into a subroutine. The macro in figure 2.8 contains subroutines, each of which controls a series of macro operations. The lines in the macro are nothing but a series of calls to macros that perform different tasks.

Using subroutines or menus to control a series of operations has definite advantages. First, you can look at the main line macro to get a

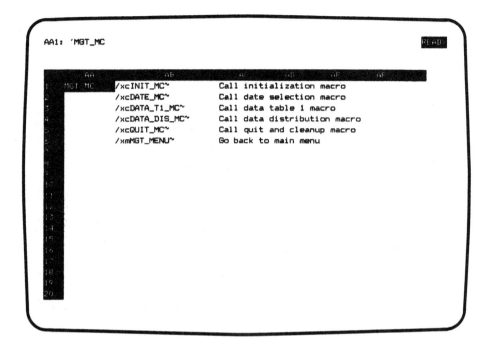

AA1: 'MGT_MC   READY

| AA | AB | AC | AD | AE | AF |

MGT_MC /xcINIT_MC~   Call initialization macro
        /xcDATE_MC~   Call date selection macro
        /xcDATA_T1_MC~   Call data table 1 macro
        /xcDATA_DIS_MC~   Call data distribution macro
        /xcQUIT_MC~   Call quit and cleanup macro
        /xmMGT_MENU~   Go back to main menu

Fig. 2.8.

quick idea of the macro's overall logic. Second, because each function is in a separate routine, you can more easily isolate problems, make changes, and test the macro's logic.

Guidelines for Storing Macros

The best way to manage a large number of macros is by creating a macro library file, available whenever you want to copy macros into your worksheets. You will, however, want to store your most frequently used macros (and those you want executed automatically) right on the worksheets where the macros are most often used. And if a worksheet contains several macros, you may conveniently store all of them in one part of the sheet. Storing the macros together makes it easier for you to find a macro for editing and also prevents you from accidentally overwriting a macro stored in an active part of the worksheet. When storing macros on a worksheet, you should consider the following guidelines.

Store macros in columns AA and AB. Because these columns are outside the part of the worksheet you normally use, your model is not likely to conflict with your macros. Keep in mind, though, that placing your macros outside the basic rectangle containing your model can consume large amounts of memory. If you are working with a large model and a relatively small amount of memory, you should be aware of this problem. In addition, placing macros outside the normal rectangle will cause the END HOME function to put the cursor at the right corner of the overall spreadsheet (including the macro area) instead of at the lower right corner of the model. Consequently, the END HOME key becomes useless.

Some users like to store their macros under the last rows of their models, in columns A and B, because these locations are out of the way. They also have another advantage: macros stored below the models use much less memory than those stored farther away from the models. Although storing macros close to your models will save memory, be careful that you don't accidentally overwrite or erase part of a macro when you make changes in the worksheet.

Another problem that can occur when you store macros involves two commands: /Worksheet Insert Row and /Worksheet Delete Row. When you use either of these commands, manually or within a macro, you may accidentally delete a row or insert a blank row in a macro. Be careful, therefore, when storing your macros.

In figure 2.9B is an example of a macro that may be affected by /Worksheet Insert Row or /Worksheet Delete Row. This macro adds extra rows, when needed, to the Cash Flow Projection, as shown in figure 2.9A. The macro located at AA1 inserts extra rows and copies the formula for the running balance to the newly inserted rows. Stored in the location shown in figure 2.9B, the macro is not affected by the /Worksheet Insert Row command (/wir).

If, however, you position the macro at AA15 and insert a row at row 15, the new row is inserted not only in the Cash Flow Projection but also in the macro itself. And the macro stops executing as soon as it reaches the new blank row. This type of macro must therefore be placed below the worksheet or above the area where insert or delete operations will occur.

Two other commands, /Worksheet Insert Column and /Worksheet Delete Column, can affect your macros. The effects, however, are different from those of /Worksheet Insert Row and /Worksheet Delete Row. /Worksheet Insert Column and /Worksheet Delete Column can create problems for the cell addresses in your macros.

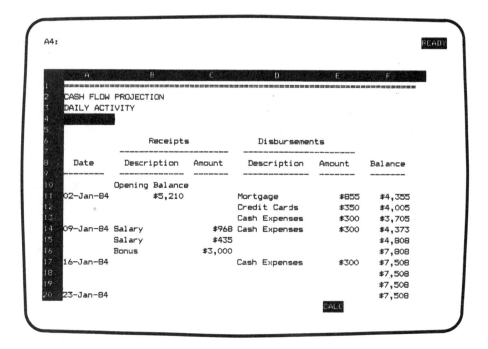

Fig. 2.9A.

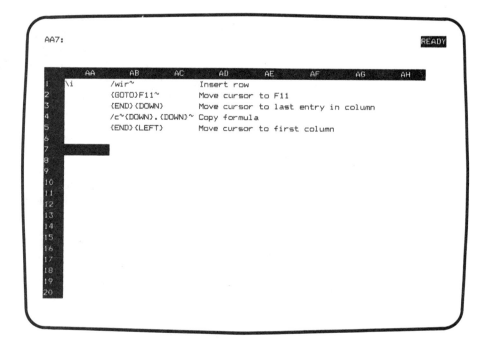

Fig. 2.9B.

To see how /Worksheet Insert Column can affect a macro, you should take another look at the macro in figure 2.9B. Line 2 of the insert macro contains the cell address F11. This line moves the cursor to cell F11, the first cell in the column that computes the running balance of the Cash Flow Projection. Then line 3 moves the cursor to the last cell in column F, above the newly created row.

Line 4 copies the formula in that last cell into the new row and the row immediately below the new one. For example, if you insert a row between rows 21 and 22, the macro line 4 copies the formula from F21 into F22 (the new row) and F23 (previously F22). After the formula is copied, line 4 moves the cursor down to the new row. Line 5 then moves the cursor back to column A.

What happens, though, if you insert a column at column F? Line 2 will still move the cursor to F11 rather than G11 (previously F11). To prevent this kind of problem from occurring because of specific cell references in macros, use range names in place of cell addresses. (See the section "Common Macro Errors" for more information.)

Once you designate an area for your macros, you should give that area a name, such as MACROS, so that you can easily get to the location by simply pressing the {GOTO} key and then entering MACROS. If you need to edit a macro, you can do it more quickly this way.

Guidelines for Documenting Macros

Professional programmers usually write programs that are self-documented, or internally documented. Such a program contains comments that help explain each step of the program. In BASIC, for instance, these comments are in REM (for REMark) statements. The REM statements in the following program explain the action taken by the other statements:

```
10 REM This program adds two numbers
20 REM Enter first number
30 INPUT A
40 REM Enter second number
50 INPUT B
60 REM Add numbers together
70 C=A+B
80 REM Display Result
90 Print C
```

For the same reasons that professional programmers document their programs, you should document your 1-2-3 macros. Comments should be placed next to each macro, in the column to the right. For example, in figure 2.10 the macro name is in column A, the macro is in column B, and the documentation is in column C.

Including comments in your macros will make them much easier to use. Comments are especially useful when you have created complex macros that you will want to change. Without documentation, you may have a difficult time remembering exactly what each step of the macro does.

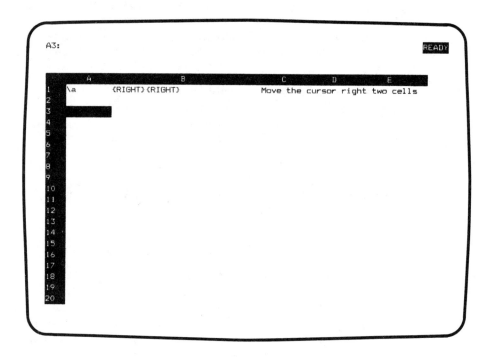

Fig. 2.10.

Guidelines for Naming Macros

As previously mentioned, once you have entered in your worksheet a macro as a label (or a series of labels), you must give the macro a name. A range containing a macro is assigned a name just as every other range is assigned a name. The only difference is that the name you assign to a macro must meet certain special conditions: the name must be only one character (an alphabetical character or a 0), and the name must be preceded by a backslash (\ ). Table 2.1 shows several legal and illegal macro names.

Legal Names	Illegal Names
\a	\abc
\b	abc
\0	\?
\x	\1

Table 2.1

Suppose, for example, that you have created the macro shown in figure 2.11, and you must now decide on a name. Although you can give the macro any one-letter name, you can also choose a name that in some way describes the macro. Obviously, selecting a descriptive one-letter name can be difficult. In this case, you may choose the name \c (for currency) or \f (for format). Probably the best name for the macro is \$, but because the symbol $ is not a letter, \$ is not legal.

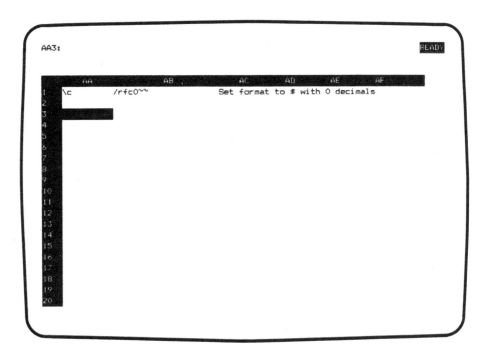

Fig. 2.11.

If you decide to name the macro \c, you then use the /**R**ange Name Create command. Next, you enter the name you have selected (\c) and press ENTER. When 1-2-3 prompts you for a range, you again press ENTER if the cursor is currently on cell AB1, which is the first macro line.

Some macros require more than one row in a spreadsheet. Look at the simple two-line macro in figure 2.12. To name this macro, you assign a name to only the first cell in the range that contains the macro. In this case, you assign the name \w to cell AB1. You can also assign this name to the entire range AB1..AB2, but the process takes a little more time.

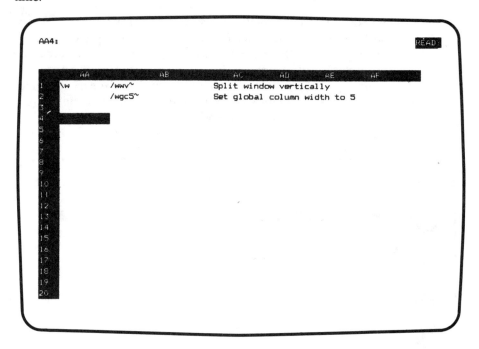

Fig. 2.12.

1-2-3's /**R**ange Name command is remarkably flexible. For example, one cell can be part of several different named ranges.

A more convenient way to name macros is to use the /**R**ange Name Labels Right command. When you use this command, you place the cursor on the cell containing the range name (AA1 in this case). Then you select /**R**ange Name Labels Right and press ENTER. 1-2-3 assigns the name in the cell where the cursor is located to the cell directly to the right.

The /**R**ange Name Labels command can be used in several ways. If you are documenting your macros properly, you will already have the names in the sheet; therefore, using the Labels option is a simple and convenient way to name the macros. If you import macros from an external library file, you can use the Labels command to assign names quickly for the imported macros.

Executing a Macro

All macros are executed, or invoked, by typing Alt followed by the letter name for the macro. For example, if the macro you want to use is named \a, you invoke it by pressing simultaneously the Alt key and the letter *a*. (The \ represents the Alt key.)

As soon as the command is issued, the macro starts to execute. If no errors occur and no special instructions are built into the macro, it will continue to run until it is finished. You will be amazed at the macro's speed. Commands are issued faster than you can see them.

Many macros can be stored in a single cell. Some that are particularly long or include special commands must be split into two or more cells, as illustrated by the example in figure 2.12. Splitting a macro presents no problem. When 1-2-3 starts executing the macro, the program continues in the first cell until all the keystrokes stored there are used. 1-2-3 then moves down one cell and continues execution. If the cell below is blank, the program stops. But if that cell contains more macro commands, 1-2-3 will continue reading down the column until the first blank cell is reached.

Common Macro Errors

1-2-3 macros have no ability to discern errors in the code. For instance, you will immediately recognize that the symbol {GOTI} is a misspelling of {GOTO}. But a macro cannot make this distinction. When the macro tries to interpret the misspelled word and fails, the macro will deliver an error message. You must therefore be extremely careful when you build your macros so that they are free of errors. Even misplaced spaces and tildes can cause difficulty for 1-2-3.

No matter how careful you are, however, some errors are going to slip through. The greatest problem that beginners have with macros is forgetting to include all the required ENTER keystrokes (~) in the macros. Another problem with 1-2-3 macros is that cell references included within macros are always absolute. These references do not change when cells are moved about or deleted from the worksheet. For example, the simple macro

/re~A6~

erases the contents of cell A6. But if you move the contents of cell A6 to cell B6, the macro reference will remain A6. A macro is a label. Unlike cell formulas, the cell references within macro cells will not change when such operations as moving, copying, inserting, or deleting are performed.

As previously suggested, one way to avoid the problem of cell references in macros is to use range names. For example, the range erase macro (/re~A6~) can be changed to /re~SALES~. If you assign the name SALES to A6 and use this range name in the macro, your macro will always operate correctly, even if the contents of A6 have been moved to another location in the worksheet.

Debugging a Macro

When you become a true 1-2-3 macro enthusiast and begin making your own macros, you'll discover that editing them is a regular part of macro creation, particularly when your macros are fairly complex. In macros, as in computer programs, errors are called bugs. Eliminating bugs from a macro is known as debugging.

Like macros or programs written in other programming languages, 1-2-3 macros often must be debugged before they can be used. The STEP function, included in Version 1A of 1-2-3, can simplify the task of debugging macros. When 1-2-3 is in STEP mode, all macros are executed one step at a time. 1-2-3 literally pauses after executing each keystroke stored in the macro. Thus, the user can follow along, step by step, as the macro executes.

Let's step through a macro that contains a bug and see how 1-2-3's STEP mode works. Suppose you have created the date entry macro shown in figure 2.13. This macro, as previously mentioned, completes four operations: (1) prompts you for the date, (2) formats the cell for DATE format, (3) adjusts column width, and (4) moves the cursor down.

If you use STEP mode while you run this macro, you can see each part of the command being executed. To use STEP mode, you press simultaneously the Alt and F1 keys and then invoke the macro by pressing Altz. When 1-2-3 is in STEP mode, the mode indicator will change to SST.

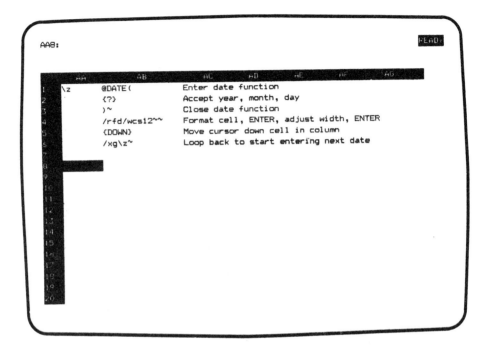

Fig. 2.13.

To step through each part of the macro, you press any key or the space bar. In the control panel, 1-2-3 will display each part of the macro as it is processed. (See fig. 2.14.) When reaching the second line, the macro will pause for you to enter the date. After entering the date, you press ENTER and then continue to step through the next lines of the macro. It will begin the /Range Format Date operation, then stop. STEP mode lets you see exactly where the macro stops execution. (See fig. 2.15.) In the example, the macro will stop after /rfd in line 4. A quick check of this line indicates that the tildes (~~) required to complete the range format operation are missing after the /rfd.

If the macro you are checking is not visible on your worksheet as you are stepping through the macro, you can use the /Worksheet Window command to make the macro visible. Suppose, for example, that you are testing a macro that you have just created for accumulating values on the worksheet. The macro is located at AA1, and the values to be accumulated begin at cell A1. (See figs. 2.16 and 2.17.) If you want to see the macro as it accumulates (in STEP mode) totals on the worksheet, use the /Worksheet Window command to divide the display screen.

61

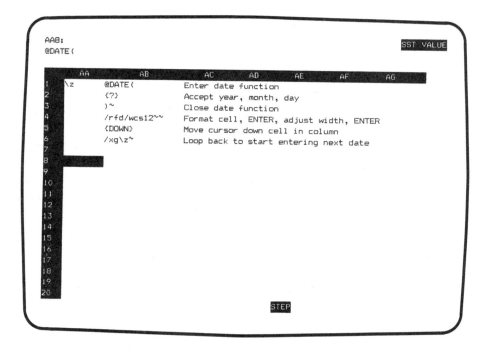

Fig. 2.14.

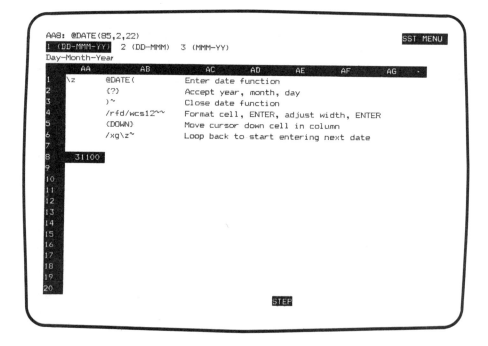

Fig. 2.15.

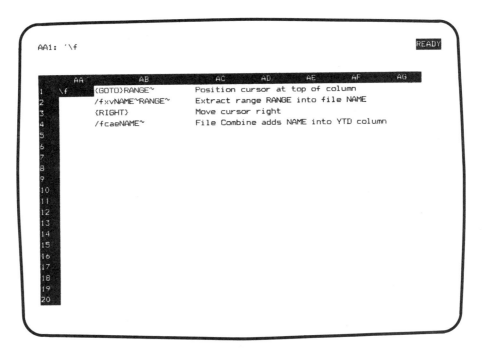

Fig. 2.16.

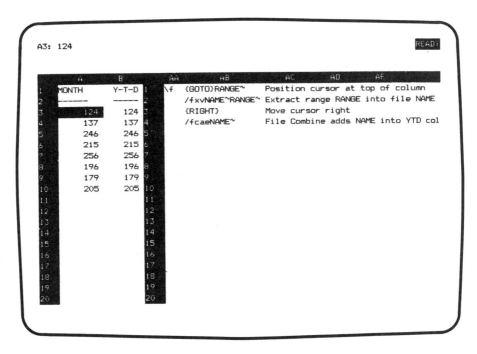

Fig. 2.17.

Using STEP mode enables you to pinpoint easily the location of an error that may occur in a macro. Once the error is identified, you can exit STEP mode by again typing Alt F1. Then you can abort the macro by pressing {ESC} and proceed to edit the macro.

Editing a Macro

Editing a 1-2-3 macro is as simple as editing the contents of any cell in your worksheet. You don't need to rewrite the whole cell; you need to change only the element that is in error.

To eliminate the error in the date macro in figure 2.13, you begin by making sure that you are in READY mode. If you are not, you press {ESC} a few times to return to READY mode. Next, you move the cursor to the cell containing the error—AB4 in the example. Press the {EDIT} key (F2 on the IBM PC and PC-compatibles). When 1-2-3 is in EDIT mode, you position the cursor below the second slash. (See fig. 2.18.) Then you type ~~ and press ENTER. In your worksheet the macro should appear as shown in figure 2.19.

Although editing complex macros can be more difficult than editing a simple macro like this one, the concept is exactly the same. You just use 1-2-3's cell editor (F2) to correct the cell that contains the error.

Conclusion

In the following chapters, you will find many macros illustrating the special features discussed in this chapter. The remaining chapters contain the actual macro library. Divided according to applications for 1-2-3 users, the chapters are filled with macros to help you enter data and make changes in the worksheet, accomplish data management tasks, complete file operations, perform tasks for printing and graphics, and create special worksheet models.

You will want to use many of the macros in the library not only by themselves but also in combination with other macros. For example, you may want to combine two or three macros into one macro controlled by the /xm command. You may also want to make long macros that contain some of the shorter ones described in the macro library. Whether you are making your own macros or modifying those presented in the library, the guidelines and tips presented in this chapter will make your task easier.

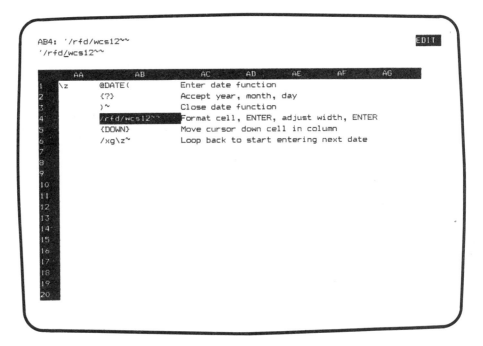

Fig. 2.18.

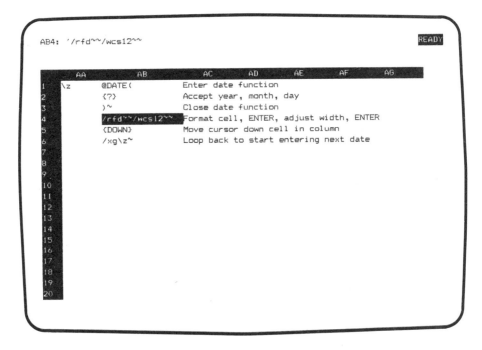

Fig. 2.19.

3

Worksheet Macros

Although the following chapters contain macros for many 1-2-3 applications—such as printing, graphics, and data management— this chapter presents macros for worksheet operations. The following types of macros are included:

1. Cursor-movement macros

2. Macros for entering data

3. Date entry macros

4. Macros for changing a worksheet

5. Macros for worksheet calculation

6. Macros for password protection

Worksheet macros range from those that reduce the number of keystrokes for 1-2-3 command operations to macros that provide operations not usually a part of 1-2-3's program capabilities. One macro, for example, transposes rows and columns. Such an operation is not included in 1-2-3 but is now available in Symphony.

The macros in this chapter also vary in complexity. Generally, the cursor-movement macros are easy to use in your own worksheet applications. Presented later in the chapter are more sophisticated macros that are much longer and more difficult to duplicate. If you are not familiar with 1-2-3 macros, you may want to begin by duplicating those in the first three sections. But whether you are a new user or an experienced one, you will find many valuable macros to add to your macro library.

Cursor-Movement Macros

These macros reduce the number of keystrokes needed to move the cursor in your 1-2-3 worksheets. Cursor-movement macros perform such operations as jumping the cursor across a number of rows or columns and speeding up the entry of formulas. Such macros can be invaluable for creating spreadsheets or data bases. Specifically, this section contains the following kinds of macros:

1. Macros for jumping the cursor across cells

2. Macro for moving the cursor to the next row

3. Macro for moving the cursor to Home

4. Macro for entering formulas

Macros for Jumping the Cursor across Cells

As mentioned in Chapter 1, macros can reduce keystrokes for any frequent operation. 1-2-3 users typically create macros for command operations from the 1-2-3 menu. But macros can also be tremendous "keystroke savers" for moving the cursor around the worksheet. The cursor-movement macros in figure 3.1 enable you to jump cells—left, right, up, or down, respectively—by row or column. To invoke each macro, you press simultaneously the Alt key and the letter key indicated by the macro name.

Macro for Moving the Cursor to the Next Row

Another cursor-movement macro is helpful for entering data across rows that are many columns wide. Suppose, for example, that you are entering data into the data base shown in figure 3.2. After you have entered data across all columns, the macro will move the cursor to the next row.

To move the cursor from cell H3 to cell A4, you invoke the macro shown in figure 3.3.

Macro for Moving the Cursor to Home

For worksheets that will be used by several people, the macro in figure 3.4 can prevent confusion when a new user retrieves a worksheet file.

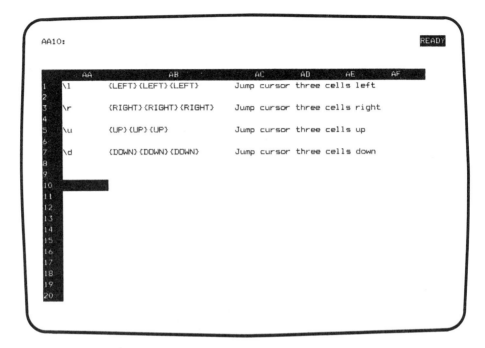

Fig. 3.1.

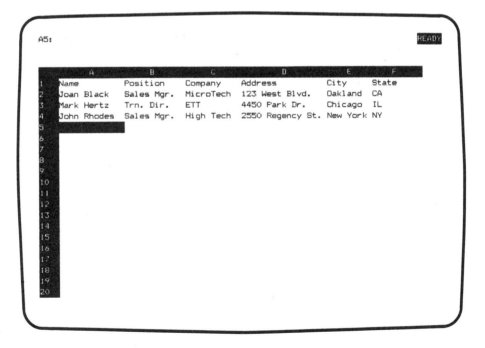

Fig. 3.2.

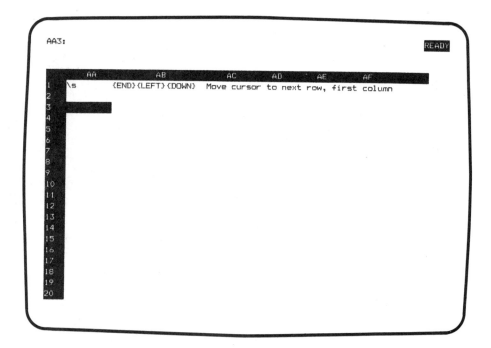

Fig. 3.3.

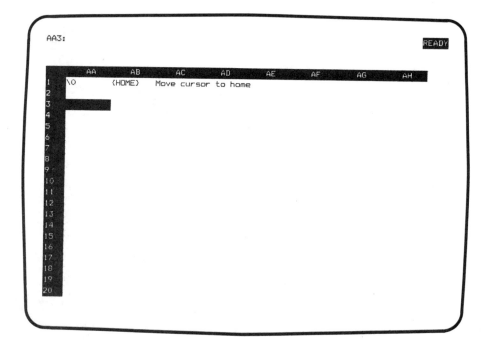

Fig. 3.4.

Or for the individual who, at the beginning of a worksheet session, likes to have the cursor located at the Home position, this macro will do the trick.

When a worksheet file is first loaded, the macro automatically moves the cursor to the Home position. You can also change the macro to jump to any location at the beginning of a worksheet session. Remember that the \0 is the macro name especially reserved for macros you want automatically loaded as soon as you have retrieved a file.

Macro for Entering Formulas

Besides using macros to jump the cursor across a worksheet, you can use a macro to speed up the entry of formulas. Suppose, for example, that you want to add the columns of numbers shown in figure 3.5.

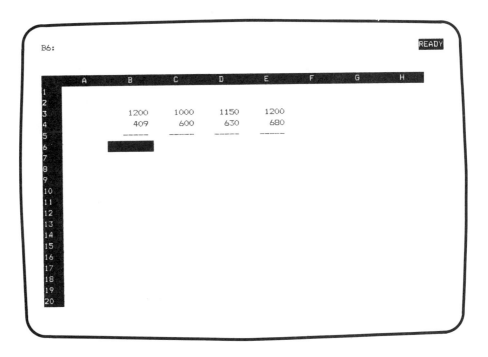

Fig. 3.5.

The pointing macro in figure 3.6 will enter automatically the formula for each column of numbers. To use this macro, you move the cursor to the cell where the formula should appear. You begin by placing the cursor in cell B6. Next, you press Altc, and the macro will enter the

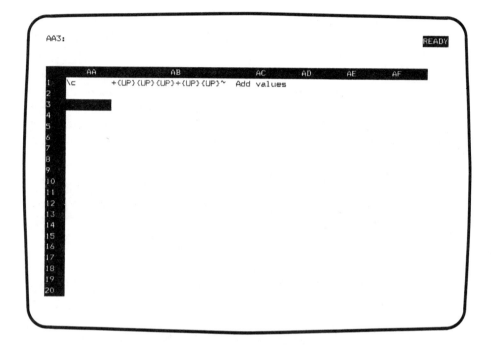

Fig. 3.6.

formula +B3+B4. To enter formulas for the other columns, you move the cursor to each appropriate cell and again invoke the macro.

The \c macro works with each formula individually. If, however, you want a macro that will continue to run, entering formulas for all four columns, you need to make the changes shown in the macro in figure 3.7.

This macro performs the same operation as that of the previous pointing macro. But after this macro has entered a formula into a cell, the cursor moves to the right, and the macro again begins to enter a formula into that cell. After the macro has entered formulas into the appropriate cells, you can stop the macro by pressing Ctrl Break.

The macro in figure 3.7 can also be easily adapted for entering formulas that subtract, multiply, or divide numbers. Changing the macro to perform any of these operations requires changing the first line of the macro. If, for example, you want the macro to subtract, you can make the changes shown in the macro in figure 3.8.

Fig. 3.7.

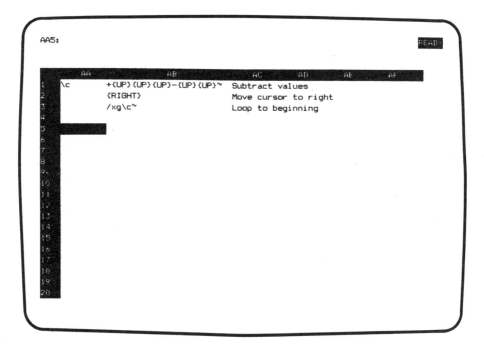

Fig. 3.8.

Macros for Entering Data

In addition to reducing the number of keystrokes required in an operation, 1-2-3 macros are particularly useful for entering, changing, and validating data in a worksheet. This section contains the following types of macros:

1. Macro for entering labels

2. Macro for creating headings

3. Numeric keypad macro

4. Enhancements for the numeric keypad macro

5. Numeric keypad and cursor-movement macros

6. Macro for changing labels to values

7. Macro for changing values to labels

8. Macro for validating numbers

9. Another validation macro

The first macro can be used for entering labels or other frequently used words or phrases. The second macro enters column headings into a worksheet. Next is a numeric keypad macro that simplifies use of the numeric keypad on IBM PCs and PC-compatible computers. This macro is also presented in versions that move the cursor, display prompts, format each number, or test each number for a condition you set.

The final three macros are helpful in changing or validating the data you enter into your worksheets. If, for example, you load numeric data that writes only a text file and you need to change the numeric data to values, a macro is available for this operation. If, however, you need to change values to labels, another macro will easily transform the values. The final macro in this section shows how to validate any number you have entered into a worksheet.

Macro for Entering Labels

This macro enters labels and other commonly used words or phrases into the worksheet. Suppose, for example, that the word *Sales* occurs a number of times in a given sheet. The word may sometimes occur by itself and other times be displayed with other words, as in the phrase "Sales expense." The macro in figure 3.9 will enter the word *Sales* into the current cell.

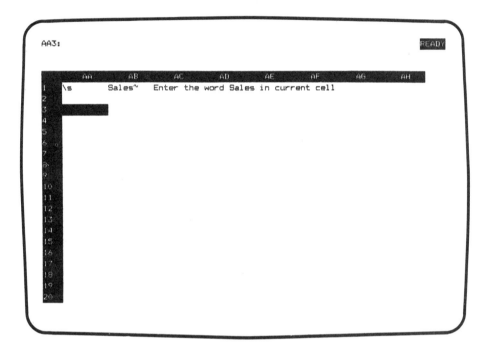

Fig. 3.9.

Notice that an extra space appears at the beginning of the macro, before the label prefix ('). When the macro is invoked, this space separates the word *Sales* from any other word in the cell. Suppose you want to enter the phrase "Sales expense" into cell A21. To use the macro, you position the cursor at cell A21, invoke the macro, and type the phrase at the keyboard. Finally, you press ENTER to close out the cell.

To enter the phrase "Monthly Sales (Regional)" into the cell, you type the word *Monthly*. Next, you invoke the macro. Then you type *(Regional)* and press ENTER to complete the macro.

The macro for entering labels will save time in setting up a large worksheet. You may want to create several "common word" macros like the one in figure 3.9 and use them to enter labels or other recurring text into your worksheets.

Macro for Creating Headings

The simple macro in figure 3.10 creates a row of column headings in the worksheet. Let's assume that you frequently make worksheets containing the twelve months as column headings. This macro will enter

75

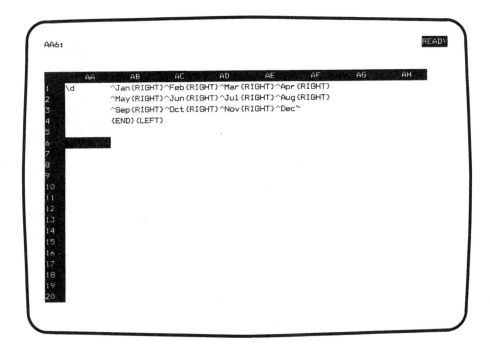

AA6:   READY

| | AA | AB | AC | AD | AE | AF | AG | AH |

1 \d   ^Jan{RIGHT}^Feb{RIGHT}^Mar{RIGHT}^Apr{RIGHT}
2   ^May{RIGHT}^Jun{RIGHT}^Jul{RIGHT}^Aug{RIGHT}
3   ^Sep{RIGHT}^Oct{RIGHT}^Nov{RIGHT}^Dec~
4   {END}{LEFT}

Fig. 3.10.

automatically the name of a month in each of twelve consecutive columns.

Essentially, the macro moves across a row and inserts the name of one month into each cell before moving on. Notice particularly that each label is preceded by the circumflex (^) for centering. To use the macro, you position the cursor at the cell for the first label, then press Altd. The macro will enter the month label in each column.

You can also create a macro for entering labels in consecutive rows. The macro in figure 3.11, for example, will enter automatically the labels for the Income Statement shown in figure 3.12.

Numeric Keypad Macro

This macro can help solve a common problem for owners of IBM PCs and PC-compatible computers. On the keyboard the numeric keypad is used for both entering numeric data and moving the cursor. Individuals who are accustomed to a ten-key adding machine may find that the keypad is awkward to use.

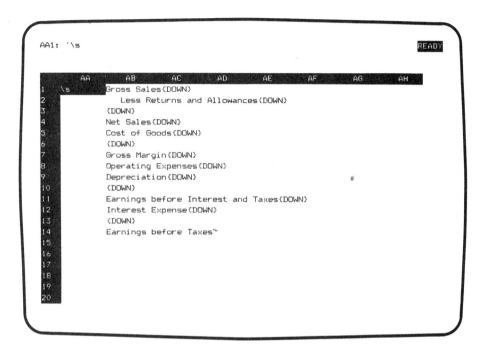

Fig. 3.11.

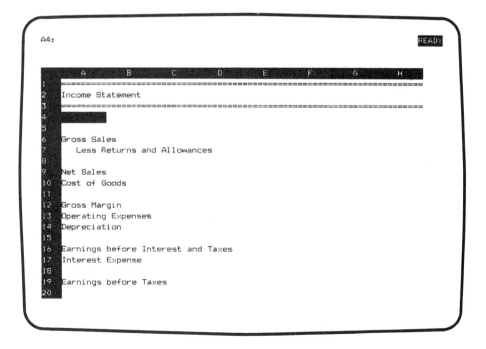

Fig. 3.12.

Let's consider a simple example of this problem. Suppose you want to use the keypad to enter the numbers shown in the worksheet in figure 3.13.

Without the aid of a macro, you would have to follow these steps to enter the numbers into the sheet:

{GOTO}B3	Position the cursor on cell B3
{NUM}	Convert keypad to numeric entry
123	Enter first number
{NUM}	Release Num Lock to convert keypad to cursor movement
{DOWN}	Move cursor down one cell
{NUM}	Convert keypad to numeric entry
234	Enter second number
{NUM}	Convert keypad to cursor movement
{DOWN}	Move cursor down one cell
{NUM}	Convert keypad to numeric entry
345	Enter last number
{NUM}	Convert keypad to cursor movement

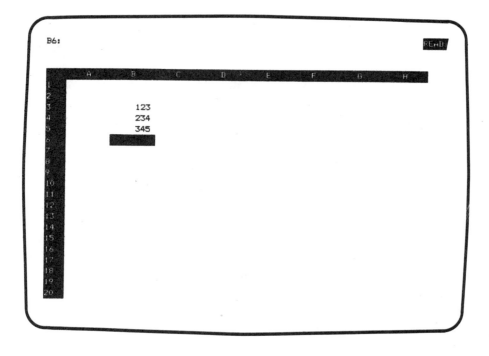

Fig. 3.13.

Obviously, using the numeric keypad can be a cumbersome process. The macro in figure 3.14, however, automatically moves the cursor as you use the numeric keypad. All you have to do is enter the data and press ENTER.

To use this macro, you press simultaneously the Alt key and the letter *k*, then enter the data. Afterward, you press ENTER, and the cursor moves down to the next cell. The macro will continue to operate until you press Ctrl Break. If you want to use the numeric keypad for moving the cursor, press the Num Lock key.

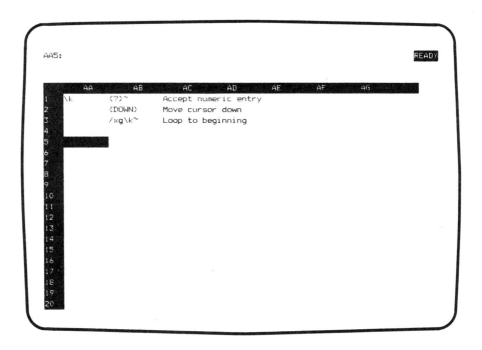

Fig. 3.14.

Enhancements for the Numeric Keypad Macro

The numeric keypad macro can be changed in several ways to include additional operations. For instance, you can change line 2 so that after each entry the cursor moves up, left, or right. (See figs. 3.15 and 3.16.) Most likely, you'll want to move the cursor down or to the right.

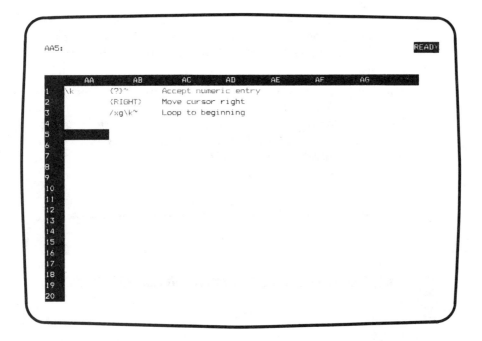

Fig. 3.15.

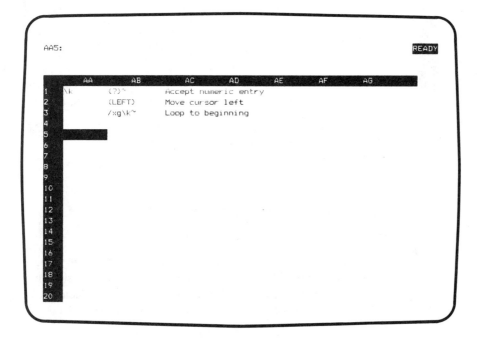

Fig. 3.16.

You can also modify the macro so that a prompt appears, asking you to enter a number. (See fig. 3.17.) To add the prompt, you simply substitute a /xn command in place of the {?} in the first line of the macro. When you invoke the macro, it will then prompt you for a number, as shown in figure 3.18. The number you enter will appear in the current cell, before the cursor jumps down to the next cell.

Another version of the macro in figure 3.17 lets you enter a number after the prompt and then moves the cursor to the cell where you want the number located. (See fig. 3.19.) To use this version of the macro, you must first assign the name TARGET to the cell where you initially entered your number after you invoked the macro. From the cell named TARGET, the macro copies the entry to the cell where you have moved the cursor.

If you use the numeric keypad macro for entering amounts in dollars and cents, another version, shown in figure 3.20, will automatically enter the decimal points. To use this macro, you simply press Altk, then press Num Lock. After you press Altk and Num Lock, the macro will wait for you to enter a number. After the number is entered, 1-2-3 switches to EDIT mode. In this mode, the cursor moves two digits to the left and places the decimal point there. Then the macro moves the cursor down one cell and loops back to begin again.

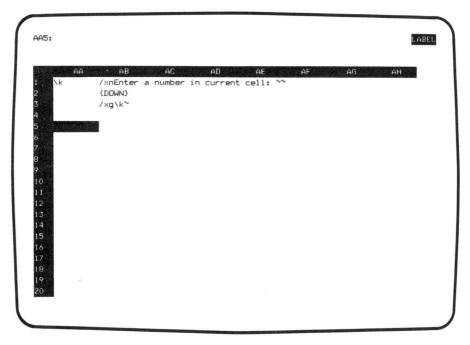

Fig. 3.17.

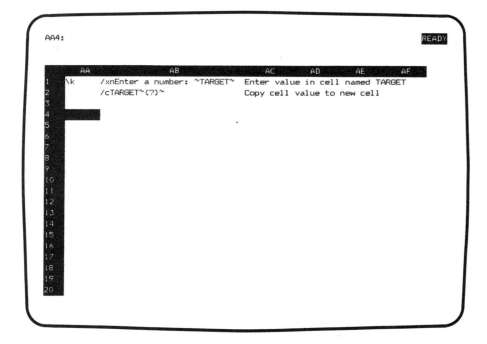

```
AA5:                                                      CMD EDIT
Enter a number in current cell:

          AA        AB        AC        AD        AE        AF        AG        AH
1    \k        /xnEnter a number in current cell:  ~~
2              {DOWN}
3              /xg\k~
4
5
6
7
8
9
10
11
12
13
14
15
16
17
18
19
20                                                            NUM
```

Fig. 3.18.

```
AA4:                                                      READY

          AA        AB                  AC        AD        AE        AF
1    \k    /xnEnter a number:  ~TARGET~   Enter value in cell named TARGET
2          /cTARGET~{?}~                  Copy cell value to new cell
3
4
5
6
7
8
9
10
11
12
13
14
15
16
17
18
19
20
```

Fig. 3.19.

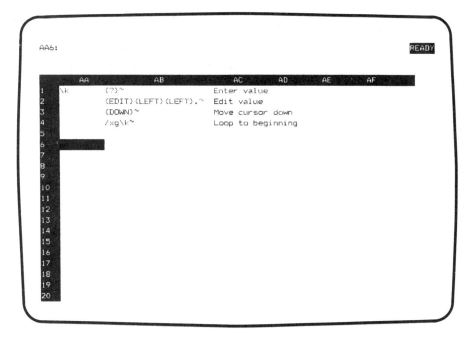

Fig. 3.20.

Figure 3.21 shows a version that enters decimal places. For instance, when you enter the digits 567, they are converted to 5.67 on the worksheet.

If you want numbers to be converted to values with three decimal places, you simply change the first line of the numeric keypad macro to

```
{?}{EDIT}/1000{CALC}~
```

You can also enhance the numeric keypad macro by having it test the numbers you are entering into each cell. Perhaps you want to test each number to make sure that it is less than 1,000,000. The macro in figure 3.22 will perform this test.

Numeric Keypad and
Cursor-Movement Macros

The basic numeric keypad macro will help you use the numeric keypad more efficiently. If, however, you need to enter long columns or many rows of data, you can speed up the process by combining this

Fig. 3.21.

Fig. 3.22.

basic macro with one of the cursor-movement macros shown later in figures 3.25 and 3.26.

Let's assume that you are entering the numbers in the worksheets shown in figures 3.23 and 3.24. For either worksheet, you begin by invoking the numeric keypad macro. If you are entering numbers down a column, as in figure 3.23, this macro will move the cursor down. If you are entering numbers across rows, as in figure 3.24, the same macro will move the cursor to the right.

After entering the last number in a column or row, you press Ctrl Break to quit the numeric keypad macro. Next, you use the appropriate cursor-movement macro to jump the cursor to the beginning of a new column or row. To jump the cursor after you enter data in cell C20 (see fig. 3.23), you use the macro shown in figure 3.25. To jump the cursor after you enter data in cell H4 (see fig. 3.24), you use the macro shown in figure 3.26. Then after the cursor has moved to the beginning of a new cell, you press Ctrl Break to stop the cursor-movement macro. To repeat the process, you again invoke the numeric keypad macro.

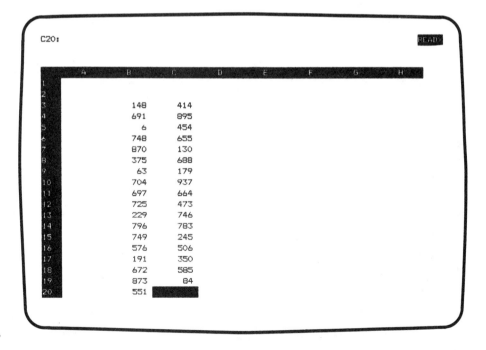

Fig. 3.23.

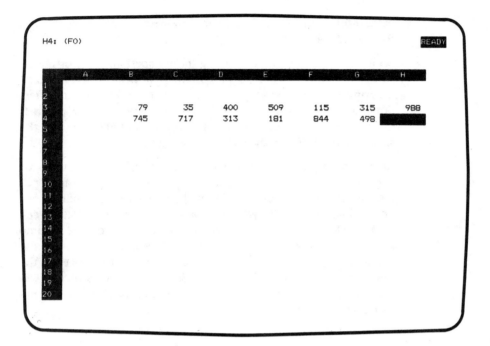

Fig. 3.24.

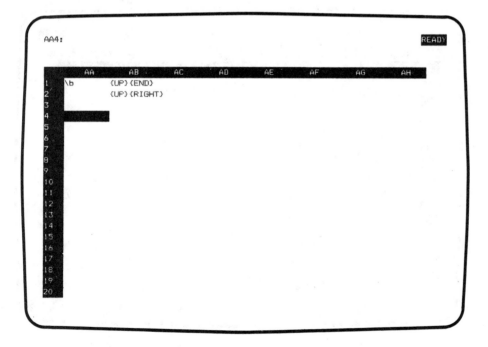

Fig. 3.25.

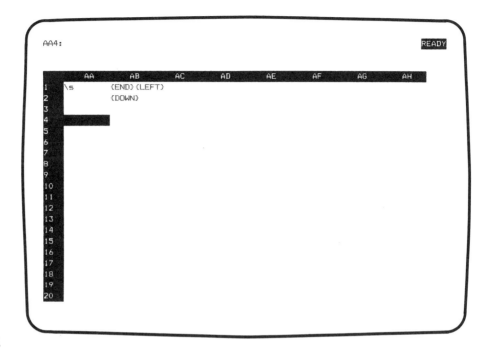

Fig. 3.26.

Macro for Changing Labels to Values

If you use 1-2-3 to load numeric data from another program, such as a word-processing program that writes only a text file, the numbers are imported into 1-2-3 as labels. To convert these labels into values, you must edit each cell by deleting the label prefix, thus turning the label into a number. This process can be fairly tedious if you have much data to convert. The macro in figure 3.27, however, will transform a whole row or column of numbers into values.

The labels-to-values macro converts data by moving from left to right. To invoke the macro, you place the cursor in the first cell in the row. You must also enter the @NA function into the cell immediately to the right of the last cell you want transformed. @NA enables you to end the macro loop. When you press Altn, the macro proceeds through the whole row of numbers and transforms each cell, thus converting labels to values.

In addition to assigning a name to the macro, you must remember to assign the range name END to line 7 of the macro (cell AB7 in fig. 3.27). If you want the macro to transform cells by moving down a col-

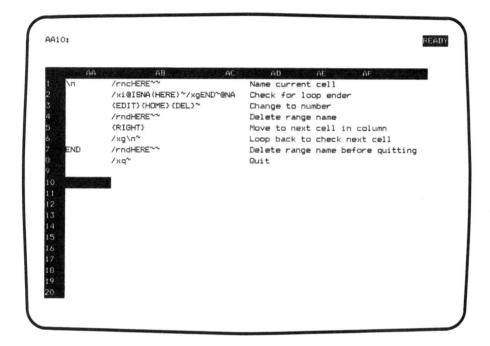

AA10:   READY

	AA	AB	AC	AD	AE	AF
1	\n	/rncHERE~~		Name current cell		
2		/xi@ISNA(HERE)~/xgEND~@NA		Check for loop ender		
3		{EDIT}{HOME}{DEL}~		Change to number		
4		/rndHERE~~		Delete range name		
5		{RIGHT}		Move to next cell in column		
6		/xg\n~		Loop back to check next cell		
7	END	/rndHERE~~		Delete range name before quitting		
8		/xq~		Quit		

Fig. 3.27.

umn, you simply edit line 5 by changing {RIGHT} to {DOWN}, as shown in figure 3.28.

Macro for Changing Values to Labels

If you want to change values to labels, you can easily make a macro to perform this operation. The macro will be especially valuable when you have used the /Data Fill command to enter as values a series of data base field names. The macro in figure 3.29 will change the entries from values to labels.

Like the macro for changing labels to values, this macro requires that you begin by placing the cursor on the first cell in the row. The macro also requires that the function @NA be entered in the cell immediately to the right of the last cell you want transformed. You must assign the range name ENDL to line 7 in the macro. And in line 5, you must change {RIGHT} to {DOWN}. The macro will then convert the numbers in a column to labels by moving down each cell.

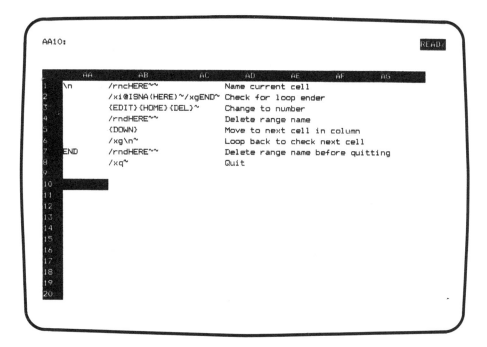

Fig. 3.28.

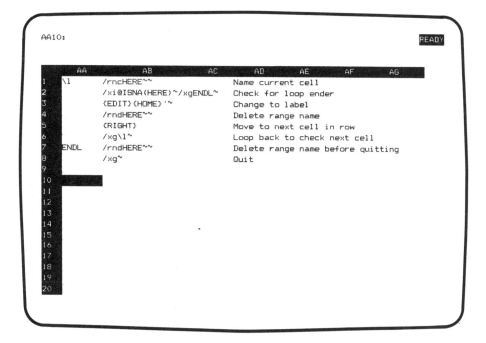

Fig. 3.29.

Macro for Validating Numbers

This macro tests whether a numeric entry satisfies a condition you have provided in the macro. Suppose you want to confirm that the numbers you have entered are less than 100. The macro in figure 3.30 will perform the test.

You will most likely want to use this macro as part of another one, such as the numeric keypad macro. See again "Enhancements for the Numeric Keypad Macro" for a combination of these two macros.

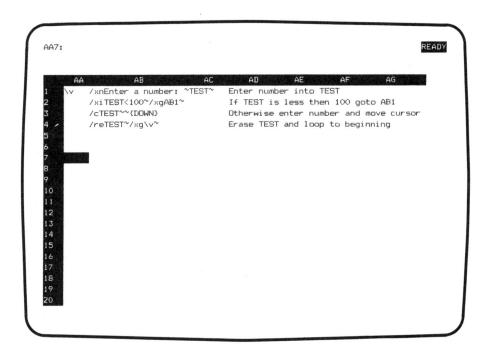

Fig. 3.30.

Another Validation Macro

Figure 3.31 shows another macro for testing the numeric data entered into your worksheet. This validation macro can be used to edit or validate data entered under macro control.

Here's how this powerful and flexible macro works. First, the macro goes to a cell you have designated for inputting the conditional value. In figure 3.31 this cell is D29. The second line provides the condition

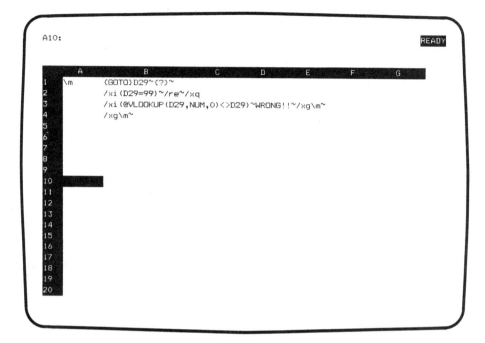

```
A10:                                                           READY

      A          B          C          D          E       F       G
1  \m        {GOTO}D29~{?}~
2            /xi(D29=99)~/re~/xq
3            /xi(@VLOOKUP(D29,NUM,0)<>D29)~WRONG!!~/xg\m~
4            /xg\m~
5
6
7
8
9
10
11
12
13
14
15
16
17
18
19
20
```

Fig. 3.31.

for quitting execution of the macro. This line says, "If the value equals the designated value (99 in the macro), then erase the cell contents in D29 and quit." The macro then uses the @VLOOKUP function. The *x* value of the @VLOOKUP (with an offset of 0), is the actual value being input, which is compared to the values in the range NUM.

Although this validation macro is simple to use, it is extremely fast. And the macro is reliable on a worksheet containing as many as two hundred items.

Date Entry Macros

Entering dates into a worksheet can become tiresome, especially when you are creating worksheets for managing cash flow or your checkbook. The first macro in this section automates the process of entering dates. The second macro lets you place a date in a worksheet and retains the date in the sheet when you save it.

Macro for Entering Dates

This macro can be used whenever you need to enter a series of random dates into a column. Suppose you are entering dates into a checkbook-manager spreadsheet, as shown in figure 3.32.

The macro in figure 3.33 lets you enter a series of dates into a column without your having to enter the @DATE function, move the cursor down, or format and adjust the width of the cells.

After you invoke the macro by pressing Altz, the macro pauses for you to enter the year, month, and day. Next, you press ENTER, and the macro continues to format the cell and adjust its width. Finally, the cursor moves down the column, and you begin again by entering the next date.

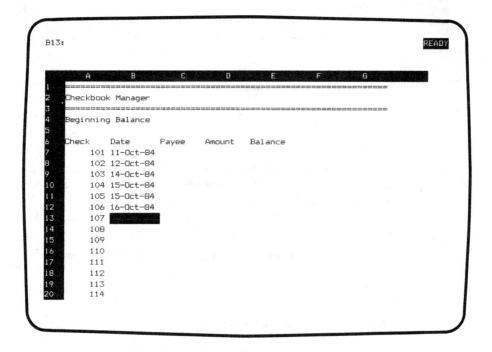

Fig. 3.32.

Macro for Dating the Worksheet

A variation of the date macro automatically enters the current date into your worksheet. This macro solves the problem of using the @TODAY function to date worksheets. Typically, if you use @TODAY

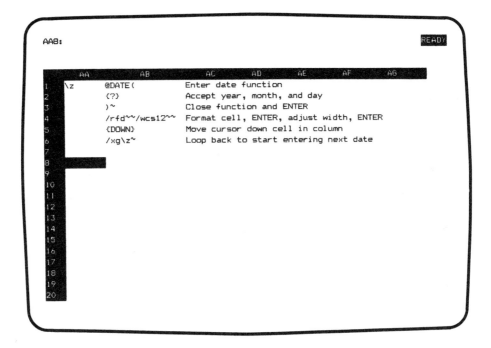

```
AA8:                                                                  READY

       AA          AB          AC       AD       AE       AF       AG
1    \z        @DATE(         Enter date function
2              {?}            Accept year, month, and day
3              )~             Close function and ENTER
4              /rfd~~/wcs12~~ Format cell, ENTER, adjust width, ENTER
5              {DOWN}         Move cursor down cell in column
6              /xg\z~         Loop back to start entering next date
7
8
9
10
11
12
13
14
15
16
17
18
19
20
```

Fig. 3.33.

for dating a worksheet, the date will be changed when, after a save, you reload the worksheet into memory. 1-2-3 automatically recalculates, changing the date before you view it.

The macro in figure 3.34 provides a solution to the problem. This macro automatically dates the worksheet, thus ensuring that the current date will remain in the sheet.

This date macro assumes that the range name DATE (see line 1 of the macro) has been assigned to a single cell somewhere in the sheet. The macro goes to the range with the name DATE and there inserts the value of @TODAY. Line 3 contains the formula-to-value conversion. This line converts the contents of the DATE cell (derived from the @TODAY function) to the actual numeric value of the @TODAY function. The conversion is what keeps the date from being automatically changed the next time the sheet is loaded.

The cell DATE can be formatted in any way you choose; the macro in figure 3.34 uses day-month-year format. If you want to use one of the other date formats, you can edit line 4 (cell B4) by deleting a tilde and adding the {RIGHT} cursor-movement command. (See the examples in fig. 3.35.)

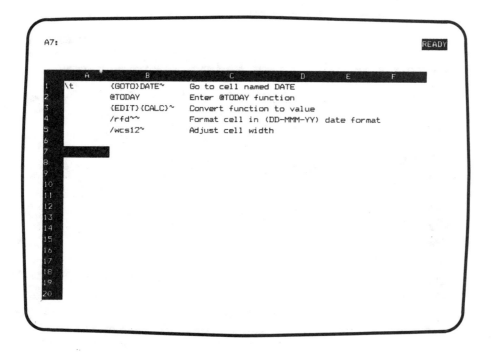

```
A7:                                                              READY

        A           B                C             D        E         F
1    \t     {GOTO}DATE~       Go to cell named DATE
2           @TODAY            Enter @TODAY function
3           {EDIT}{CALC}~     Convert function to value
4           /rfd~~            Format cell in (DD-MMM-YY) date format
5           /wcs12~           Adjust cell width
6
7
8
9
10
11
12
13
14
15
16
17
18
19
20
```

Fig. 3.34.

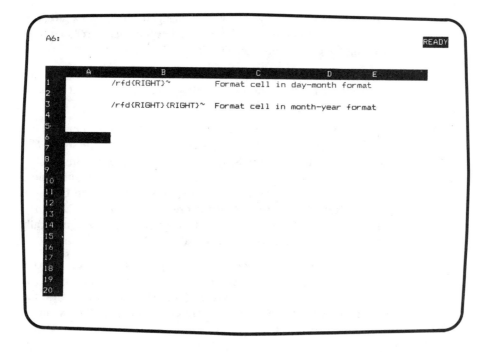

```
A6:                                                              READY

        A           B                C             D        E
1           /rfd{RIGHT}~           Format cell in day-month format
2
3           /rfd{RIGHT}{RIGHT}~   Format cell in month-year format
4
5
6
7
8
9
10
11
12
13
14
15
16
17
18
19
20
```

Fig. 3.35.

Another variation of the date entry macro provides a further convenience. Although the macro in figure 3.34 may work well to ensure that your worksheets are dated correctly, the cursor does not return to the original location where you invoked the macro. The version in figure 3.36 dates the worksheet and leaves the cursor in its original position.

This macro uses the /**Data F**ill command for entering the value of the @TODAY function into the cell named DATE. Notice that /**Data F**ill enters into the cell the value of the function and not the function itself, thus eliminating the need for the {EDIT}{CALC} macro. /**Data F**ill uses the value of the @TODAY function as the start value. The last two tildes after @TODAY select the defaults for the other /**Data F**ill options: **Step** and **Stop**.

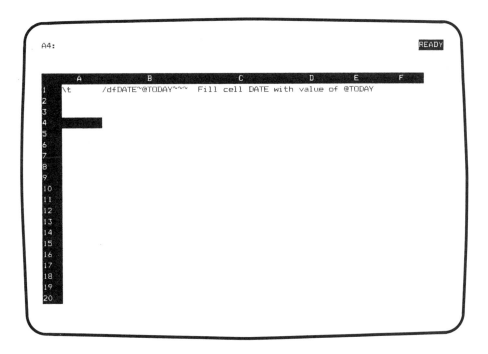

Fig. 3.36.

Macros for Changing the Worksheet

When you are creating and updating 1-2-3 worksheets, the macros presented thus far are useful for reducing the number of keystrokes needed to move the cursor around a worksheet and for entering labels, values, and dates. This section contains macros for many formatting and "cutting and pasting" operations that can be performed on the data entered in your worksheets. Macros for formatting, changing data, and changing the worksheet display include the following:

1. Format macros

2. Macro for converting decimals to fractions

3. Macro for changing zeros to dashes

4. Indent macro

5. Label justification macro

6. Macro for using /Worksheet Insert or Delete with /Worksheet Protection

7. Macro for transposing rows and columns

8. /Worksheet Titles macro

9. Macro for creating windows

Format Macros

A simple but handy macro to use alone or with other macros is the range format macro. Figure 3.37 contains several such macros. All of them reduce keystrokes when your worksheet has many columns of values appearing in three or more formats, such as Currency, General, and Percent. With these macros and variations of them, you can easily format a range of numbers by pressing simultaneously the Alt key with the key for the macro name, and then entering the range.

Macro for Converting Decimals to Fractions

If you create reports containing numbers that should be represented as integers with fractions, the macro presented here will convert decimals into fractions. The macro works by converting the original value into a label displayed as an integer and fraction. Once the number is converted, it cannot be processed as a value. This macro is useful for graphs, tables, or text that should contain fractions.

The macro in figure 3.38 converts decimal fractions that are exactly divisible by 16. Such a macro can be extended or simplified to suit par-

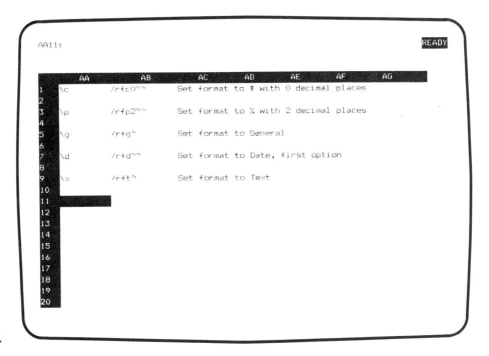

AA11:   READY

	AA	AB	AC	AD	AE	AF	AG
1	\c	/rfc0~~	Set format to $ with 0 decimal places				
2							
3	\p	/rfp2~~	Set format to % with 2 decimal places				
4							
5	\g	/rfg~	Set format to General				
6							
7	\d	/rfd~~	Set format to Date, first option				
8							
9	\x	/rft~	Set format to Text				
10							
11							
12							
13							
14							
15							
16							
17							
18							
19							
20							

Fig. 3.37.

ticular needs, of course. For example, fractions up to 64ths can be accommodated, or the limit can be set at 8ths.

The time needed to run the program is determined by the number of /xi statements to be read. The macro shown here is relatively fast when creating fractions in 16ths. Twenty numbers can be processed in approximately 50 seconds by this particular macro.

The macro contains four important range names. Including the macro name itself, the range names and cells are the following:

\C	AB1
C	AB2
F	AB7
P	AB25
Q	AB29

To run the macro, you position the cursor at the cell where the first number to be changed is located, then press Altc. Once the macro begins executing, the first line (line 1 in fig. 3.38) assigns the name H to the current cell, and the second line calls the principal subroutine F. This subroutine is a series of /xi statements that test the decimal por-

97

```
AA1:  '\c                                                                    READY

        AA            Hb              AC        AD        AE        AF
1   \c      /rncH~{BS}~              Name the current cell H
2   C       /xcF~                    Call subroutine F
3           /rncH~{BS}~              Name the current cell H
4           /xiH<>0~/xgC~            If the current cell is not blank
5           /xq~                          call subroutine C, else quit
6
7   F       /xi@MOD(H,1)=0~/xcP~{EDIT} %~/xcQ~/xr
8           /xi@MOD(H,1)=.0625~/xcP~{EDIT} 1/16%~/xcQ~/xr
9           /xi@MOD(H,1)=.125~/xcP~{EDIT} 1/8%~/xcQ~/xr
10          /xi@MOD(H,1)=.1875~/xcP~{EDIT} 3/16%~/xcQ~/xr
11          /xi@MOD(H,1)=.25~/xcP~{EDIT} 1/4%~/xcQ~/xr
12          /xi@MOD(H,1)=.3125~/xcP~{EDIT} 5/16%~/xcQ~/xr
13          /xi@MOD(H,1)=.375~/xcP~{EDIT} 3/8%~/xcQ~/xr
14          /xi@MOD(H,1)=.4375~/xcP~{EDIT} 7/16%~/xcQ~/xr
15          /xi@MOD(H,1)=.5~/xcP~{EDIT} 1/2%~/xcQ~/xr
16          /xi@MOD(H,1)=.5625~/xcP~{EDIT} 9/16%~/xcQ~/xr
17          /xi@MOD(H,1)=.625~/xcP~{EDIT} 5/8%~/xcQ~/xr
18          /xi@MOD(H,1)=.6875~/xcP~{EDIT} 11/16%~/xcQ~/xr
19          /xi@MOD(H,1)=.75~/xcP~{EDIT} 3/4%~/xcQ~/xr
20          /xi@MOD(H,1)=.8125~/xcP~{EDIT} 13/16%~/xcQ~/xr
21          /xi@MOD(H,1)=.875~/xcP~{EDIT} 7/8%~/xcQ~/xr
22          /xi@MOD(H,1)=.9375~/xcP~{EDIT} 15/16%~/xcQ~/xr
23          /xnNot an even 1/16th. Re-input & "ENTER": ^H~/xcC~
24
25  P       {RIGHT}@INT(H)~          Create a label of
26          {EDIT}{CALC}{HOME}^        the integer portion
27          {END}~/xr                  of the target cell
28
29  Q       /m~{LEFT}~              Move result back to column
30          {LEFT}{DOWN}~/xr        Reposition cursor
31
32
33
34
35
36
37
38
39
40
```

Fig. 3.38.

tion of the input and supply the fractional equivalent. Line 3 of the main part of the macro resets range H to the next cell in the column. In subroutine F, repetitive parts of each /xi command are placed in separate nested subroutines, for housekeeping purposes. Next, subroutine P creates a label from the integer portion of the value in the target cell. Subroutine Q then moves the cell pointer to the next value in the range of cells to be converted.

If a decimal does not match any of the /xi tests in subroutine F, the /xn command in line 30 invokes a message that calls for a new input (in this case, one that is divisible by 16) at the cell pointer location.

Two helpful programming tips are incorporated in this macro. First, limiting range names to a single letter reduces processing time because each letter represents a single step in program execution. And second, when you are resetting a single-cell range (as in line 1 of fig. 3.38), instead of using the **/R**ange **N**ame **D**elete command, you can simply place the cursor on the new cell where you want the range to be located and use **/R**ange **N**ame **C**reate range-name~{BS}~. If you apply these techniques in your macros, you will save substantial execution time.

When you run the macro for converting decimals to fractions, you should keep two points in mind. First, because the column to the right of the column being converted is erased, any information in the erased column will be lost. Before you run the macro, be certain to check the column on the right. Second, decimal fractions that are not even 16ths will not be accepted and will therefore remain in their current form.

Macro for Changing Zeros to Dashes

If you need to show a dash in place of a zero, particularly for easy identification of zero items in your worksheets, you can make a macro that lets you change quickly all zero entries in a column to dashes. (See fig. 3.39.)

Here's how this macro works. First, you position the cursor at the top of the column of numbers containing the zeros to be changed. Then you invoke the macro by pressing Alta. The first line of the macro creates a range named ZTEST in the current cell, where the cursor is positioned. Line 2 tests to determine whether ZTEST equals 0. If ZTEST equals 0, a label (-) is entered into that cell. The third line moves the cell pointer down to the next cell. Finally, line 4 loops back to begin the process again. The macro will continue to run until you press Ctrl Break to stop the processing.

If you want the macro to operate on a row of numbers instead of a column, you must change the {DOWN} command in line 3 to {RIGHT}. Be careful when you use the macro in a row or column containing labels. When operating on a cell that contains a label, the macro will convert the label into a dash.

Indent Macro

If you create spreadsheets containing labels listed along the left column and indented, the macro in figure 3.41 will indent every label for you. Suppose, for example, that you have created a column of row

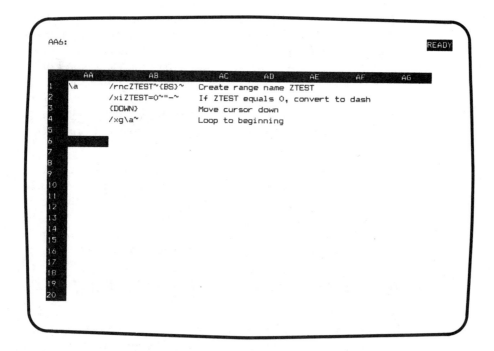

```
AA6:                                                               READY

      AA          AB              AC      AD      AE      AF      AG
 1  \a      /rncZTEST~{BS}~    Create range name ZTEST
 2          /xiZTEST=0~"-~     If ZTEST equals 0, convert to dash
 3          {DOWN}             Move cursor down
 4          /xg\a~             Loop to beginning
 5
 6
 7
 8
 9
10
11
12
13
14
15
16
17
18
19
20
```

Fig. 3.39.

headings like those shown in figure 3.40. After entering the headings, you then decide to indent all subheadings underneath the four main headings of INDICATORS OF SOLVENCY, INDICATORS OF LIQUID-ITY, FUNDS MANAGEMENT RATIO, and PROFITABILITY RATIOS. To indent each heading without the aid of a macro, you would press the {EDIT} key and add three spaces at the beginning of each heading. Indenting a large number of headings can be very tedious, but the task can be accomplished easily if you use the macro shown in figure 3.41.

When you make the macro, don't forget to add the appropriate number of spaces in the first line. In this macro, three spaces have been added. If you want the macro to indent only one space, you can change the first line of the macro by deleting extra spaces between the closing brace in {RIGHT} and the tilde (~). In this case, the first line will appear as

```
{EDIT}{HOME}{RIGHT} ~
```

To use the macro, you place the cursor on the first heading to be indented; press Alti; and, after the last heading in the list has been indented, press Ctrl Break to stop the macro.

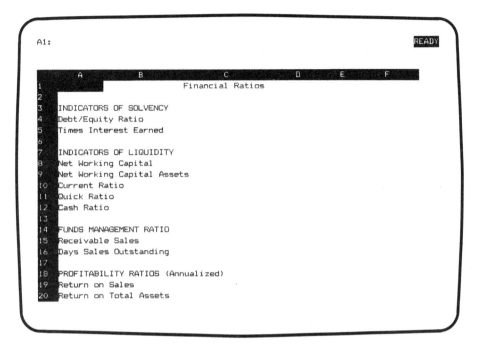

Fig. 3.40.

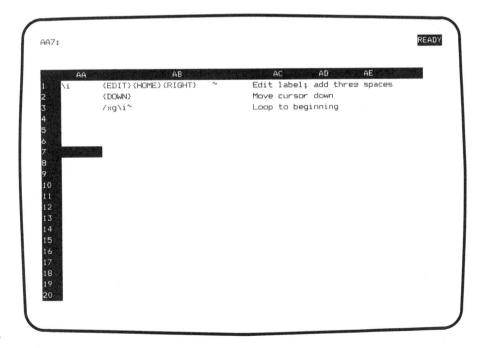

Fig. 3.41.

Once the macro is invoked, the cursor will start skipping down the column, and each label will be indented one space. If you analyze the macro, you will see that it simply "macroizes" the edit process previously mentioned. Line 2 of the macro jumps the cursor down one row. The statement in line 3 tells the macro to continue processing at the cell named \i, which is the name of the macro. Figure 3.42 shows the spreadsheet after the macro has run.

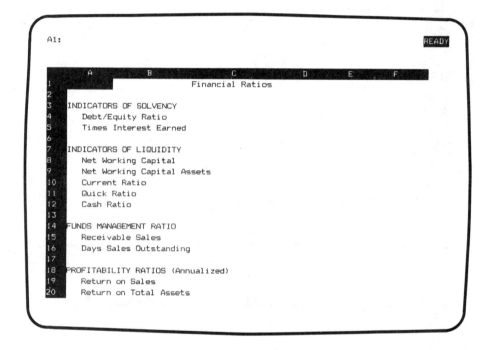

Fig. 3.42.

Label Justification Macro

If you want a macro that will center or right-justify labels entered as row headings, you just edit the first line of the indent macro. For centering labels, you change the first line to

```
{EDIT}{HOME}^
```

Or for right-justifying labels, you change the first line to

```
{EDIT}{HOME}"
```

Suppose you want a macro that will center column headings which have been entered left-justified, as those shown in figure 3.43. For this

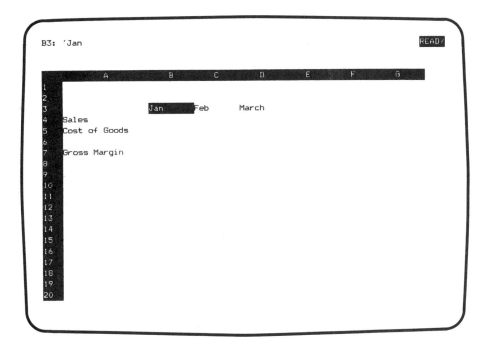

B3: 'Jan   READY

| | A | B | C | D | E | F | G |

Jan   Feb   March

Sales
Cost of Goods

Gross Margin

Fig. 3.43.

task, you can use the macro in figure 3.44. To run this macro, you move the cursor to cell B3, invoke the macro, and then press Ctrl Break when you want the macro to stop.

Macro for Using /Worksheet Insert or Delete with /Worksheet Protection

If you use the /Worksheet Global Protection command to protect your worksheet, you will have a problem in using /Worksheet Insert or /Worksheet Delete. Whenever protection is enabled in the worksheet, you'll get a "Protected cell" message if you try to use the Insert or Delete commands. The macros in figures 3.45 and 3.46, however, allow you to use these two commands whenever the worksheet is protected. As soon as you invoke either macro, protection is disabled. After the insert or delete operation is completed, protection is enabled once again.

The delete macro in figure 3.45 contains a main menu macro and three submacros. When you press Altd, you invoke the start-up macro, which displays a menu for confirming or rejecting the delete proce-

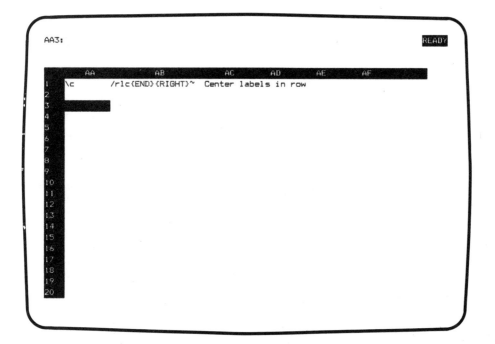

Fig. 3.44.

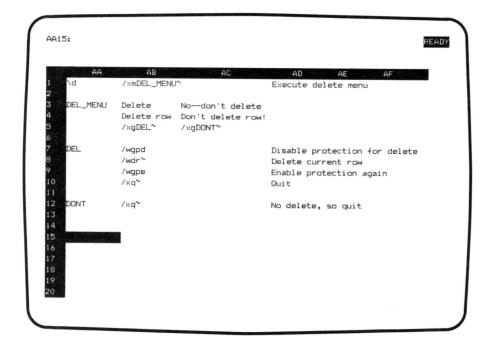

Fig. 3.45.

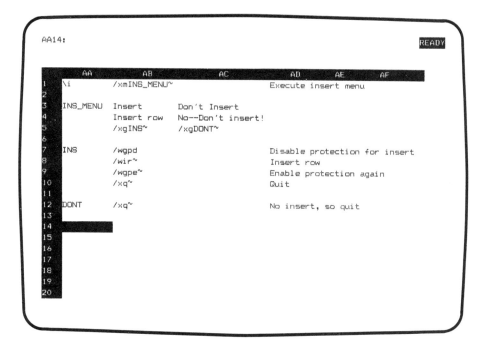

Fig. 3.46.

dure. When you select **Delete** from the menu, the delete macro disables protection, deletes the row, and then turns protection back on. If you select **No**, the macro stops.

Figure 3.45 contains a macro for deleting rows. But if you want a macro for deleting columns, you just change the second line of the delete macro to /wdc~.

The macro for inserting columns or rows is similar to the delete macro except that the insert macro has some changes. (See fig. 3.46.) To modify the insert macro so that it will insert columns, you just change the second line to /wic~.

As mentioned in Chapter 2, operations that delete or insert rows should be used with care because such operations may affect your macro. If you have stored your macro directly to the right or left of the worksheet where the row is inserted or deleted, the insert or delete operation will change the macro, and it will no longer run.

Macro for Transposing Rows and Columns

One problem in 1-2-3 is that columns and rows cannot be transposed. The macro in this section, however, overcomes this limitation. Using 1-2-3's window feature, one version of the macro will change rows to columns, and the other version will change columns to rows. (Whether or not the macro works for you may depend on your hardware.)

Let's consider the following example. Suppose you have created a template to analyze a real estate limited partnership. Typically, this kind of analysis is laid out in rows like that in figure 3.47.

Individual-investor analysis of the same project, however, is usually arranged in columns, as in figure 3.48.

The formulas for both worksheets are simple, but if you want to change rows to columns, you cannot automate the creation of formulas. To make formulas for the transposed cells, you have to enter the formulas manually. Although Symphony has a **Range Transpose** command, in 1-2-3 the best solution to the problem of transposing rows and columns is to use the macro shown in figure 3.49.

To change columns into rows, you should follow these steps. First, split the screen by using the /**W**orksheet **W**indow command. (You can select either **H**orizontal or **V**ertical from this command.) Second, in window #1, place the cursor one cell above the column of numbers to be transposed and then press the {WINDOW} key to move the cursor to window #2. Third, place the cursor on the first cell where you want a transposed number to appear. Finally, invoke the macro by pressing Altf.

To turn columns into rows, you just reverse the words {DOWN} and {RIGHT}, as in

    +{WINDOW}{RIGHT}~{DOWN}

To transpose a formula, you insert it before the first tilde, as in

    +{WINDOW}/60*107^4~

These macros work on COMPAQ equipment and IBM PCs. The macros may not work on other equipment, however. Try using the macros, and if they don't work on your machine, then try the macro in figure 3.50. This version is only a bit more complicated than the basic macro for transposing rows into columns.

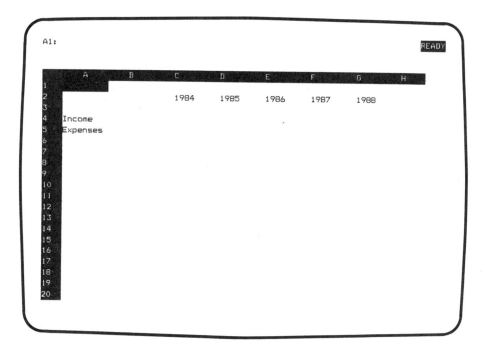

Fig. 3.47.

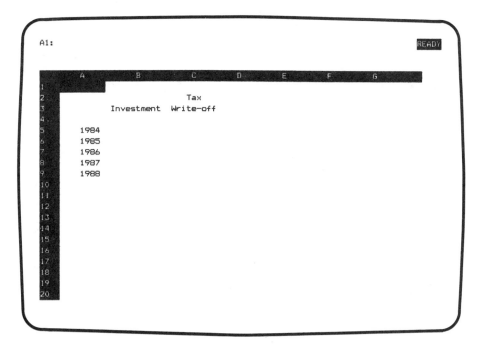

Fig. 3.48.

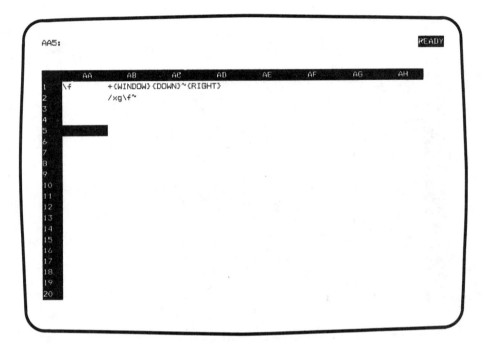

Fig. 3.49.

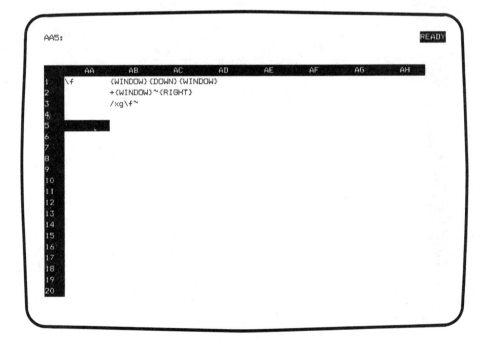

Fig. 3.50.

To simplify the steps already discussed, you can build an elaborate macro that creates the windows, initially places the cursor in the right spot, and uses a counter to stop automatically. But because such a macro is more appropriate as a tool for template builders, you will probably want to keep your macro simple and use Ctrl Break to stop the loop after you have transposed rows or columns.

/Worksheet Titles Macro

1-2-3's /Worksheet Titles command lets you freeze part of your worksheet so that it remains on screen as you move vertically or horizontally throughout the sheet. This command is especially helpful when you have a large worksheet and want to keep column or row headings in view while you move to other parts of the sheet. But if you frequently must turn the /Worksheet Titles setting on and off, the operation can become tiresome. The macro in figure 3.51 lets you create a toggle switch for turning /Worksheet Titles Horizontal on and off whenever you want.

If you want the macro to create titles vertically instead of horizontally, you simply change the last character of the third line in both the \s and UNFRZ macros from *h* to *v*, as shown in figure 3.52.

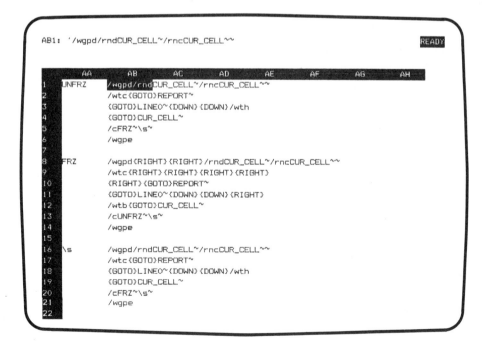

Fig. 3.51.

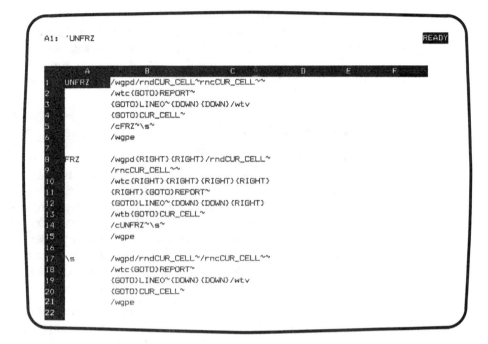

Fig. 3.52.

When you invoke the \s macro, as shown in figure 3.52, the following operations will occur:

1. The macro disables worksheet protection, deletes the existing range name CUR_CELL, and creates the range name CUR_CELL where the cursor is presently positioned.

2. The macro clears the existing /Worksheet Titles setting and moves the cursor to the beginning of the report.

3. The cursor moves to the cell where the vertical or horizontal division should be made and selects /Worksheet Titles Horizontal.

4. The cursor moves to the cell named CUR_CELL.

5. At \s the macro copies either the FRZ or the UNFRZ macro.

6. The macro enables worksheet protection.

As you can see from this macro, a number of range names working in both the macro and the worksheet must be set. These range names include the following:

\s	The macro name
UNFRZ	Range name for the macro that unfreezes titles
FRZ	Range name for the macro that freezes titles
CUR_CELL	Range name for the current cell
REPORT	Range name indicating the beginning of the report
LINE0	Range name marking the position for horizontal titles

Macro for Creating Windows

One of the advantages of Lotus' Symphony is its window capability. Being able to create windows in Symphony allows you to divide your worksheet into a number of areas and to display multiple windows on screen at the same time, or to toggle back and forth easily between windows. If, for example, your worksheet has two spreadsheets, you can create a window for each spreadsheet and have both of them on screen, or you can compare data by toggling back and forth between full-screen windows. Another advantage to using windows is that you can enter different settings in each window without interfering with those in any other window.

With the macro shown in figure 3.53, you can create in 1-2-3 a limited window capability that allows you to toggle back and forth between different areas of the same worksheet. This macro uses the /xm command, which displays on screen the selected part of the spreadsheet.

Although the macro sets border titles for each part of the worksheet, you must create a range name for the upper corner of each window. For example, the first window in the macro in figure 3.53 is named REVENUES. You should name the topmost cell in the title column, which is also the leftmost cell in the title row. Depending on the number of title rows and columns, you may have to change the number of {DOWN} and {RIGHT} commands in line 5 of the macro. This particular macro has been set for two title rows and one title column.

Of course, you can adjust the macro to suit your needs. For instance, you can add a line to change format or column widths. If you do add macro lines for one window, remember to add similar lines for the other windows so that their settings will be restored.

Macros for Worksheet Calculation

As you become experienced in using 1-2-3 macros, you'll soon discover specific applications to help you with your financial analysis

AA10:

Fig. 3.53.

needs. The following macros can simplify various kinds of worksheet calculation tasks:

1. Macro for rounding formula results

2. Accumulator macro

3. Macro for consolidating worksheets

4. Variations of the consolidation macro

5. Macro for using text with @IF

These macros range from those that generally can be used in many kinds of worksheets to macros that are particularly useful for calculating totals in balance sheets, product plans, and other types of forecasts. You'll find that many of the macros can be easily adapted to your own spreadsheets.

Macro for Rounding Formula Results

In a worksheet containing amounts that are the results of formulas, some rounding errors are likely to appear in the subtotals and totals.

Using @ROUND will solve the problem although inserting the function for every number can be time-consuming. The macro in figure 3.54 will automatically round amounts for you. This particular version assumes a rounding factor of no decimals, but you can change the macro to round to whatever decimal place you want.

You can also enhance the macro to operate on a whole range of values, by simply adding the appropriate cursor-movement commands and the /xg command so that the macro begins again with every new value. If, for example, you want to round a series of numbers in consecutive rows, you can modify the macro, as shown in figure 3.55.

After placing the cursor on the formula in the first cell to the left, you press Altr to invoke the macro. The macro will operate on all values in consecutive rows to the right, until you press Ctrl Break to stop the macro.

Accumulator Macro

One of the most popular macros for 1-2-3 users is the accumulator macro, which solves the problem of how to compute year-to-date totals efficiently. The worksheet in figure 3.56 shows a simple example of this problem. Column A holds the values for the current month, and column B shows the year-to-date amounts. If you want to add the current month data to the current year-to-date balance and then store the result (the new year-to-date amount) in column B, 1-2-3 provides no expedient way to accomplish this task. It can be done, however, with the accumulator macro.

At first, you may think that the columns can be added without the use of a macro. One solution is to put a formula such as

    B3: B3+A3

into each cell in column B. To perform the consolidation, you then just enter the current period figures and {CALC} the worksheet.

Although this circular reference approach may initially seem to work, it has one glaring weakness. Each time you {CALC} the worksheet, the formulas in column B are recomputed—even if you don't want them to be. If you accidentally press {CALC} a second time, the current figures will again be added to the year-to-date totals, thus resulting in a double count.

Several approaches may be used to solve the problem of consolidating data. But one of the best solutions is to use the accumulator macro shown in figure 3.57.

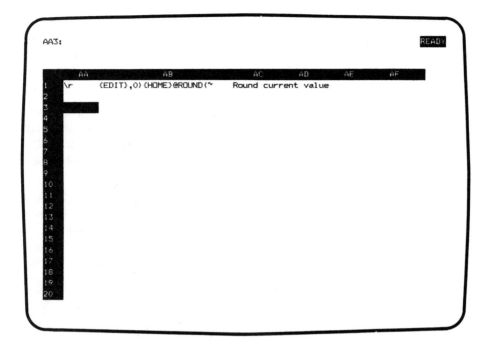

Fig. 3.54.

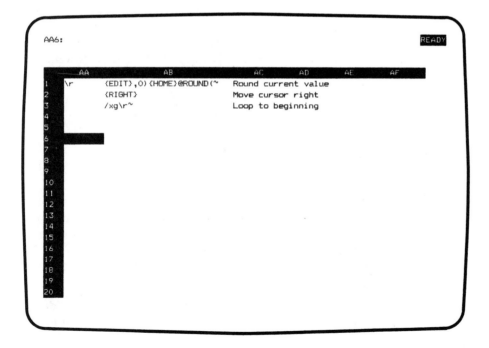

Fig. 3.55.

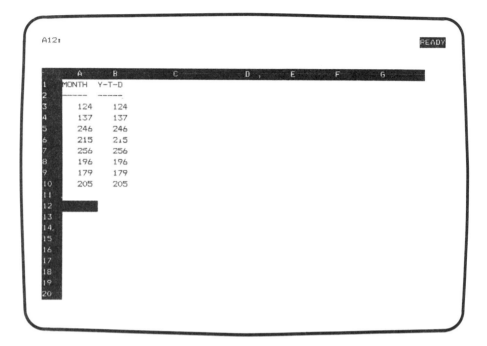

Fig. 3.56.

Fig. 3.57.

The first step in using this macro is to assign the name RANGE to the range A3..A10 (or whatever range contains the values in your first column). Afterward, here's how the macro works. When the macro is run, the first line causes the cursor to jump to cell A3, which is the first cell in the range named RANGE. Next, the macro performs a /File Extract Values on RANGE. The values in this range are stored in a file called NAME.WKS. Line 3 moves the cursor one cell to the right, where the cursor rests in cell B3. Finally, line 4 issues the /File Combine Add Entire File command, specifying NAME as the file to be added to the current worksheet.

When NAME is added to the worksheet, the values in NAME are added to the values in the worksheet. Because the cursor was moved one cell to the right, the values that were in column A are now combined with those in column B. Thus, the value in A3 is added to the value in B3, the value in A4 is added to the value in B4, and so on. When the process is completed, the worksheet will look like the one in figure 3.58.

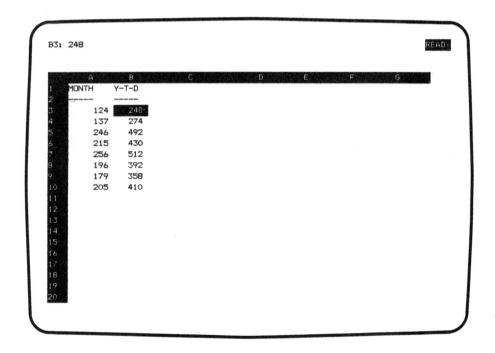

Fig. 3.58.

When you use the accumulator macro to accumulate totals, the only rule to remember is that cells B3..B10 cannot contain formulas because the /File Combine Add command ignores cells containing formulas. Because you are using the macro to consolidate the current-period data into the year-to-date data, the formulas don't need to be in column B.

Macro for Consolidating Worksheets

This macro streamlines the process of consolidating financial statements. One of the questions commonly asked by 1-2-3 users is, How can I consolidate several different worksheets into one sheet? With earlier spreadsheets, such as VisiCalc and SuperCalc, consolidation was a long and cumbersome process. Fortunately, 1-2-3 offers several commands that make the process much simpler.

In 1-2-3 the main tool for consolidating worksheets is the /File Combine command. /File Combine is used to load one file into 1-2-3 without erasing the current worksheet. (Remember that the /File Retrieve command automatically erases the contents of the worksheet before loading the new file.)

/File Combine offers several options for consolidating worksheets. First, the file can be copied into the worksheet. If the file is copied, however, it will overwrite the contents of the worksheet in every cell location where the file contains data.

Second, the file can be subtracted (using the Subtract option) from the current contents of the worksheet. In this case the value in every one of the file's cells containing a number or a formula will be subtracted from the value of the corresponding cell in the current worksheet. If, for example, cell A4 in the file contains the number 4 and cell A4 contains the number 6, then cell A4 in the consolidated worksheet will have the value 2. If cell A4 in the worksheet is blank before the consolidation, the cell will have a value of -4 after the sheets are merged.

Third, the file can be added to the worksheet. The Add option is similar to Subtract except that Add combines the values in the two worksheets. Of course, the Add option is more important in worksheet consolidation.

/File Combine also offers the choice of combining the entire file with the worksheet or combining only a named range with the sheet. The Entire command is used when you want to consolidate two worksheets in their entirety. The Named Range option extracts information from one worksheet and places that information in another sheet.

Let's see how the command works. Imagine that you are responsible for preparing a sales forecast for a small company with three product lines. You have created the three product budgets shown in figure 3.59 and the corporate budget shown in figure 3.60. Now you want to consolidate the product budgets into the summary corporate budget.

Notice in the corporate budget that the lines for Sales and Cost of Sales are blank, but the expense lines contain values. For this example, you can assume that all the company's overhead is accounted for as corporate expense and that all sales and cost of sales flow from the three product groups.

To consolidate the three worksheets into a final corporate sales forecast, you must perform the following operations: (1) assign file names to the four worksheets—PROD1, PROD2, PROD3, and CORP; (2) load the CORP worksheet; and (3) on the CORP sheet, create the macro in figure 3.61.

This macro completely automates the consolidation process. The first step moves the cursor to the Home position. If the cursor is not in cell A1 when the consolidation is begun, the product budgets will not be properly aligned on the summary sheet. The second step uses the /File

PROD1

	Qtr 1	Qtr 2	Qtr 3	Qtr 4	Total
Sales	$100,000	$12,500	$13,500	$13,000	$490,000
Cost	$40,000	$50,000	$54,000	$52,000	$19,600
Gross	$60,000	$75,000	$81,000	$78,000	$294,000

PROD2

	Qtr 1	Qtr 2	Qtr 3	Qtr 4	Total
Sales	$40,000	$37,000	$36,000	$39,000	$152,000
Cost	$19,200	$17,760	$17,200	$18,720	$72,000
Gross	$20,000	$19,240	$18,720	$20,280	$79,040

PROD3

	Qtr 1	Qtr 2	Qtr 3	Qtr 4	Total
Sales	$17,000	$22,000	$35,000	$37,000	$111,000
Cost	$13,260	$17,160	$27,300	$20,060	$86,500
Gross	$3,740	$4,040	$7,700	$8,140	$24,420

Fig. 3.59.

118

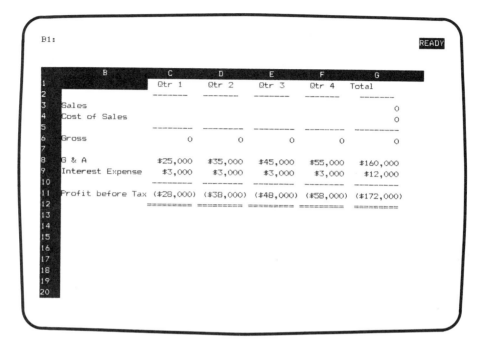

Fig. 3.60.

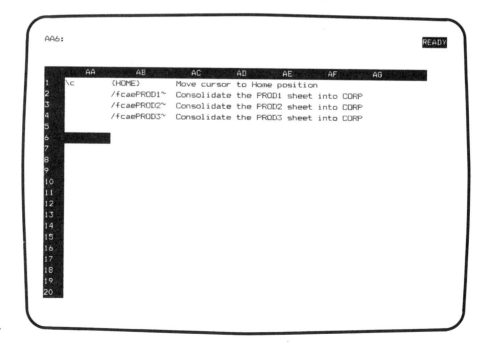

Fig. 3.61.

Combine Add Entire command to consolidate PROD1 into the summary sheet. The resulting worksheet will look like that in figure 3.62. Immediately after PROD1 has been consolidated into the summary worksheet, the macro will proceed to PROD2 and PROD3. The final worksheet appears in figure 3.63.

Several important characteristics of the Add option should be noted. First, Add converts each formula in the file into a simple number, before the formula is loaded into the new sheet. Assume, for example, that cell C4 in the file PROD1 is defined as

    C4: (C,0) +C3*.40

Because cell C3 contains the number 100,000, the current value in cell C4 is 40,000. When the /fcae command loads this number into the summary sheet, only the number 40,000 is transferred. This means that later changes in PROD1 are not automatically passed to CORP. If, say, the value in cell C3 in PROD1 is changed to 200,000, the value in cell C4 in that sheet changes to 80,000. The summary sheet is not affected by this change, however. To update the summary sheet, you must perform the entire consolidation again.

Second, the Add option will not overwrite any of the worksheet's cells containing a label or a formula. If a value in the file conflicts with a formula or a label in the worksheet, the value will be omitted from the consolidated worksheet. For instance, cell C6 in PROD1 may contain the formula

    C6: (C,0) +C3-C4

Cell C6 has a current value of 60,000. You would therefore expect that the value 60,000 will be transferred to the summary sheet during the consolidation. But cell C6 in the CORP worksheet contains a formula; consequently, when the transfer is made, the /fcae command ignores cell C6 in PROD1.

When you save the new summary sheet, you will want to use a name other than CORP (or whatever name you have used for the unconsolidated summary worksheet). Otherwise, the consolidated sheet will overwrite the blank summary sheet. If this occurs and later you need to rerun the consolidation, you'll have to re-create the blank summary sheet.

Using a macro may not save you much time if you have only three sheets to be combined. Most companies, though, have many products and divisions. Whenever you need to consolidate many sheets, a macro can accomplish the task efficiently.

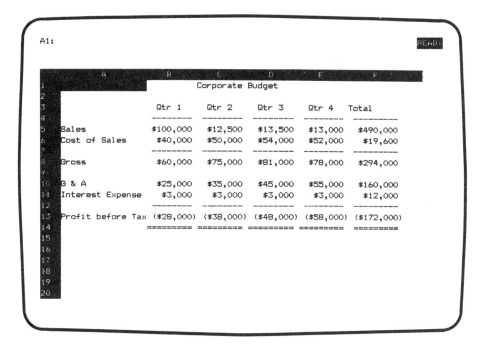

Fig. 3.62.

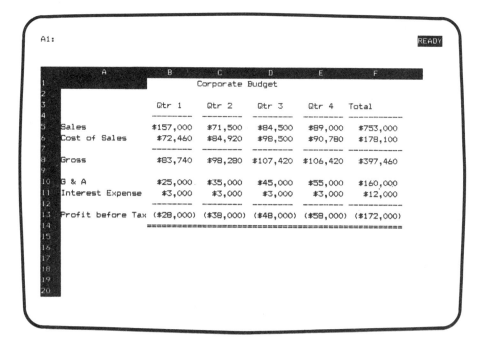

Fig. 3.63.

Whenever you want to perform what-if analysis, perhaps to measure the impact of changes in the product forecasts on the corporate forecast, a macro like the one in figure 3.61 can be especially helpful. Because changes in the product forecasts are not automatically passed through to the summary, every change in the product worksheets will require a new consolidation. Letting a macro do each consolidation is much easier than typing the commands by hand.

Variations of the Consolidation Macro

Another type of consolidation involves extracting information from subsidiary worksheets so that the information can be combined on a summary sheet. For example, the summary sheet shown in figure 3.64 loads each product line's forecast on the previous forecast. Although the final document represents an accurate consolidation, it does not show each division's contribution to sales. Figure 3.64 shows a model that presents the details of each division's revenue forecast.

In most respects this model is similar to the previous consolidation model. The main difference is that the model in figure 3.64 shows each division's sales separately. Making this model therefore requires a few more steps than are needed for making the previous model.

First, you must create range names in the summary model (called CORP2). As in the previous example, cell C4 is named SALES with the /Range Name Create command. Cell C9 is given the name CGS (Cost of Goods Sold). Range C3..F3 is named SALES in PROD1, PROD2, and PROD3. And the range C4..F4 in each worksheet is named CGS.

This variation of the consolidation macro uses these range names to load the data from each worksheet into the summary. To perform the consolidation, you then load the CORP2 model and create the macro in figure 3.65.

The macro shows two different techniques for using the /fcan command. Lines 2 through 6 load the sales data from the subsidiary worksheets. After each line is loaded, the cursor skips down one cell. Because the cursor is moved after each /fcan is performed, each product's sales forecast is placed on a different line in the model. Thus, /fcan can be used to create on the master sheet a detail of the subsidiary sheets.

The last three lines of the macro load into the summary sheet the cost-of-goods-sold data from the subsidiary worksheets. The cursor remains stationary while the three sets of data are loaded. Because the

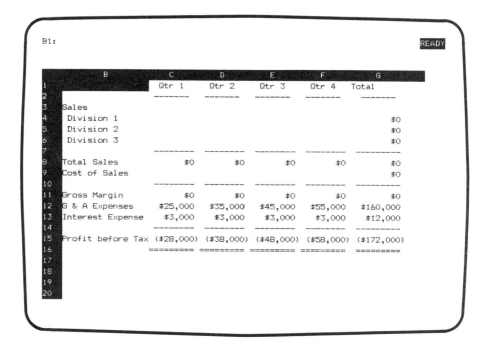

Fig. 3.64.

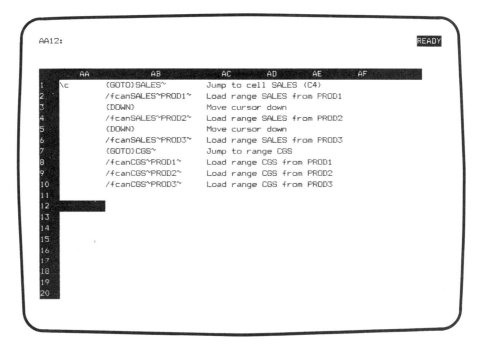

Fig. 3.65.

cursor is not moved between steps, the cost-of-goods-sold data for all three products is accumulated on one line. Figure 3.66 shows the summary worksheet after the macro has run.

```
B1:                                                              READY

          B           C         D         E         F         G
 1                   Qtr 1     Qtr 2     Qtr 3     Qtr 4    Total
 2                  -------   -------   -------   -------   --------
 3   Sales
 4     Division 1  $100,000  $125,000  $135,000  $130,000  $490,000
 5     Division 2   $40,000   $37,000   $36,000   $39,000  $152,000
 6     Division 3   $17,000   $22,000   $35,000   $37,000  $111,000
 7                  -------   -------   -------   -------   --------
 8   Total Sales   $157,000  $184,000  $206,000  $206,000  $753,000
 9   Cost of Sales  $72,460   $84,920   $98,500   $99,500  $355,540
10                  -------   -------   -------   -------   --------
11   Gross Margin   $84,540   $99,000  $107,420  $106,420  $397,460
12   G & A Expenses $25,000   $35,000   $45,000   $55,000  $160,000
13   Interest Expense $3,000   $3,000    $3,000    $3,000   $12,000
14                  -------   -------   -------   -------   --------
15   Profit before Tax $56,540  $61,000  $59,420   $48,420  $225,460
16                  =======   =======   =======   =======   ========
17
18
19
20
```

Fig. 3.66.

Suppose that you have many subsidiary schedules to consolidate and that they cannot all fit on a single floppy disk. The consolidation macro will need a statement allowing you to change disks in the middle of the consolidation. The following routine (extracted from a longer consolidation macro) does the trick nicely:

```
/fcaePROD12~
/fcaePROD13~
/xmMessage~
     Change
     Insert disk containing file PROD14 and press ENTER
     /fcaePROD14~
     /fcaePROD15~
```

This routine contains a message menu that is activated by the /xm command, which delivers the message in the fourth and fifth lines. To move the macro to the message, however, you must assign the name

MESSAGE to the first cell (containing the word *Change*) in the menu. The next line contains an explanation of this message. After you read the message, change disks, and press ENTER, the macro will continue the consolidation with worksheet PROD14.

Note a word of caution when using this macro. The message menu does not verify that you have inserted the correct disk into the drive. Presumably, 1-2-3 does not have the ability to test a disk for a file from within a macro. If the wrong disk is inserted into the drive, the macro will be aborted. Always check to make sure that you have inserted the correct disk.

These consolidation macros are examples of what are called "golden macros"—those that are simple and elegant, yet accomplish important tasks quickly and efficiently. The consolidation macros are relatively simple, but they may save much time in consolidating worksheets.

Macro for Using Text with @IF

1-2-3 has no string arithmetic capabilities. (The program's upgraded version, Symphony, does offer them.) Without such capabilities, 1-2-3 cannot, for example, return a string in response to a conditional statement. 1-2-3 specifically does not allow you to use text in @IF statements. The /xi command, however, lets you make a macro with limited capability for returning text in response to an @IF statement.

Suppose, for instance, that you have created a data base like the one in figure 3.67. The data base lists the original, closing, and high prices of stocks. Suppose further that you want to return text indicating whether you should "sell" or "hold" the stock.

To return a string response in the ACTION column, you can use the macro in figure 3.68. In this macro, the /xi command compares the contents of cell D2 to a constant (105 in this case). If the value in D2 is greater than the constant, control of the macro is sent to cell AB3, which moves the cursor to cell E2 and enters the label HOLD. If the value in cell D2 is not greater than the constant, the macro moves the cursor to cell E2 and enters the label SELL.

Macros for Password Protection

One of the oldest techniques for ensuring the security of data stored in computers is to create passwords that users must enter before they can access data. Most mainframe and minicomputer systems require that you enter a password before you log onto the system. Some mi-

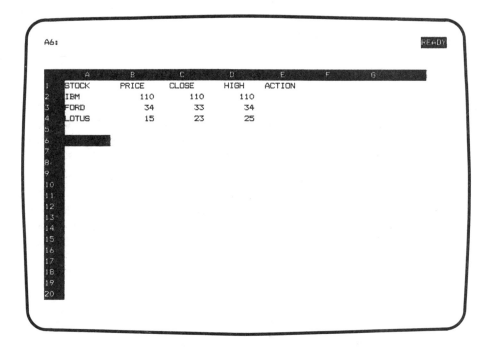

Fig. 3.67.

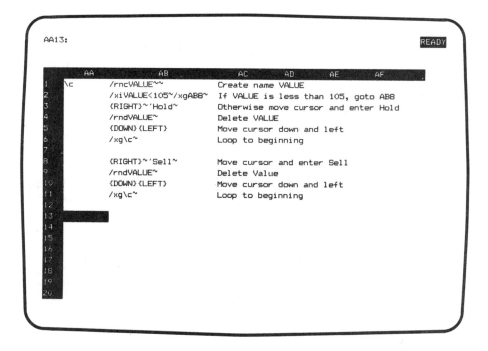

Fig. 3.68.

crocomputer programs (most notably accounting systems) also offer password protection. 1-2-3, however, does not offer built-in password protection for models. But password protection is possible through the use of macros. The two macros in this section show you how to use passwords to protect the valuable information in your 1-2-3 models.

Password-Protection Macro

The macro in figure 3.69 lets you create passwords for restricting the use of your models. Let's work through this basic macro one step at a time.

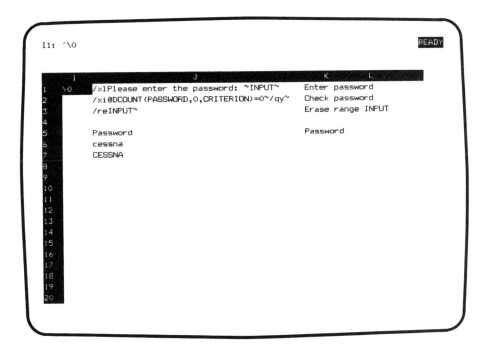

Fig. 3.69.

First, you should notice the special name given to the macro: \0. This is the only nonalphabetical macro name accepted by 1-2-3. Whenever a worksheet containing a macro with this name is loaded into 1-2-3, the \0 causes a macro to execute automatically. Because of this feature, you can be reasonably sure that anyone who wants to use the model must first encounter the password macro.

In line 1 of the macro, the /xl command requests that the user input the password for this worksheet. The word entered will be stored in cell K6, which has been named INPUT with the /Range Name command.

The second line compares the word entered to the correct password, which is stored in a simple 1-2-3 data base. Line 2 needs careful study. The line can be translated as "If the number of records in the first column of the data base named PASSWORD (located at cells J5..J7) that matches the criterion in the range K5..K6 (named CRITERION) is 0, then immediately quit from 1-2-3." In other words, if no record in the data base PASSWORD matches the phrase in INPUT, then exit from 1-2-3.

A couple of techniques are used in this second line of the macro. First, the range INPUT (K6) is a subset of the range CRITERION (K5..K6). Thus, the word entered in response to the /xl command is automatically entered in the criterion range and is immediately used to compute the @DCOUNT. Second, @DCOUNT is used in the macro because 1-2-3 cannot easily compare one text string to another. Because you cannot directly compare the two strings (the phrase entered by the user and the correct string), you must instead have 1-2-3 count (@DCOUNT) the number of records in the data base that match the criterion exactly.

Remember to store both uppercase and lowercase versions of the password. Because 1-2-3 is strict in its rules for matching, the program will reject the correct password entered in uppercase letters if the password stored is in lowercase. By storing both versions of the password, you can eliminate this problem. If for some reason, however, the password is entered with a combination of upper- and lowercase letters, 1-2-3 will reject the password.

Variation of the Password-Protection Macro

Most password systems allow the user to make several attempts to enter the correct password before forcing the user out of the system. You can easily modify the password-protection macro to allow three or more attempts to enter the password. The macro in figure 3.70 provides this capability.

The first line of this expanded macro uses the /Data Fill command to increment a counter that has been established in the model. In the example, cell J9 (named COUNTER) has been designated as the counter.

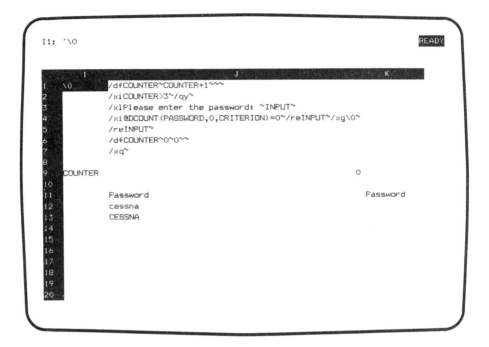

Fig. 3.70.

Line 1 can be translated as "Fill the range COUNTER with the value (COUNTER+1)." Each time this line is executed, the value in cell COUNTER is increased by one.

Line 2 in the macro uses the value in COUNTER to decide whether to force the user out of the system or permit another entry of the password. If the value in COUNTER is greater than three (indicating that the user has tried and failed three times to enter the correct password), the macro immediately issues the /Quit Yes command, thus forcing the user out of 1-2-3. If the count is less than three, the macro moves on to line 3, and the user is given another chance to enter the password.

Line 3 in this macro is identical to the first line in the previous macro. (See fig. 3.69.) But because this variation is longer, the named range INPUT has been moved to cell K12. The ranges CRITERION and PASSWORD have also been moved. PASSWORD is now located in the range J11..J13, and CRITERION is located at cells K11..K12.

Line 4 in this macro is similar to the second line of the basic macro except that in the variation, line 4 contains some new statements. If no records are found that match the password entered by the user (@DCOUNT=0), the macro erases the INPUT range and loops back to the beginning. At this point, the first statement adds one (1) to the value in COUNTER, and the second statement tests to see whether another attempt should be allowed.

If the password entered by the user matches one of the words in the PASSWORD data base, the macro moves on to line 5, which erases the range INPUT. Line 6 simply resets the value in COUNTER to 0. The COUNTER is then ready for the user to load and use the model again.

Limitations

Although the password-protection macro and its variation can be handy, they do have limitations. First, you can load a model containing either macro without knowing the correct password. You simply use the /File Combine All command. \0 macros do not execute when loaded with /fca; therefore, the password macros will not be effective. Expert 1-2-3 users who are determined to access your data will eventually discover this option.

Another limitation is that the variation of the password-protection macro (see fig. 3.70) does not restrict the number of times a user can attempt to enter the model by using the /fr command. Many advanced password systems refuse to permit a user to keep trying to enter the correct password after failing a certain number of times. With the variation presented here, you can issue the /fr command as many times as you want and continue guessing.

Finally, using these password-protection macros can be an irritating experience. Passwords are easily forgotten or mistyped, and being restricted from your own model can be extremely frustrating. The best advice is to delay password protection until after you have finished building and debugging your models. Then use a password only if your models contain sensitive information. Be sure to keep a log of your passwords so that you don't forget the key to an important model.

Conclusion

In many ways, the macros for worksheet operations are the most fundamental macros in the library. With the aid of these macros, you can create many types of 1-2-3 worksheets. In this chapter, you have learned how to reduce the number of keystrokes needed to move the cursor around a worksheet. You have discovered ways to simplify the tasks of entering labels, numbers, and formulas; of formatting cells; and of changing a worksheet. And you have learned how to create macros for more sophisticated operations, such as accumulating totals, consolidating worksheets, and protecting your valuable models by using passwords.

In the next chapters, you will learn how to create macros for the specific 1-2-3 operations of data management, graphics, and printing. You will also discover many useful macros for specific applications, such as managing client files and creating worksheet instructions.

4
Macros for
Data Base Management

As most users know, 1-2-3 is highly acclaimed as an electronic spreadsheet program. Its data base commands and functions, however, are not among the program's strong features. Limited data search capabilities, an inability to use string functions, and an inability to save data query settings for more than one data base on the same worksheet are some of 1-2-3's weaknesses.

Nevertheless, some data management capability is available in 1-2-3, and users have found the program sufficient for small-scale data processing tasks. If you want to get the most out of 1-2-3 for data management applications, building a library of data management macros is a good way to expand the program's capabilities. Macros can simplify the task of manually creating a data base in a 1-2-3 worksheet area. And macros can expand the capability of 1-2-3's data commands and data management functions. Included in this chapter are the following macros:

1. Macro for creating data input forms

2. Macro for creating a data base from a ratios model

3. Macro for storing data table settings

4. Macro for storing data query settings

5. Macro for performing a label lookup

6. /Data Find macro

7. Macro for converting numeric field names to labels

8. Macro for comparing character strings

9. /Data Query Extract macro

Macro for Creating Data Input Forms

In 1-2-3, creating a data base involves entering records into a worksheet area in the same way that you enter numbers and labels into a spreadsheet. Lotus, in fact, emphasizes the benefits of its fully integrated data management capabilities. But using the worksheet for creating a data base in the same way that you create, say, a financial spreadsheet has its disadvantages.

One of the major problems in using 1-2-3 for data management is that the program has no data input forms for adding records into a data base. Being able to enter data automatically into a data base without having to move the cursor to every cell, however, is a tremendous convenience. A macro can provide such a capability.

For creating data input forms, you can make a fairly simple macro that will provide prompts for the records you enter. Suppose, for example, that you want to create a data base like the one shown in figure 4.1.

For this task, you can use the macro in figure 4.2, which will perform the following operations: (1) prompt you for each record, (2) enter the record, and (3) loop back to begin entry of a new record.

The first step in creating a data input form is to enter the field names into the data base. In the example in figure 4.1, these field names are NAME, ADDRESS, CITY, STATE, ZIP CODE, and TELEPHONE. After you have created the data base headings, the next step is to enter the macro.

When you invoke the macro by pressing Alta, the cursor moves to the cell in the upper left corner of the data base. If the data base begins at A1 (see fig. 4.1), the first line of the macro will be {HOME}. Next, the cursor moves to the empty cell immediately beneath the last entry in the first column of your data base. If you are entering your first record, the cursor moves to the empty cell below NAME. Appearing in the control panel will be the first prompt, which waits for you to enter a name. (See fig. 4.3.)

After entering the name, you press ENTER, and the next prompt will appear. The macro will continue to present a prompt for each item in a record. Once you have completed the record, the macro begins

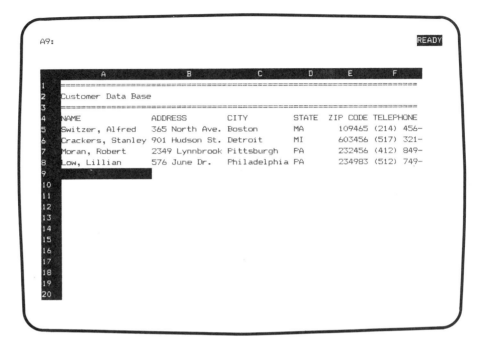

Fig. 4.1.

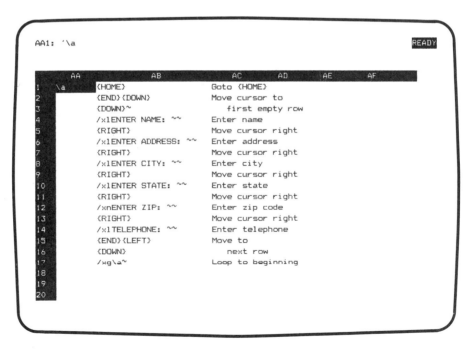

Fig. 4.2.

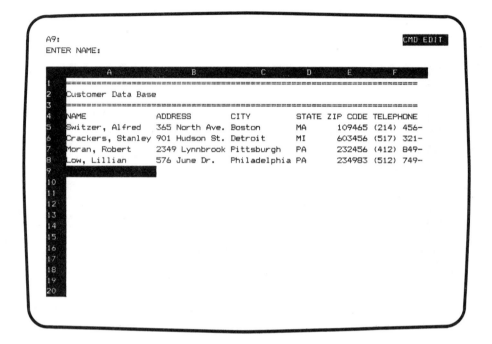

```
A9:                                                    CMD EDIT
ENTER NAME:

            A              B              C        D     E       F
1   ==========================================================================
2   Customer Data Base
3   ==========================================================================
4   NAME           ADDRESS        CITY        STATE ZIP CODE TELEPHONE
5   Switzer, Alfred    365 North Ave. Boston      MA     109465 (214) 456-
6   Crackers, Stanley  901 Hudson St. Detroit     MI     603456 (517) 321-
7   Moran, Robert      2349 Lynnbrook Pittsburgh  PA     232456 (412) 849-
8   Low, Lillian       576 June Dr.   Philadelphia PA    234983 (512) 749-
9
10
11
12
13
14
15
16
17
18
19
20
```

Fig. 4.3.

again by prompting you for data for a new record. When you have finished entering all the data, you press Ctrl Break to stop the macro and return to READY mode.

This data input form macro can be easily changed to work with data bases that do not begin at A1 or with those that have different fields. If, for example, your data base begins at A50, you just change the first line to

　{GOTO}A50

If, however, you want to use the macro with data bases beginning at various locations, you change the first line to

　{GOTO}{?}~

And if you want to use the macro with a data base containing different field names, you need to edit only the /xl and /xn commands so that the appropriate prompts will be presented.

When you use the data input form macro, keep two points in mind. First, if you want to enter numeric data into the data base so that you can perform calculations on it, remember to use /xn. And second, using /xl to enter numbers will enter them as labels.

The data input form macro is a helpful, timesaving tool, especially when you are entering hundreds of records. This macro is only one example of many simple macros that are available to simplify data base operations in 1-2-3.

Macro for Creating a Data Base from a Ratios Model

The data input form macro is useful for entering new records into a data base. If you want to create and update a data base from data already entered into other parts of a worksheet, you will need a different macro, one that automatically creates and updates a data base for you.

This macro enables you to develop a data base from selected items in reports that you update periodically. Suppose, for example, that you update monthly a Balance Sheet, an Income Statement, and a Financial Ratios Report, such as those shown in figures 4.4, 4.5, and 4.6.

```
C2:                                                                    READY

       A        B        C        D        E        F        G        H
1  ============================================================================
2  Balance Sheet          ▮▮▮▮▮▮▮
3  ============================================================================
4                                                              Common
5    Assets                                      31-Jul-83     Size
6
7  Cash                                          $275,000       8%
8  Marketable Securities                          35,000        1%
9  Accounts Receivable                1,256,000
10    Allowance for Doubtful Accounts    8,000
11    Net Accounts Receivable                    1,248,000      39%
12 Inventory                                      359,000       11%
13 Prepaid Expenses                               70,000        2%
14 Other                                          23,000        1%
15                                              -----------
16    Total Current Assets                       2,010,000      62%
17
18 Property, Plant, and Equipment      956,700
19    Accumulated Depreciation         123,700
20    Net Property, Plant, and Equipment         833,000        26%
```

Fig. 4.4.

137

A53:   READY

```
        A       B       C   D E F      G          H         I
50  ================================================================
51  Income Statement
52  ================================================================
53                                                          Common
54                               31-Jul-83     Y-T-D        Size
55
56  Gross Sales                  $732,730   $4,923,677      100%
57     Less Returns and Allowances   4,167      66,666       1%
58                               ---------  ----------
59  Net Sales                     728,563   4,857,011       99%
60  Cost of Goods                 468,947   3,386,720       64%
61                               ---------  ----------
62  Gross Margin                  259,616   1,470,291       35%
63  Operating Expenses            201,042   1,105,625       27%
64  Depreciation                   12,016      72,096        2%
65                               ---------  ----------
66  Earnings before Interest and Taxes  46,558  285,550      6%
67  Interest Expense                7,043      46,535        1%
68                               ---------  ----------
69  Earnings before Taxes          39,515     246,035        5%
70  Income Taxes                   10,342      62,816        1%
71                               ---------  ----------
72  Earnings after Taxes           29,173     183,219        4%
73  Cash Dividends                      0      76,389
74                               ---------  ----------
75  Net Income                    $29,173    $106,830        4%
76                               =========  ==========
77
78
79
80
81
82
83
84
85
86
87
88
89
```

Fig. 4.5.

Suppose also that you want to create a data base containing totals from the Balance Sheet, Income Statement, and Financial Ratios Report. Finally, you want to update the data base monthly. The macro in figure 4.7 will automatically enter values into the data base and re-sort all records in ascending order each time you add data to the data base.

Although this macro is long because of the number of entries added to the data base, only five operations are performed:

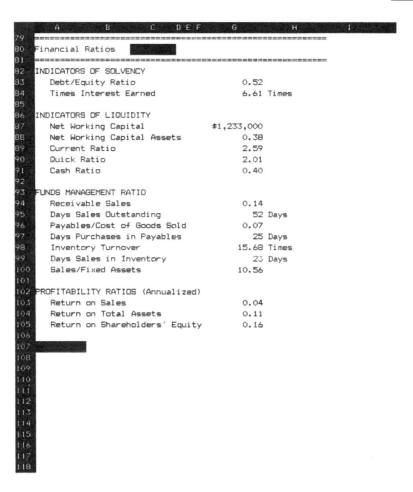

Fig. 4.6.

1. Positioning the cursor in the data base

2. Entering values

3. Converting values

4. Formatting cells in the data base

5. Sorting data base records in order

Here's how to make the data base macro. First, the data base depends on a number of range names from the Balance Sheet, Income State-

139

AA1: '\d   READY

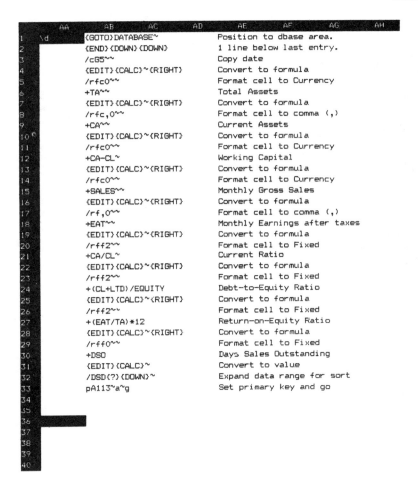

	AA	AB	AC	AD	AE	AF	AG	AH
1	\d	{GOTO}DATABASE~			Position to dbase area.			
2		{END}{DOWN}{DOWN}			1 line below last entry.			
3		/cG5~~			Copy date			
4		{EDIT}{CALC}~{RIGHT}			Convert to formula			
5		/rfc0~~			Format cell to Currency			
6		+TA~~			Total Assets			
7		{EDIT}{CALC}~{RIGHT}			Convert to formula			
8		/rfc,0~~			Format cell to comma (,)			
9		+CA~~			Current Assets			
10		{EDIT}{CALC}~{RIGHT}			Convert to formula			
11		/rfc0~~			Format cell to Currency			
12		+CA-CL~			Working Capital			
13		{EDIT}{CALC}~{RIGHT}			Convert to formula			
14		/rfc0~~			Format cell to Currency			
15		+SALES~~			Monthly Gross Sales			
16		{EDIT}{CALC}~{RIGHT}			Convert to formula			
17		/rf,0~~			Format cell to comma (,)			
18		+EAT~~			Monthly Earnings after taxes			
19		{EDIT}{CALC}~{RIGHT}			Convert to formula			
20		/rff2~~			Format cell to Fixed			
21		+CA/CL~			Current Ratio			
22		{EDIT}{CALC}~{RIGHT}			Convert to formula			
23		/rff2~~			Format cell to Fixed			
24		+(CL+LTD)/EQUITY			Debt-to-Equity Ratio			
25		{EDIT}{CALC}~{RIGHT}			Convert to formula			
26		/rff2~~			Format cell to Fixed			
27		+(EAT/TA)*12			Return-on-Equity Ratio			
28		{EDIT}{CALC}~{RIGHT}			Convert to formula			
29		/rff0~~			Format cell to Fixed			
30		+DSO			Days Sales Outstanding			
31		{EDIT}{CALC}~			Convert to value			
32		/DSD{?}{DOWN}~			Expand data range for sort			
33		pA113~a~g			Set primary key and go			
34								
35								
36								
37								
38								
39								
40								

Fig. 4.7.

ment, and Financial Ratios Report. All values added to the data base must be assigned range names. The names used in the model in figures 4.4, 4.5, and 4.6 are listed in table 4.1.

After assigning all the range names, you then create the data base, using the appropriate command lines for entering records into each data base field. After you invoke the data base macro shown in figure 4.7, the macro moves the cursor to the cell named DATABASE (A111 in the example). Next, the cursor moves to the cell directly beneath the

Worksheet Item	Range	Range Name
Current Assets	G16	CA
Total Assets	G25	TA
Total Current Liabilities	G35	CL
Long-Term Debt	G37	LTD
Total Stockholders' Equity	G45	EQUITY
Gross Sales	G56	SALES
Days Sales Outstanding	G95	DSO
Data Base	A111	DATABASE

Table 4.1

last record in the first column (A). Third, the date from the Balance Sheet is copied to the data base and converted to a formula. The cursor then moves right, formats that cell, and enters the "Total Assets" from the Balance Sheet. The entry is converted to a formula, and the cursor moves right again.

The same process for adding "Total Assets" to the data base is then used for adding each of the other formulas to the data base. After all formulas have been entered into the data base, its records are sorted in ascending order.

Although the data base macro can be long, it is simple to make and easy to use. If you need to create a data base from data in your worksheet, this macro will accomplish the task efficiently.

Macro for Storing Data Table Settings

A feature not included in 1-2-3 but provided in Symphony is the capability of saving settings. Unlike 1-2-3, Symphony enables you to save many kinds of settings, such as print settings or data management settings. You can retrieve these settings at any time as long as you have remembered to name them. In 1-2-3, however, a macro can store settings so that they are available whenever you need them.

Among the settings you can store with the aid of a 1-2-3 macro are data table definitions. Usually, you can have only one data table active at a time; when you create a new table, you destroy the definition of a previous table. If you want to use several data tables and switch back and forth among them, you must create new settings from the keyboard whenever you want to use another table. You can, however, store data table definitions by using the macro in figure 4.8.

This data table macro provides two choices: table 1 or table 2. Each option causes the macro to issue a set of commands that defines and computes a data table. After you have made your selection, the macro activates a predefined graph that goes with the table. Thus, the macro not only allows you to store two different data table definitions, but also creates automatically a graph from each definition.

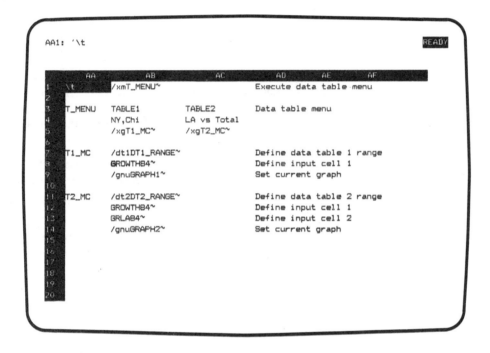

Fig. 4.8.

Macro for Storing Data Query Settings

Data query settings can also be conveniently stored with the aid of a macro. Although these settings can be saved in Symphony, 1-2-3 provides no capability for naming or saving data query settings. The macro in figure 4.9 lets you name and save these settings.

This macro is created especially for querying two data bases. When you invoke the macro, you have two choices from the menu: (1) to perform the query operation on the first data base, or (2) to perform the query operation on the second data base. Input, Criterion, and Output settings are contained within the macro.

If you want to add more items to the menu, you can extend it to include query settings, such as Q3_MC or Q4_MC, for other data bases as well. All you do is add choices to the macro's menu and provide subsidiary macros for your other data query settings.

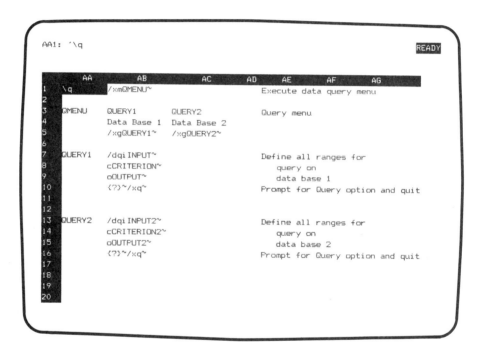

Fig. 4.9.

Macro for Performing a Label Lookup

1-2-3 does not have the capability of using a label as the argument for the @VLOOKUP or @HLOOKUP functions, or using a label as an element in the lookup table. But you can make a macro that will perform label lookup.

143

Let's assume that you want to print the report shown in figure 4.10, with all department names entered. Suppose also that you have an existing Department Name Table. (See fig. 4.11.) Because the report in figure 4.10 lists budgets according to code, you will need to enter the corresponding department names.

The procedure for performing a label lookup requires three steps. First, you define the Input, Output, and Criterion ranges for the Department Name Table. (See fig. 4.11.) Second, you assign the range name CODE to the Code field in the Criterion range and assign the range name NAME to the Name field in the output range. Third, you make the macro as shown in figure 4.12.

This macro contains two parts. The first part counts the number of rows in the report. The second part is a loop that the macro runs through once for each row in the report. Each time through the loop, the macro copies the Department Code for that row to the Code field of the Criterion range (see fig. 4.11) and executes the /Data Query operation. (This code assumes that the last type of query executed was a /Data Query Extract.)

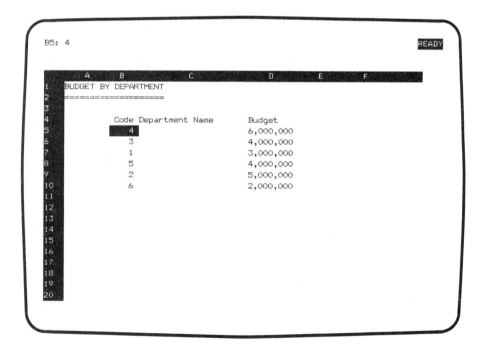

Fig. 4.10.

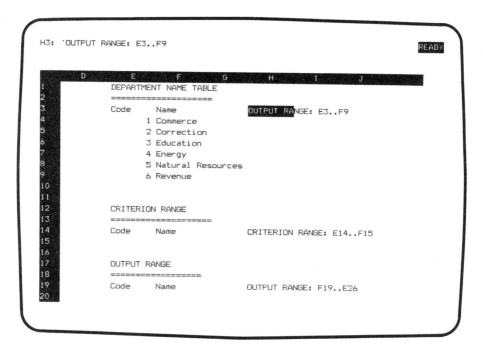

Fig. 4.11.

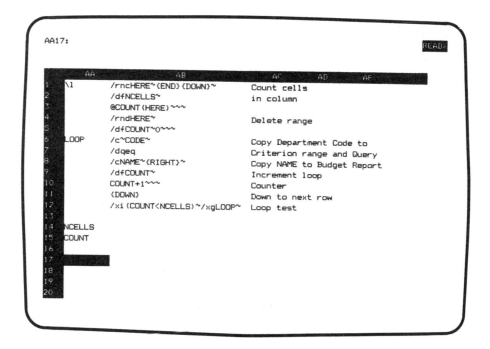

Fig. 4.12.

As a result of the query, the corresponding Department Name from the table is extracted and placed in the Name field at F20 in the Output range. The macro then copies this name into the Department Name column in the report and continues to the next row. After the macro has processed through the last row, the macro moves out of the loop and ends.

To execute the macro, you place the cursor on the first Department Code in the report and press Altl. When the macro has finished executing, it will have copied all the labels into the report, as shown in figure 4.13.

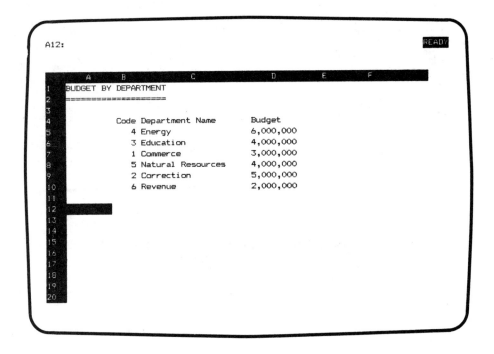

Fig. 4.13.

/Data Find Macro

Another limitation of 1-2-3 data management capabilities is found in the /Data Find command. /Data Find cannot be used to update a record in a data base. Updating a record requires a complicated series of steps. First, you must use the /Data Query Extract command to extract from the data base the record you want to change. Second, you must change the record. Third, you must delete the old record from the data base. Finally, you must copy the updated record to the position where the old record was deleted. Changing even one record obviously requires many operations.

Unfortunately, 1-2-3's regular data commands provide no other way for changing a record. One solution to this problem is to use the macro shown in figure 4.14. This macro is appropriate if, for example, you want to change a record in the data base shown in figure 4.15.

Changing a record in this data base requires the following steps. First, you create the macro. Second, before the macro is executed, you create range names for each record in the data base. Although this step sounds like a laborious task, it is actually quite easy if you use the /Range Name Labels command. (And if you use a /Range Name Labels macro, the task is even easier.) For example, you can name every cell in the range B8..B13 by issuing the /Range Name Labels Right command and specifying the range A8..A13. Each cell in B8..B13 will then have the name of the corresponding cell in column A. (Cell B8 is named A, cell B9 is named B, and so on).

Third, you press Altd to invoke the macro. When the macro is executed, the user's response to the prompt "Enter the desired

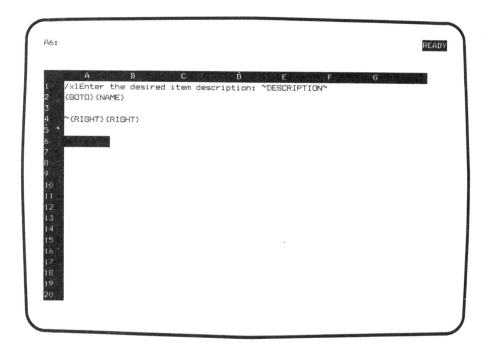

Fig. 4.14.

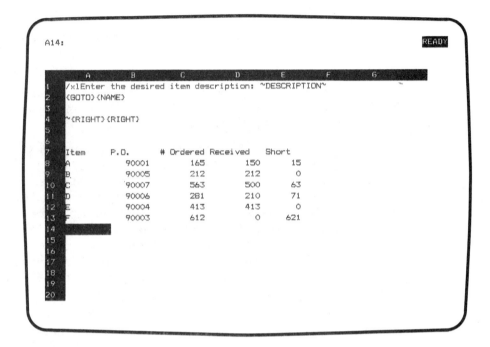

```
A14:                                                              READY
          A        B        C        D        E        F      G
   1  /xlEnter the desired item description: ~DESCRIPTION~
   2  {GOTO}{NAME}
   3
   4  ~{RIGHT}{RIGHT}
   5
   6
   7  Item     P.O.      # Ordered Received   Short
   8  A        90001        165      150       15
   9  B        90005        212      212        0
  10  C        90007        563      500       63
  11  D        90006        281      210       71
  12  E        90004        413      413        0
  13  F        90003        612        0      621
  14
  15
  16
  17
  18
  19
  20
```

Fig. 4.15.

item description: " is copied to cell A3, which has been given the name DESCRIPTION. Next, the macro issues the command {GOTO}{NAME}, which uses the label in cell A3 as the name to jump to. Once the record is found, the macro moves the cursor two cells to the right so that you can update the file.

This macro compensates greatly for your inability to edit entries with the /Data Find command. And for simple searches, the macro works almost as well as /Data Find.

Several limitations of the macro are worth noting, however. First, for the macro to operate properly, the data base's field that you use for naming each record cannot have duplicate entries. In other words, if each cell in the adjacent column has a distinctive name, the macro will work fine. But if duplicate names are in the key field, only the last of the duplicate names will retain the proper range name. For example, if cell A13 in figure 4.15 contains the label A, only cell B13 will have the name A; cell B8 will have no name at all. Obviously, such duplication can cause problems for the macro.

Second, the macro does not allow searches on more than one criterion as /Data Find does. Because each record is identified by a single range name, only that name can be used to locate a given record. To modify the macro so that it will allow more complex searches, you need to change the first lines to

```
{GOTO}TOP~
/rnlr.{END}{DOWN}~
```

The first line causes the cursor to jump to the cell named TOP, which should be the first cell in the column that will be used to name the data base (A8 in the example). Then the /**R**ange **N**ame **L**abels **R**ight command is used to name every cell in the column to the right. From here, the macro proceeds as previously described. Adding these two lines to the macro ensures that the proper names have been assigned to the proper cells before every query of the data base.

Macro for Converting Numeric Field Names to Labels

Another 1-2-3 macro can solve the problem of using numbers as data base field names. Let's assume that you want to create a data base which will record the depreciation expense for all your fixed assets for 1984 to 1988. Each asset will constitute a record. The data base will contain several information fields and 5 yearly fields. (See fig. 4.16.)

Look at the field names in row 1. The first two names, in cells A1 and B1, are labels; and the years in C1, D1, and so on, are numbers. The numbers in the range C1..G1 were entered with the /**D**ata Fill command. The Fill range is C1..G1, the Start value is 1984, the Step value is 1, and the Stop value is 1988.

Let's say that you want to perform a /**D**ata **Q**uery **E**xtract on the data base. First, you must designate the necessary ranges. Because you will want to search the data base by using "Asset Name" as your criterion, you enter that heading in cell A7. Cell A8 holds "Telephones," the actual criterion. Next, you create the Output range by simply copying the field headings from row 1 into row 10. Finally, you issue the /**D**ata **Q**uery **E**xtract command. What do you think happens? Figure 4.17 shows the results of the query.

Notice that only the "Asset Name" and "Cost" are extracted. Why? The field headings in cells C1 to G1 are numbers instead of labels, and 1-2-3 requires that all data base field names be labels. If you use values

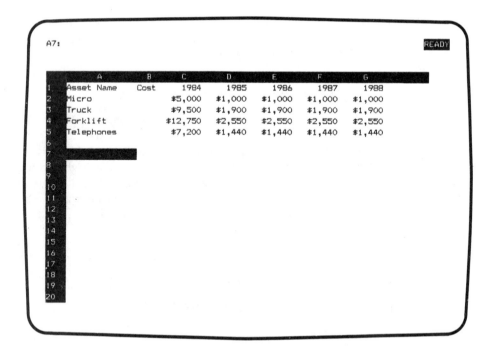

Fig. 4.16.

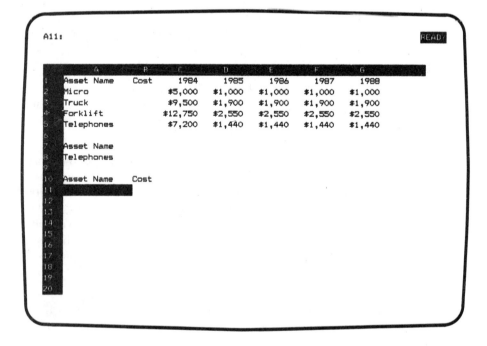

Fig. 4.17.

as field names, you cannot use the /**Data Query** command and the data base statistical functions on the fields with value headings.

This rule is not much of a problem unless you have a data base that logically needs numeric field headings; a data base storing yearly information is one example. Or you may have a problem if you want to perform calculations using the headings in a data base. In such cases, you'll want to enter the headings as values. Unfortunately, 1-2-3 won't let you do this.

One solution to the problem is to use the macro in figure 4.18. You can enter the headings as numbers and then use the macro to convert values to labels. This macro edits a numeric entry, moves the edit cursor to the Home position (the first character in the entry), adds a label prefix to the entry, closes the entry, and moves one space to the right. The second line causes the macro to loop back to the beginning. Every number in a row of entries is converted to a label, which can then be used as a field heading.

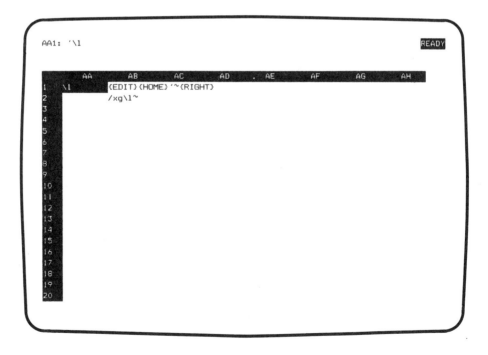

Fig. 4.18.

Macro for Comparing Character Strings

Although 1-2-3 is powerful and flexible when dealing with numbers, it has little capability when working with character strings. Despite this weakness, you can perform string operations by using macros. The macro in figure 4.19 compares character strings in a data base. •

To use the macro, you first enter the characters you wish to compare into two specially designated input cells (K1 and K2 in fig. 4.19). You then move the two input cells to a mini-data-base area and place them in the same column. (This area is the Input range for the mini-database.) Next, you move the first input cell to the Criterion range. Finally, you set up an Output range large enough to contain only one or two cells. At this point, you are ready to perform a query on the data.

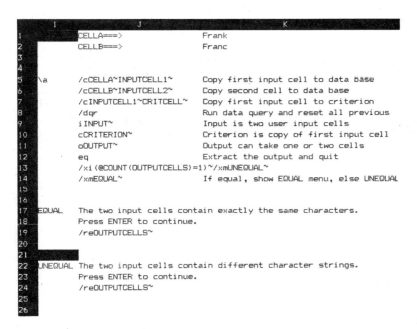

Fig. 4.19.

Two possible outcomes can result from the query. If the values in the two input cells are the same, the query extracts the data from both cells and moves the data to the Output range. If, however, the values in the two input cells are different, the query extracts the data from only one cell and moves the data to the Output range. An @COUNT of the Output range then identifies whether data was extracted from one or two cells. Depending on the value of the @COUNT, the macro returns either an EQUAL or an UNEQUAL message to the control panel.

Here's how each line of the macro works. The first two lines copy the input values from CELLA and CELLB to the Input range in the data base area of the worksheet. The third line of the macro copies to the Criterion range the first entry in the Input range. (See fig. 4.20 for the data base ranges. Notice that "Col" is a field name heading; you can use any field names as long as they are the same as the range names in the Input, Criterion, and Output ranges.) Don't forget to assign the following range names:

CELLA	K1
CELLB	K2
INPUTCELL1	L4
INPUTCELL2	L5
CRITCELL	M4
INPUT	L3..L5
CRITERION	M3..M4
OUTPUT	N3..N5
OUTPUTCELLS	N4..N5
EQUAL	J17
UNEQUAL	J22

Line 4 of the macro then resets all the data query settings. Lines 5, 6, and 7 set the Input, Criterion, and Output ranges, respectively. Line 8 starts the Extract to write to the Output range all the records that correspond to the criterion. Finally, the /xi statement in line 9 counts how many entries are in the Output range. If the count is 1, then the EQUAL menu is displayed (starting in cell J17). Otherwise, the UNEQUAL menu is displayed (starting in J22).

One of the nicest features of this macro is that it accomplishes something generally thought to be impossible in 1-2-3. With the macro, you can compare strings in a data base.

When you are making and using 1-2-3 macros, keep in mind that you shouldn't always accept the program's apparent limitations. First try to pin down exactly what it is that you want a particular macro to do. Then determine whether 1-2-3's macro capability can help you achieve your goal.

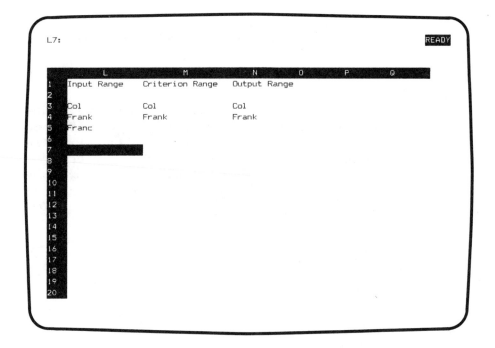

Fig. 4.20.

/Data Query Extract Macro

As mentioned in the previous chapters, you can make macros for any frequently used command operation or series of operations. And if you use 1-2-3 for data management, macros can save you considerable time. The /Data Query Extract macro is one of many useful macros that can automate data base operations.

Let's assume that you have created the data base shown in figure 4.21. Suppose also that you often extract parts of the data base and store the extracted information in a file separate from the one in which the original data base is stored.

To extract three months of data from this data base, you must perform the following operations:

1. Enter the Criterion range for extracting the data you want.

2. Set the Input range.

3. Set the Criterion range.

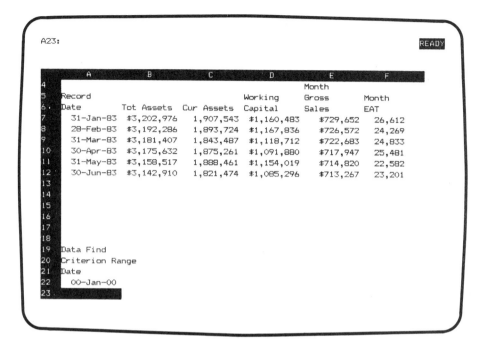

Fig. 4.21.

4. Set the Output range where you want the extracted data to be located.

5. Perform the /**Data Q**uery **Extract** operation.

6. Store the data in the Output range in a separate file.

If you find that you frequently use 1-2-3 to perform these operations, a macro can simplify your task substantially. The data query extract macro in figure 4.22 will perform all these operations for you. In addition, the macro allows you to edit the formula entered as the criterion, and the macro erases the Output range after it has been stored in a separate file.

To make and use this macro, you should complete the following steps. After creating the data base or adding new data to it, you enter the criterion for extracting data. Suppose, for example, that you want to extract from the data base shown in figure 4.21 all records for March, April, and May. To enter the criterion for extracting records for these months, you create a Criterion range containing the formula

+A7>@DATE(83, 2, 28)#AND#+A7<@DATE(83, 6, 30)

As indicated by the cursor position in figure 4.21, this formula is entered into cell A22.

After entering the criterion, you then create all the range names used in the macro. The data query extract macro uses the following range names:

CRITERION	A22
FIELDS	A6..J4
EXTRACT	A24
INPUT	A6
RANGE	A21..A22
OUTPUT	A26..J50

Next, you enter the macro as it appears in figure 4.22 and name the macro \q.

After entering the criterion, creating range names, and entering the macro, you are ready to run the macro and extract the data you want. When you invoke the macro, it performs five different operations. First, it allows you to edit the criterion. If, for instance, you use the

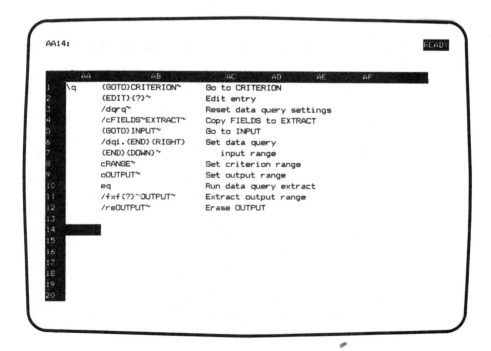

Fig. 4.22.

macro repeatedly and extract different information each time, the first line allows you to update or change the criterion. If, though, your criterion remains the same—for example, extracting all customers whose outstanding bills are over $200—you can delete lines 1 and 2 from the macro.

Second, the macro copies the field headings from your data base to the Output range, which is the area where extracted records will be placed. FIELDS is the range name for the original data base headings, and EXTRACT is the name of the range where the headings should be copied.

The third operation performed is the /Data Query Extract. Input, Criterion, and Output ranges are set, and records are extracted. INPUT is the beginning cell of the Input range. The macro sets the Input range by moving the cursor to the last record in the data base. CRITERION is the Criterion range, and OUTPUT is the Output range. When you name the range OUTPUT, be sure to provide enough space for all the records you want to extract; otherwise, the macro will stop, and 1-2-3 will display the message "Output range not large enough" at the bottom left of your screen.

When the records are extracted, they are placed below the Criterion range in A25..J29. (See fig. 4.23.)

Fourth, all new records are extracted and moved to a separate file named EXTRACT. Finally, the Output range is erased so that you can extract a different set of records if you want.

Although this macro has a specific application, you can easily adapt the macro to fit a data base you have created. Remember that you can delete lines 1 and 2 if you will not be changing your criterion.

Conclusion

When compared to stand-alone data base programs, 1-2-3 is limited in its data management capability. This chapter has shown how 1-2-3 macros can significantly increase that capability. Whether you want to simplify the job of creating data bases or perform operations not included in 1-2-3's data commands and functions, macros can help you accomplish many data management tasks.

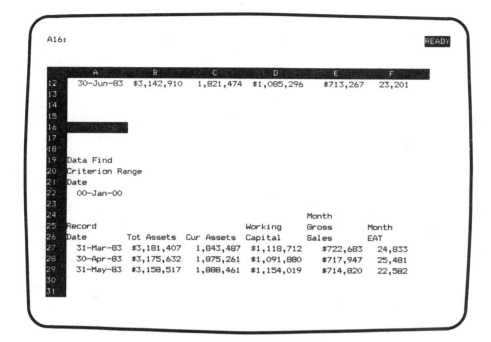

Fig. 4.23.

5

Macros for File Operations

No matter how much time you save when using macros or how greatly they simplify your worksheet operations, your energies will be wasted if you lose your data, forget to save it, or can't save it. The macros in this chapter will help you avoid common problems that may occur when you save data and manage files, even if you are an experienced user.

These file operation macros vary from simple ones that automatically save worksheets to complex macros that manage disk space. The following macros are included:

1. Macro for saving worksheets

2. Macro for backing up worksheets automatically

3. Macro for managing files

4. Macro for using subdirectories (for systems with a hard disk)

5. Macro for managing disk space

6. Macro for saving files to one or two disks

7. Macros for /File Xtract and /File Import

Macro for Saving Worksheets

As you add new 1-2-3 files to your data disks, the list of file names you must wade through becomes longer. This increase in the number of file names becomes a problem when you want to save updated versions of your worksheet, print, or graph files. A macro can save a 1-2-3 file for you by reading the file name from a designated cell in your worksheet.

The macro in figure 5.1 is fairly simple. First, the macro goes to the cell containing the name of the file. In this example the file name is placed in cell A1. Second, the macro copies the contents of cell A1 — the file name—to cell AB5 in the macro. Third, the macro begins the file save operation. When 1-2-3 asks for the file name, the name given is the one that has been copied from cell A1 of the worksheet. Finally, the macro ends by selecting **Replace**, which replaces the current file.

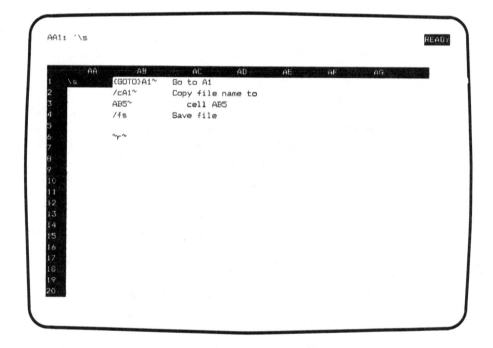

Fig. 5.1.

When you use this macro, keep in mind the following points. First, if you store the macro in a special macro library file so that you'll have the macro available for copying into the worksheet, you should copy the macro to the same worksheet location as that in the library file. In other words, if the file save macro is stored in AA1 in your library file, you should copy the macro to AA1 in your worksheet. Second, the location of the file name should be stored in the same cell in every worksheet. In the example here, A1 was chosen as the location for the file name; therefore, each file name for each of the other worksheets should be stored in A1.

One way to avoid having to copy the macro to the same location in every worksheet and storing the file name in the same cell in each worksheet is to use range names for both the macro and the file name. Figure 5.2 shows a version of the file save macro that substitutes range names for the original cell addresses. However, when you copy the macro from its library file into a worksheet, you will need to assign the two range names after the macro has been copied into the worksheet.

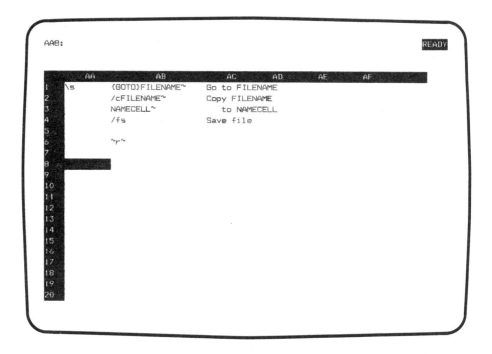

Fig. 5.2.

In this version of the macro, the cell where the file name is stored has been named FILENAME, whereas the cell in the macro where the file name is read has been named NAMECELL.

You may want to make another change to the original file save macro in figure 5.1. You can stop the macro before it begins the replace operation. In the original macro, no condition is provided that causes the macro to stop before it begins to replace the previously saved file. If you begin executing the macro and then decide to retain the previously saved file, the only way to save it is by trying to stop the macro (by pressing Ctrl Break) before the replace operation begins.

You can, however, modify the macro so that it pauses, providing you with the opportunity to cancel the file save operation or to continue by replacing the previously saved file. Changing the last line, r~, to {?}

161

will stop the macro so that it will wait for your input. You can then select either Cancel or Replace and press ENTER before proceeding. (See fig. 5.3.)

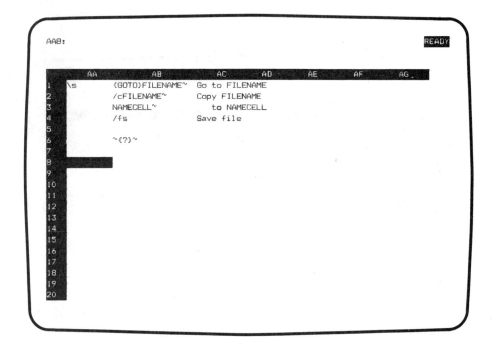

Fig. 5.3.

Macro for Backing Up Worksheets Automatically

As you become an avid 1-2-3 macro user, you'll soon discover the practical benefits of using macros for developing worksheets. But 1-2-3 macros can benefit you even in ways you have never imagined. For instance, a macro can save you from the horror of losing hours or possibly even weeks of work. The macro in figure 5.4 will automatically make backup copies of your worksheets. If you use this macro, you'll never need to worry about losing your only disk copy of a file.

Here's how the macro works. First, you need to create the macro and name it, making sure that you have assigned \0 to the macro. Because you are using the name \0, the macro will run automatically when the worksheet is retrieved. The macro first prompts you to change disks

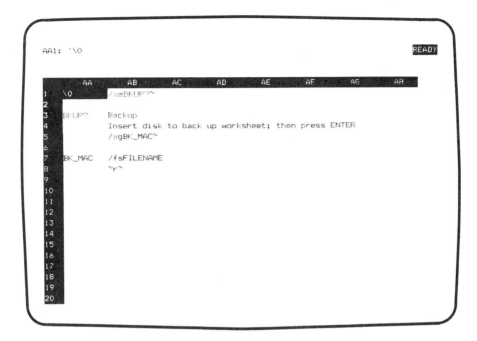

Fig. 5.4.

and then uses the /**F**ile **S**ave command to create the backup copy. If you want to stop the macro before it makes the backup file, you just press Ctrl Break.

The macro in figure 5.4 is designed to work with a specific file. When the file save operation begins in line 1 of the BK_MAC subroutine, the macro saves only the file provided in this line. If, however, you want to use the macro for many worksheets, you can make the changes shown in the macro in figure 5.5.

If you substitute {?} for the file name, the macro will stop. You can therefore use the macro to save any current worksheet. And you can store this file save macro in your macro library and copy the macro into a worksheet as soon as you create it.

Macro for Managing Files

For users who create many worksheet, graph, and print files on a single disk, retrieving any one of these files requires digging through many levels of file names. With the macro in figure 5.6, you can set up a list of file names on a special worksheet and have that worksheet automatically loaded whenever you begin a 1-2-3 session.

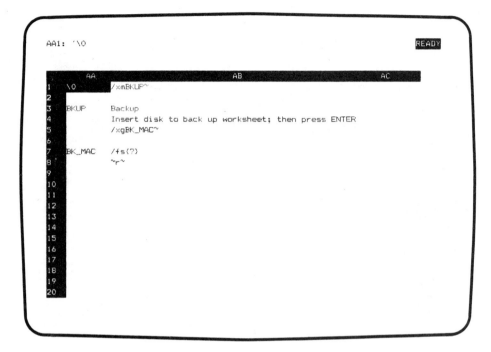

Fig. 5.5.

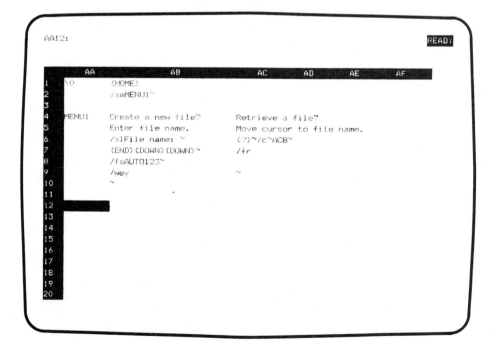

Fig. 5.6.

Here's how you can create both the worksheet and the macro for managing files. First, you begin with a new worksheet, reserving as many columns as needed to list the file names for your 1-2-3 worksheet files (.WKS). In the sample worksheet in figure 5.7, column A has been reserved for file names. Because the first file name is entered in A1, the macro begins by moving the cursor to A1, or {HOME}. Second, you type into the worksheet the file names currently stored on your disk. Third, you enter the macro shown in figure 5.7 into an area that won't interfere with the file name list. Fourth, you name the macro \0. You must use \0 so that your macro will be invoked automatically, as soon as the file containing your file list and macro is loaded.

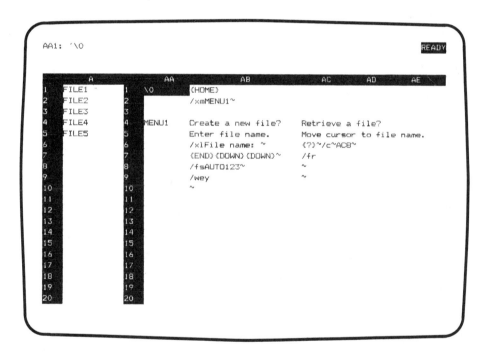

Fig. 5.7.

A final step is necessary if you want your file list to be automatically loaded whenever you begin a 1-2-3 session. You must assign the name AUTO123 to the file. (When you name the file AUTO123, the extension *.WKS* will be added by the program.) AUTO123.WKS is the file name especially reserved for automatically loaded worksheets.

After you complete the steps for setting up the file list and the macro, the following process takes place. As soon as you begin a 1-2-3 session, your file list worksheet will be loaded. Once the worksheet is loaded, the macro will begin running. The macro first moves the cursor to {HOME}. Two options are then provided by the macro menu: (1) to create a new file and add the name to your file list, or (2) to retrieve one of the files from the list.

Whenever you select the "Create a new file" option, the macro first allows you to add the new name to the current list. Second, the macro updates the AUTO123.WKS file with the new name included. Finally, the macro erases the present worksheet so that you can begin a new one.

Two major benefits of using this macro are evident. You can have a complete list of file names displayed as soon as you begin a 1-2-3 session, and retrieving a file doesn't require scrolling through many menu levels. When you create your list of file names on the worksheet, you should remember to type each file name exactly as it appears in 1-2-3's file menu. You should include only the first part of the file name without the .WKS extension and also make sure that the file name contains exactly the same characters that it has in 1-2-3's file menu.

Using \0

As already indicated, the \0 name should be used whenever you want to invoke a macro automatically, as soon as 1-2-3 loads the worksheet file. Because you cannot have more than one macro named \0 in a single worksheet file, you may want to use \0 for selected macros, such as the one for automatically backing up files. You may also want to reserve the name \0 for macros in worksheets that will be used by other people, to assure that certain operations will be performed, no matter who uses the worksheet.

Macro for Using Subdirectories (for Systems with a Hard Disk)

If you are using a hard disk system and want to automate the process for setting up subdirectories of 1-2-3 files, the macro in figure 5.8 will accomplish the task. This macro lets you divide either worksheet or graph files.

If you assign the name \0 to the macro, it will be invoked automatically, as soon as the worksheet file is loaded. When the macro begins running, the following process takes place. The first line allows you to

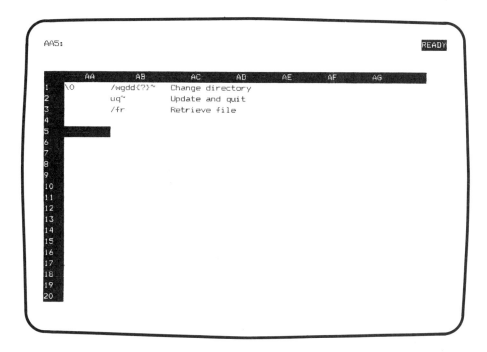

Fig. 5.8.

change directory path names. Because of the {?} in the first line, the macro pauses with the current path name displayed in the control panel. (See fig. 5.9.)

At this point, you can change the parts of the path name in order to get to the desired directory. After you have changed the subdirectory, the macro continues by making the new subdirectory the default. Finally, the macro retrieves the file menu for those files that are available in the current subdirectory.

The real power of this macro becomes apparent when you create in each subdirectory an AUTO123.WKS file for the macro. By including the macro in an AUTO123.WKS file in every subdirectory, you can easily shift from one subdirectory to another, under the 123 path. Don't forget, however, that if you are creating a new subdirectory, you first need to create the path name from the root directory.

Macro for Managing Disk Space

Checking available disk space isn't always the first thing a user thinks about when beginning a 1-2-3 session—although many users will agree that this task is an important one. If you want to be reminded of

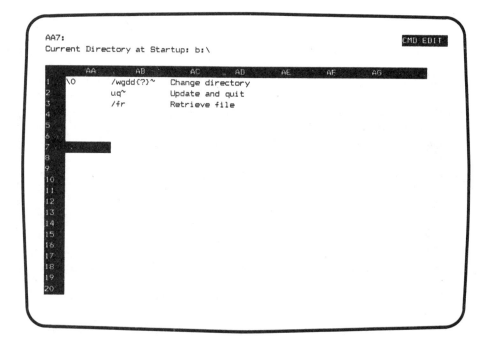

AA7:
Current Directory at Startup: b:\
```
              AA        AB        AC      AD      AE      AF      AG
  1    \0         /wgdd{?}~     Change directory
  2               uq~           Update and quit
  3               /fr           Retrieve file
  4
  5
  6
  7
  8
  9
 10
 11
 12
 13
 14
 15
 16
 17
 18
 19
 20
```

Fig. 5.9.

the disk space and the file names on your data disk, the macro in this section can assist you.

The macro in figure 5.10 provides two kinds of help. First, the macro allows you to get a list and a report of disk space for any of the three types of 1-2-3 files—.WKS, .PRN, or .PIC. Second, the macro enables you to clean out unnecessary files by automatically retrieving the /File Erase command.

Two features in this macro are important to note. First, the macro has been named \0, which will automatically invoke the macro as soon as the worksheet is loaded. If you want the macro to run at the beginning of every 1-2-3 session, then naming the worksheet AUTO123 will automatically load the file.

Second, when the macro begins to run, it will provide you with one of two options: (1) to get a list of your .WKS, .PRN, and .PIC files and a report of disk space, or (2) to begin erase operations. If you only want a list of files and a report on disk space, then you should press the {ESC} key, which will move you back to 1-2-3's READY mode. If, however, you want to begin the erase operation, the erase menu does provide a QUIT option. You can therefore move back to READY mode without

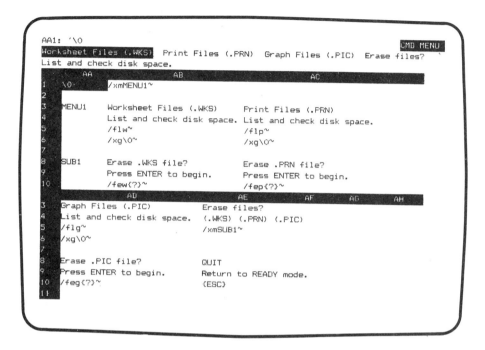

Fig. 5.10.

beginning erase for any of your files. In addition, each of the erase options—to erase .WKS, .PRN, or .PIC files—contains a second safeguard. Each erase macro allows you to back out of the erase operation after you have indicated which file you want erased.

Macro for Saving Files to One or Two Disks

Another method is available for saving backup copies of your important worksheet files. A macro can provide you with the choice of saving your files either to the disk in drive B or to disks in both drives A and B.

The macro in figure 5.11 works with DOS 2.0 and uses the macro menu command (/xm) to give you two options for saving files. If you select "Drive B" from the menu, the macro changes the default directory to drive B (or retains it) and saves the file to the disk in that drive. If, however, you select "Drives A & B" from the menu, the default directory is first changed to A, and the file is saved on drive A. Next, the macro changes the directory to B, and the file is saved on drive B.

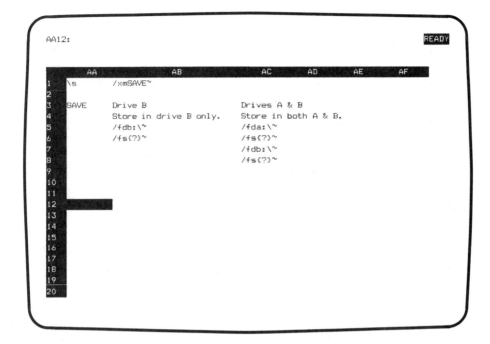

```
AA12:                                                            READY

        AA              AB              AC         AD       AE        AF
1   \s          /xmSAVE~
2
3   SAVE        Drive B                 Drives A & B
4               Store in drive B only.  Store in both A & B.
5               /fdb:\~                 /fda:\~
6               /fs{?}~                 /fs{?}~
7                                       /fdb:\~
8                                       /fs{?}~
9
10
11
12
13
14
15
16
17
18
19
20
```

Fig. 5.11.

If you are using DOS 1.1 instead of DOS 2.0, you'll need to use the macro shown in figure 5.12.

Macros for /File Xtract and /File Import

The /File Xtract and /File Import commands may be used frequently, although perhaps not as often as /File Save and /File Retrieve. You may, for example, need to divide your worksheet or import text from files created by programs outside 1-2-3. For these tasks, the macros presented here will be valuable additions to your macro library.

The file extract macro can be created in different versions. First, the macro in figure 5.13 is designed to save formulas when data is extracted from one file and moved to another.

You can modify this macro so that it extracts a specified range whenever you run the macro. Suppose, for example, that you update a worksheet monthly and that you want to extract the same range to another file every month. Each of the versions in figure 5.14 contains a particular range to be extracted and moved to another file.

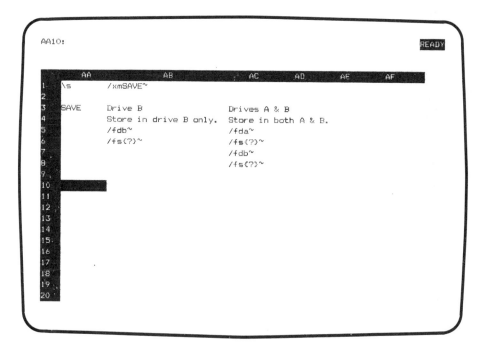

Fig. 5.12.

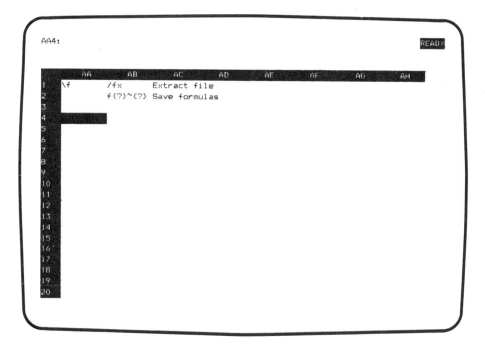

Fig. 5.13.

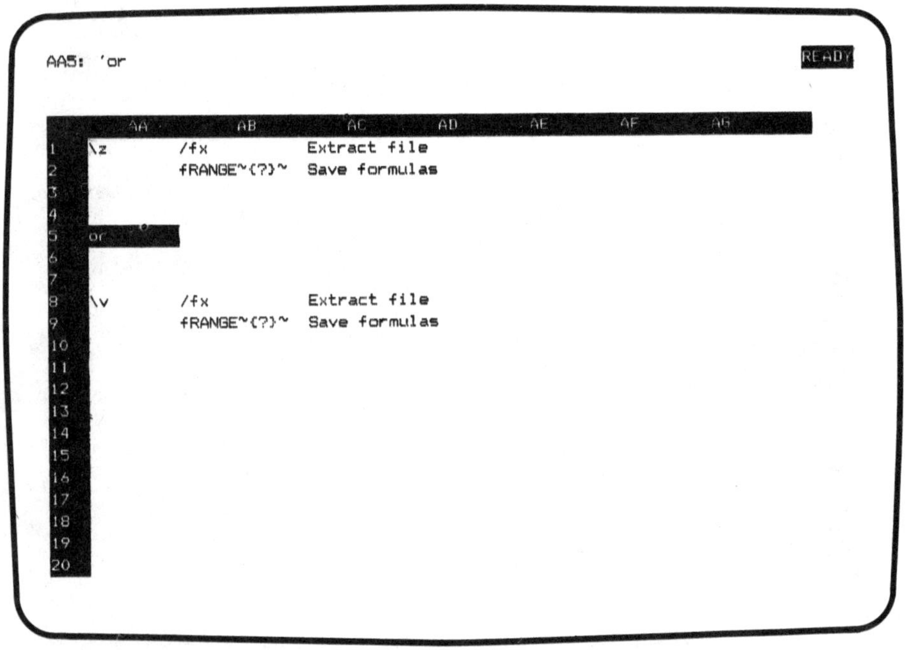

```
AA5: 'or                                                      READY

        AA          AB          AC          AD        AE        AF        AG
   1   \z          /fx         Extract file
   2               fRANGE~{?}~ Save formulas
   3
   4
   5   or
   6
   7
   8   \v          /fx         Extract file
   9               fRANGE~{?}~ Save formulas
  10
  11
  12
  13
  14
  15
  16
  17
  18
  19
  20
```

Fig. 5.14.

File import macros can also be modified in various ways. First, you can make a file import macro which imports text so that the macro enters each line of the file as a single label. (See fig. 5.15.)

You can also change the macro so that it treats each line as numbers and quoted labels. (See fig. 5.16.)

Finally, the file import macro can be changed (see fig. 5.17) to import the same specified file whenever you use the macro.

Although the file extract and file import macros are simple, they can be helpful when you are saving or adding data from other files to your 1-2-3 worksheets.

Conclusion

Developing good file management habits should become a regular part of creating 1-2-3 worksheets. These habits will ensure that you don't forget some necessary tasks, such as making a backup copy of each worksheet file or checking available disk space. The macros in this chapter can help make file management an important part of using

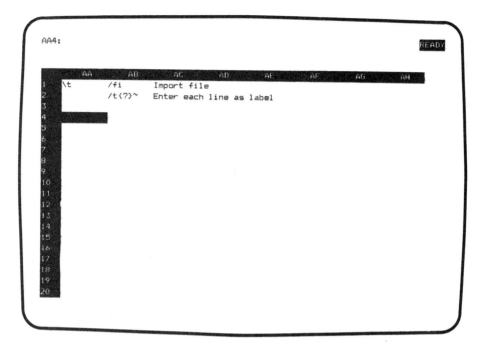

Fig. 5.15.

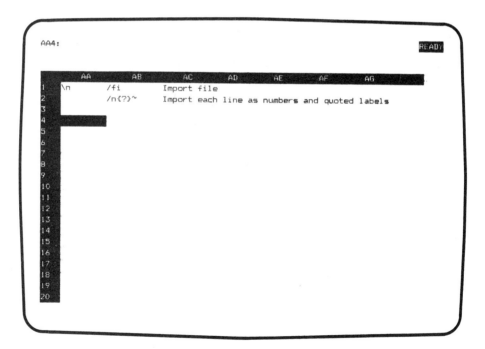

Fig. 5.16.

Fig. 5.17.

1-2-3. In fact, if you save some of these macros in the AUTO123.WKS file and use the name \0 for selected macros, 1-2-3 will automatically take care of certain tasks, such as making backup files or checking disk space. In addition, the macros in this chapter can help you manage subdirectories and conduct file extract or file import operations.

6

Macros for Printing

Imagine the convenience of being able to print 1-2-3 worksheets or graphics by pressing only one two-keystroke combination. Manually entering print settings and selecting commands for each worksheet to be printed can be time-consuming tasks. Once again, macros can reduce the keystrokes required and thus save time spent in producing reports and graphics.

This chapter presents macros ranging from those that enable you to store print settings to those that let you print range names. The following macros are included:

1. Macro for printing worksheets

2. Macro for printing multiple copies of worksheets

3. Macro for printing worksheets from different files

4. Macro for printing divider lines in data bases

5. Macro for printing range names

6. Self-modifying print macro

7. Macro for printing amortization schedules

8. Macro for printing form letters

9. Macro for printing labels

Many of these macros can be used for various types of worksheets and applications. At the end of the chapter are a few macros that are written for special applications, such as printing amortization schedules, form letters, and labels.

Macro for Printing Worksheets

A good way to begin using print macros is to make a simple one for printing most of your worksheets. If you often use the same print settings when printing worksheets and you don't need to change margins, set borders or headings, or change page length, this macro will print the worksheets for you. All you have to do is press Altp and designate the range you want printed. (See fig. 6.1.)

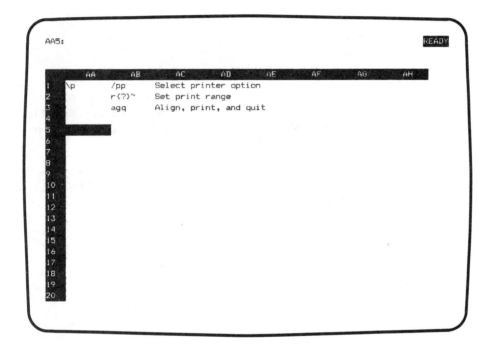

Fig. 6.1.

You can also modify the macro so that you can include special settings or even change settings. If, for example, you print reports with different left and right margin settings, the macro in figure 6.2 will do the job.

Unlike the basic macro in figure 6.1, this macro pauses for you to enter the range, then selects the /Options Margins Left command. The macro pauses for you to enter the left margin, then selects the Margins Right command so that you can enter the right margin. Afterward, the macro prints the worksheet.

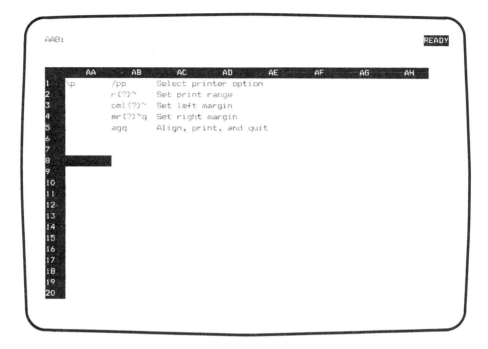

Fig. 6.2.

Macro for Printing Multiple Copies of Worksheets

This macro shows how 1-2-3's macro capability can be used to automate the process of printing multiple copies of a large report. Suppose, for example, that you have just created a large worksheet and that you are now ready to print a report. Because of the size of the worksheet, you estimate that the printing of one copy of the report will take 15 minutes. To print more than one copy, you must enter the /Print Printer Go command after each printing. If you want to print, say, three copies of a long report, the waiting time can be quite long.

1-2-3's macro capability provides a solution to this problem. To print multiple copies of the same report, you can use a print macro with a counter that automatically prints the number of reports you need. Such a macro is shown in figure 6.3.

Here's what you do to make the macro work. First, you use the /Range Name Create command to assign the name COUNTER to cell AA1.

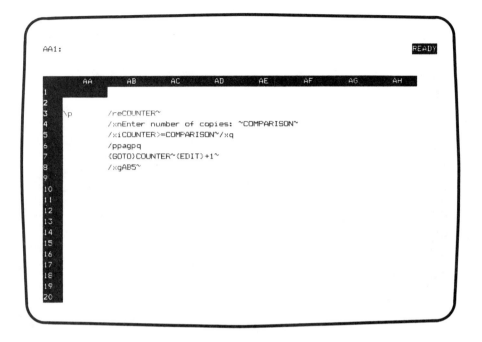

AA1:   READY

```
          AA        AB        AC        AD        AE        AF        AG        AH
 1
 2
 3    \p       /reCOUNTER~
 4             /xnEnter number of copies: ~COMPARISON~
 5             /xiCOUNTER>=COMPARISON~/xq
 6             /ppagpq
 7             {GOTO}COUNTER~{EDIT}+1~
 8             /xgAB5~
 9
10
11
12
13
14
15
16
17
18
19
20
```

Fig. 6.3.

Next, you give the name COMPARISON to cell AA2. Finally, you activate the macro, named \p, by typing Altp.

After the macro is invoked, it prints your report and keeps count of the number of printings. The first line of the macro erases cell AA1. Line 2 uses 1-2-3's /xn command to let you enter the number of copies to be printed. If you want three copies, you enter that number in response to the prompt "Enter number of copies: ". Afterward, the /xn command stores the number in cell AA2, COMPARISON.

The third line contains a conditional statement. Line 3 says that if the value in cell AA1 (COUNTER) is greater than or equal to the value in cell AA2 (COMPARISON), then quit the macro (/xq); otherwise, continue the macro on the next line. On the first pass through the macro, COUNTER will have a value of 0, and COMPARISON will have a value of 3. Because 3 is greater than 0, the macro will continue.

Line 4 prints the current worksheet. The single letters in this line perform several important functions. The first four letters, *ppag* (for /**P**rint **P**rinter **A**lign **G**o) actually print the report. The next letter, *p*, stands for **P**age and forces the printer to do a form feed, aligning the paper for the next copy of the report. Finally, the *q* (**Q**uit) allows the macro to exit from the Print menu.

This set of commands is used when a print range has already been established. You can change the macro, however, so that it will stop to let you enter the print range. (See the variation of the macro at the end of this section.)

The statement in cell AB5 increments the value in COUNTER by 1. After the first report is printed, COUNTER will have a value of 0 + 1, or 1. Finally, line 6 loops the macro back to the beginning. This line tells the macro to go to cell AB5 and continue processing. If the new value in COUNTER is still less than the value in COMPARISON, the macro will print the report again. The macro continues until the value in COUNTER equals the value in COMPARISON. When these values are equal, the macro stops, having printed the exact number of reports requested.

One of the problems with this print macro is that it won't allow the user to designate a print range from within the macro. The user must designate the range, exit from the print menu, and then run the macro. If, however, you make the changes shown in the macro in figure 6.4, you will be able to designate the print range. The new line, in row 3, issues the /Print Printer Range command and then pauses for the user to enter the appropriate range. After the range is entered, the macro issues the Quit command to exit from the Print menu. At this point, the macro continues on, as previously described.

Because the new line is located above the loop, the macro requests a print range for only the first copy of the report. The same range is used for all subsequent copies.

This relatively simple variation of the print macro is an excellent example showing how macros can be used to automate tedious or time-consuming tasks. The modified macro, in fact, offers increasing benefits: the more copies of a report you want to print, the more time and hassle the macro saves. Most likely, you will want to include this useful macro in your library and use it in nearly every worksheet.

Macro for Printing Worksheets from Different Files

Another timesaving macro prints worksheets from different files. If, for example, all your files in a certain application share the same format—specifically, the same column width (see fig. 6.5)—you can build a relatively simple print macro to print the separate files.

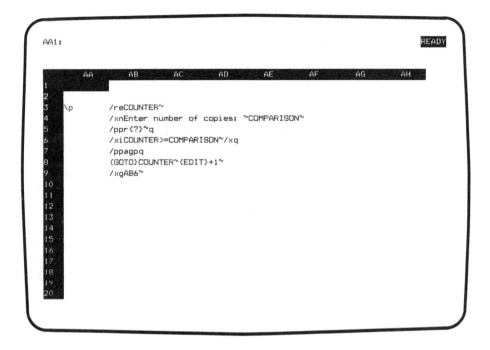

AA1:   READY

```
          AA        AB      AC       AD      AE       AF       AG      AH
1
2
3    \p        /reCOUNTER~
4              /xnEnter number of copies: ~COMPARISON~
5              /ppr{?}~q
6              /xiCOUNTER>=COMPARISON~/xq
7              /ppagpq
8              {GOTO}COUNTER~{EDIT}+1~
9              /xgAB6~
10
11
12
13
14
15
16
17
18
19
20
```

Fig. 6.4.

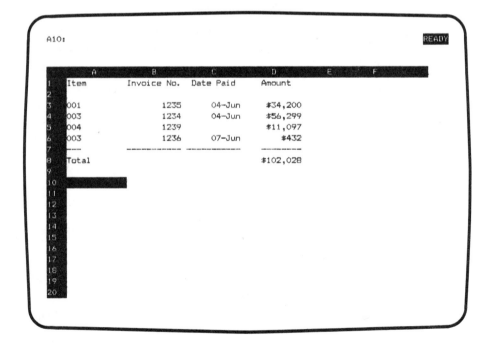

A10:   READY

```
          A           B         C          D       E        F
1    Item        Invoice No.  Date Paid   Amount
2
3    001           1235       04-Jun     $34,200
4    003           1234       04-Jun     $56,299
5    004           1239                  $11,097
6    003           1236       07-Jun        $432
7    -----       ----------  ---------   --------
8    Total                               $102,028
9
10
11
12
13
14
15
16
17
18
19
20
```

Fig. 6.5.

Let's assume that you have three files named PG1, PG2, and PG3. To print all three files consecutively, you begin by creating a new file called PRINT. In this file, you must first make sure that all column widths are the same as those in your active files (PG1, PG2, and PG3). Next, you make the macros as shown in figure 6.6.

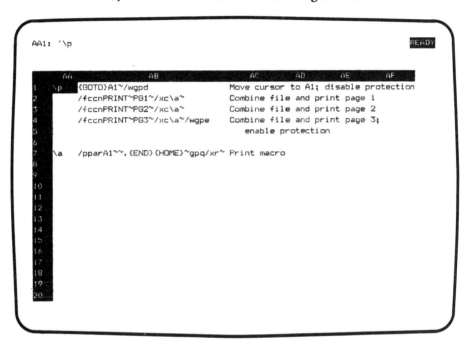

Fig. 6.6.

When you invoke the \p macro, here's what happens. The first line of the macro (AB1) positions the cursor at A1, then unprotects the worksheet. If you've named each print range PRINT, lines 2 through 4 of the macro successively combine the various files for printing. Then the macro calls the subroutine \a to print each file. After \a executes, it returns control to the main print macro, \p. These routines are repeated as many times as necessary. Finally, line 4 reprotects the worksheet. And that's all there is to it!

This print macro can be modified in two ways. First, you can further speed up the printing process by naming the macro \0. Printing will then begin immediately after you have retrieved the PRINT file. Second, if you want to print more than three files, you can add extra lines in the main macro by supplying only the respective name for each file. (See fig. 6.7.) Remember, however, that all files must contain the same column widths.

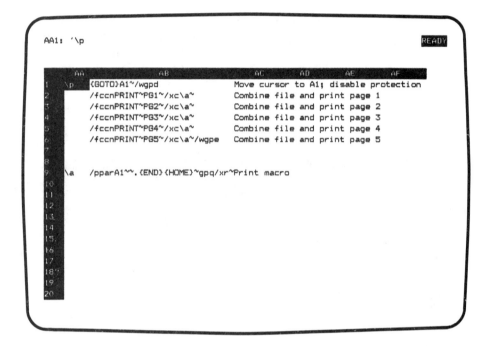

Fig. 6.7.

If you have a copy of ProKey, the macro processor from RoseSoft, the procedure for copying multiple files is even easier. Using ProKey, you simply make a macro that will do the following:

1. Load a file

2. Print a particular print range

3. Load the next file or quit

With the help of ProKey, you don't have to format column widths; the macro can print various files, each with different formats, while you attend to more important tasks. ProKey also allows the loading of one file after another, which is a feature that 1-2-3 doesn't have. With 1-2-3, you must combine files as previously outlined.

ProKey works best when you want to change the flow of control on the spot (for example, when you want to skip one page in a report or include another page). Using ProKey lets you "get outside" of 1-2-3 to control the printing order. (For a further discussion of ProKey, see Chapter 7.)

Macro for Printing Divider Lines in Data Bases

If you create a data base, 1-2-3 requires that you place the field headings in the row immediately above the records, with no intervening rows. You can only use the /Data Query command on the data base if field names are located immediately above the records. You can make a macro, however, that lets you change the format of the headings for printing reports and then restores field names to their original locations.

Suppose, for example, that you have created a data base like the one in figure 6.8. If you want to print the data base with a divider line separating the field names from the records, the macro in figure 6.9 will perform the task and restore the field names.

Notice that the main part of the macro (lines 1-3) only places a divider line into the data base and removes the line after the data base has been printed. This part of the macro does not contain the actual printing commands. They are located in the submacro named PRINT_DB

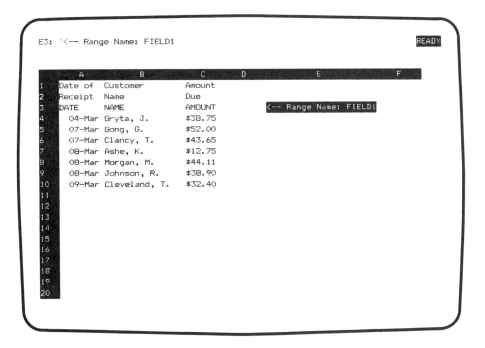

Fig. 6.8.

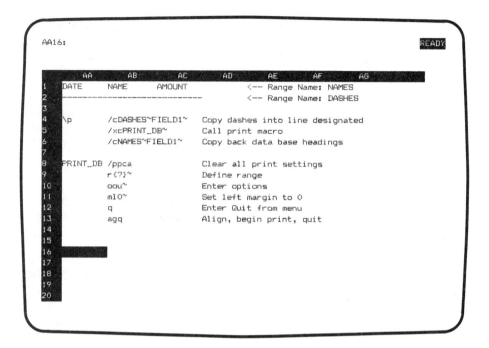

```
AA16:                                                              READY

        AA        AB        AC        AD      AE      AF      AG
1   DATE      NAME      AMOUNT             <-- Range Name: NAMES
2   ·------------------------------------   <-- Range Name: DASHES
3
4   \p        /cDASHES~FIELD1~    Copy dashes into line designated
5             /xcPRINT_DB~        Call print macro
6             /cNAMES~FIELD1~     Copy back data base headings
7
8   PRINT_DB  /ppca               Clear all print settings
9             r{?}~               Define range
10            oou~                Enter options
11            ml0~                Set left margin to 0
12            q                   Enter Quit from menu
13            agq                 Align, begin print, quit
14
15
16
17
18
19
20
```

Fig. 6.9.

(lines 4-9). The /xc command in line 2 of the main macro calls this submacro. After printing is completed, the \p macro continues by copying back the original data base headings.

As demonstrated in Chapter 4, you can use macros to solve many of the limitations of 1-2-3's data management capabilities. The macro for printing divider lines in data bases provides yet another tool for improving 1-2-3 data management capabilities.

Macro for Printing Range Names

Although several print utilities are available for printing all range names that appear in a 1-2-3 worksheet, you can accomplish the same result with a macro. You can produce a complete list of range names, then print, or save and print, the list. Such a list is particularly helpful when you need to debug and document 1-2-3 worksheets and macros.

For example, when you are writing large template worksheets containing many macros, you may find that the original range names have been deleted by changes you have made. Finding which names have been deleted or changed can be a long and difficult task. The macro in figure 6.10 can solve this problem. If you insert this macro into any

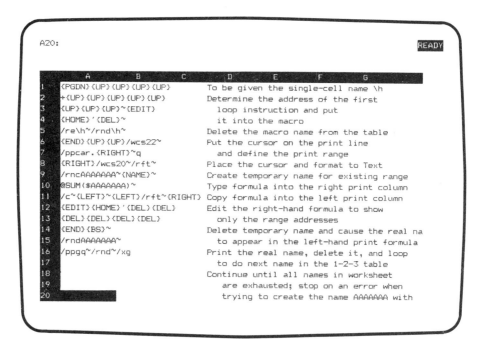

A20:   READY

	A	B	C	D	E	F	G
1	{PGDN}{UP}{UP}{UP}{UP}			To be given the single-cell name \h			
2	+{UP}{UP}{UP}{UP}{UP}			Determine the address of the first			
3	{UP}{UP}{UP}~{EDIT}			loop instruction and put			
4	{HOME}'{DEL}~			it into the macro			
5	/re\h~/rnd\h~			Delete the macro name from the table			
6	{END}{UP}{UP}/wcs22~			Put the cursor on the print line			
7	/ppcar.{RIGHT}~q			and define the print range			
8	{RIGHT}/wcs20~/rft~			Place the cursor and format to Text			
9	/rncAAAAAAA~{NAME}~			Create temporary name for existing range			
10	@SUM($AAAAAAA)~			Type formula into the right print column			
11	/c~{LEFT}~{LEFT}/rft~{RIGHT}			Copy formula into the left print column			
12	{EDIT}{HOME}'{DEL}{DEL}			Edit the right-hand formula to show			
13	{DEL}{DEL}{DEL}{DEL}			only the range addresses			
14	{END}{BS}~			Delete temporary name and cause the real na			
15	/rndAAAAAAA~			to appear in the left-hand print formula			
16	/ppgq~/rnd~/xg			Print the real name, delete it, and loop			
17				to do next name in the 1-2-3 table			
18				Continue until all names in worksheet			
19				are exhausted; stop on an error when			
20				trying to create the name AAAAAAA with			

Fig. 6.10.

worksheet at any location, name the macro, and execute it, you will get a complete listing of all range names and their current locations in the worksheet.

After you run the macro, it produces a list of range names, appearing as a hard-copy column of @SUM formulas. (See fig. 6.11.) If you leave the range names in the @SUM form, the list can be easily read; however, you may want to edit the list, as shown in figure 6.12.

The first eight lines (1-8) of the macro are setup commands; they make the macro executable from any location in the worksheet. The next ten lines (9-18) constitute the loop that actually produces the range name list. Because the macro is a type of file extract, the cursor will be located at position A1 (as shown in fig. 6.10) whenever the macro is inserted into another worksheet. This feature lets the user name the routine (/**Range Name Create** \h) as soon as the macro is retrieved, and then execute the macro. Be careful not to move the cursor after using /**File Retrieve**, or the macro will not work properly.

The first five macro lines enter the proper loop address (A9 in this case) into the correct location (A17) without adding extra range names to the list to be printed. Line 5 erases line 1 so that line 1 can be used for the print range, and deletes the macro name from both the

185

```
@SUM($ACTOUT)
@SUM($BHRS)
@SUM($DEPT)
@SUM($DESC)
@SUM($DUEDATE)
@SUM($ENTRIES)
@SUM($ESTIN)
@SUM($ESTOUT)
@SUM($ESTJOB)
```

Fig. 6.11.

```
@SUM($ACTOUT)
@SUM($BHRS)
@SUM($DEPT)
@SUM($DESC)
@SUM($DUEDATE)
@SUM($ENTRIES)
@SUM($ESTIN)
@SUM($ESTOUT)
@SUM($ESTJOB)
```

Range	Name
AE6	ESTIN
AE12	ESTOUT
AE13	ACTOUT
AJ11	ENTRIES
AJ18	DUEDATE
AJ38	DEPT
AJ39	DESC
AJ42	BHRS
AK14	ESTJOB

Fig. 6.12.

1-2-3 table and the list to be produced. Lines 6, 7, and 8 set up the print command and format the print range to Text. This step is vital to the entire routine. Any text-formatted formula that refers to a single range of cells having two names will redisplay the second name if the first name is deleted. (See also the discussion of lines 12, 13, and 14.)

Here's how the loop works. Line 9 creates a temporary name on the first range name in the 1-2-3 table. (This step is necessary so that 1-2-3 will make range locations accessible in the macro.) The macro then types into the print range an @SUM formula that uses the temporary name. The formula is written with absolute references so that it can be copied. You can use the formula without absolute references by changing line 11 so that the formula is retyped. Either way, the formula displays the temporary range name after completion of line 11.

Lines 12-15 are important for producing the actual range names. Lines 12, 13, and 14 change the right-hand formula to show only cell locations. Line 15 deletes the temporary name and causes 1-2-3 to find the other name (the real name) in the 1-2-3 table and to display the real name in the left-hand print column. The result is that the range name and its current address are entered in the cells previously defined as PRINT RANGE.

Line 16 prints the real range name from the 1-2-3 table, then deletes from the table the first name found that is identical to the name just printed. This action moves all other range names up one position in the table and prepares the loop (beginning in line 9) to apply the temporary name to the next name in the loop's next execution. The remainder of line 16 and lines 17 and 18 return execution of the macro to the beginning of the loop by using the /xg command followed by the return address (created in lines 1-4).

When the macro has finished creating the range name table, the routine terminates in an error because line 9 does not have an existing range to apply to the temporary name AAAAAAA, and 1-2-3 reads line 10 as an illegal range. The macro can be made to halt on something other than an error condition; in any case, once you get the list you need, you simply retrieve the file again and continue with your debugging.

There's one important point to remember when using this macro. Although the macro does provide the range names you need for debugging, *do not* save your worksheets after running the macro. The old worksheet will have no valid range names remaining, column widths may have been changed, and the print command will have been reset.

Self-Modifying Print Macro

This self-modifying macro incorporates features of the macro that prints worksheets and also uses the /Copy command to bring in new macro statements as they are needed. Although self-modifying macros can get quite complex, the print macro in this section is simple and useful.

The macro in figure 6.13 can help you streamline the process of printing worksheets, particularly when you are printing multipage printouts and need extra pages added at the end. The techniques presented here allow you to predefine the output and then invoke a print macro to print standard forms and additional options. After printing begins, the printer can run unattended.

To use the macro, you first assign a range name to each output page to be printed. Using range names is advantageous because once the print macro is developed, modifications to the print ranges can be made easily through the /Range Name Create command, instead of having to move the cursor to the print macro and do extensive editing.

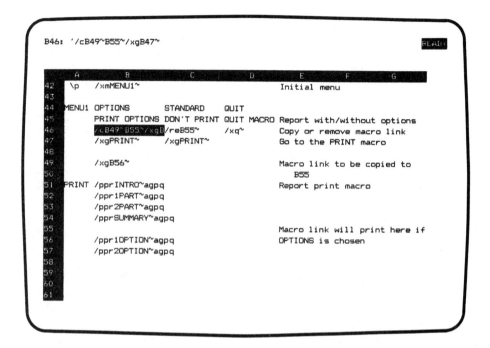

B46:   '/cB49~B55~/xgB47~   READY

```
      A          B           C          D        E         F          G
42   \p    /xmMENU1~                               Initial menu
43
44  MENU1 OPTIONS        STANDARD      QUIT
45        PRINT OPTIONS DON'T PRINT QUIT MACRO Report with/without options
46        /cB49~B55~/xgB/reB55~       /xq~      Copy or remove macro link
47        /xgPRINT~     /xgPRINT~                Go to the PRINT macro
48
49        /xgB56~                                Macro link to be copied to
50                                                 B55
51  PRINT /pprINTRO~agpq                          Report print macro
52        /ppr1PART~agpq
53        /ppr2PART~agpq
54        /pprSUMMARY~agpq
55                                               Macro link will print here if
56        /ppr1OPTION~agpq                       OPTIONS is chosen
57        /ppr2OPTION~agpq
58
59
60
61
```

Fig. 6.13.

You must assign a range name to each page of the report you want printed. The range you enter for each name should cover the appropriate range for printing. If, for example, PG1 includes A1..E44, then you should enter that range when creating the name. In the macro in figure 6.13, range names such as INTRO, SUMMARY, PART1, and PART2 designate different pages of the report.

When you look at the macro, you will see that MENU1 gives you the choice of quitting the macro or printing your report with or without options. The trick here is to use a macro link. The link consists of a /xg statement that is copied from cell B49 into the space between the commands for printing a standard report form and the commands for optional forms. The actual menu options included in MENU1 are listed in figure 6.14.

If you choose the macro hierarchy that includes the options, the macro link is invoked so that both standard and optional forms are printed. Under the STANDARD macro hierarchy, the macro erases the contents of cell B55, thus causing the print macro to stop after the last standard form has been printed.

Within the print macro itself, the *agpq* option (**Align Go Page Quit**) is included in each print command in case any of the ranges assigned

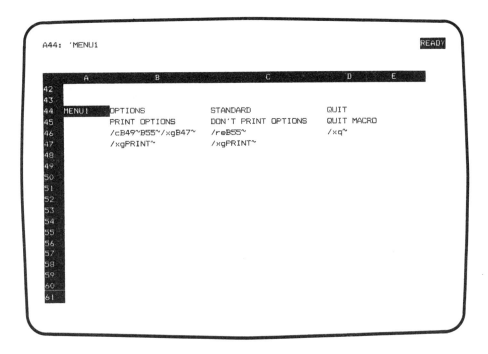

A44: 'MENU1   READY

	A	B	C	D	E
42					
43					
44	MENU1	OPTIONS	STANDARD	QUIT	
45		PRINT OPTIONS	DON'T PRINT OPTIONS	QUIT MACRO	
46		/cB49~B55~/xgB47~	/reB55~	/xq~	
47		/xgPRINT~	/xgPRINT~		
48					
49					
50					
51					
52					
53					
54					
55					
56					
57					
58					
59					
60					
61					

Fig. 6.14.

are not 66 lines long. Shorter ranges can cause the printer to get out of alignment.

The print macro in figure 6.13 can be modified with as many options as necessary for the printing tasks you frequently perform. For example, a number of options have been added to the macro as indicated in figure 6.15. In this macro the options have been expanded to include the printing of any combination of options, or none at all. If 1OPTION is chosen, the macro link is inserted as before. But the space between the fifth and sixth lines of the print submacros causes the macro to stop after 1OPTION.

The actual menu options included in this macro are listed in figure 6.16, and the actual options included in MENU2 are shown in figure 6.17.

2OPTION inserts a different macro link, thus providing a branch between MENU1 and the second option only. If BOTH OPTIONS is chosen, both macro links are inserted. With the STANDARD branch, the macro erases cell B55, as indicated in figure 6.16.

If you need to print a complex spreadsheet and you want to scroll through each print range before printing, the macro allows you to do

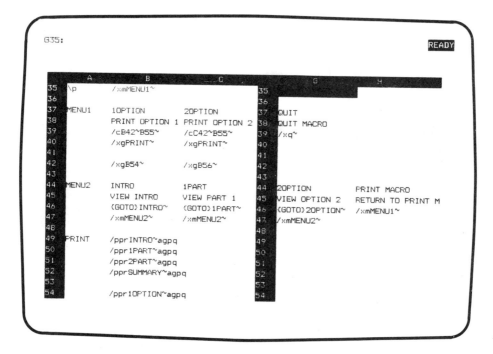

Fig. 6.15.

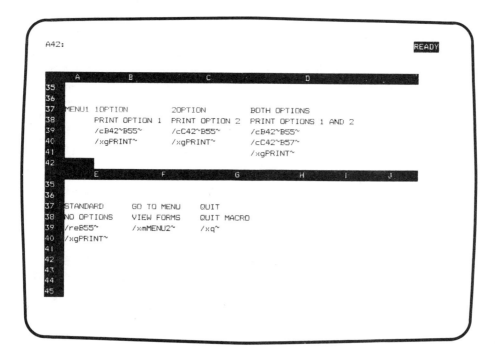

Fig. 6.16.

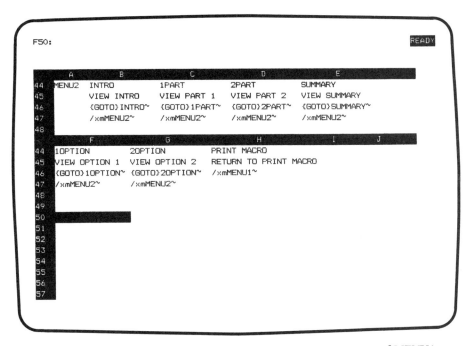

Fig. 6.17.

the scrolling. If you select the GO TO MENU option of MENU1, you can scroll through each print range before printing. The last line of each option in this menu is /xmMENU2~, which causes the macro to loop, letting you scroll through each print range in turn. To leave the macro to make a correction, you press {ESC}. Otherwise, the PRINT MACRO option takes you back to MENU1 for the appropriate print command.

This self-modifying print macro can be changed in several ways. First, you can add an additional menu that lets you print multiple copies of the entire report. A counter should be added within a loop, for counting the number of proposals printed. Second, you can add before the print macro a reminder for the user to check the printer for paper alignment, margins, etc. Whatever modifications you decide to make, the techniques presented here should meet some of your printing needs.

Macro for Printing Amortization Schedules

As previously suggested, print macros can be used for specific applications, such as printing amortization schedules. The macro in this section shows not only how to print the schedules, but also how to make a print macro for reports of varying length. This print macro is particularly useful for models built to accommodate the largest possible application.

The Loan Amortization Schedule in figure 6.18 is a simple example of such a model. It handles up to 30 years of monthly payments and is intended to be saved with most of the cells blank. After retrieving the model, you enter the three input items under the report title and also the first date in the date column. Then you just recalculate and print your spreadsheet.

The whole process could be accomplished quickly if printing didn't require many keystrokes. Because printed schedules usually have more than one page, you must enter settings so that column headings will be printed on every page. And because schedules will vary in length, you must set a different print range unless you use a macro that enters a range for the whole model. If your model does not handle a full 30 years, for example, you will end up with totals being printed in row 374.

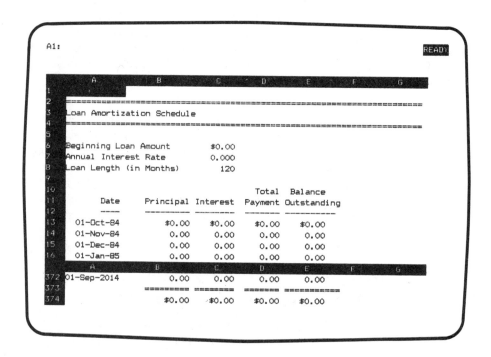

Although neither the concept nor the actual keystrokes necessary to print each individual schedule are extremely complicated, the operation still requires setting and clearing borders, specifying and printing three or more ranges, and completing several other operations. A much easier alternative to entering all print settings manually is to create a macro that will do these tasks for you.

The print macro in figure 6.19 is capable of printing schedules of different lengths. Specifically, the macro adjusts printing to the length of the loan schedule.

```
F1:                                                              READY

           F              G              H      I      J      K
1
2   Last Payment Row ( = Loan Length + 12)-->        132
3                       ( = C8 + 12)
4
5   Print Macro: Altp
6   =====================
7
8   {GOTO}G16~
9   +I2{CALC}{HOME}'~
10  {HOME}
11  /ppcb
12  rA1..E9~
13  ag
14  obrA10..A12~q
15  rA13..E
16
17  ~g
18  cb
19  rA373..D374~
20  gpq
```

Fig. 6.19.

Here's how the macro works. The last payment row is calculated in cell I2 (or manually entered). The formula in cell I2 says to take the length of the loan and add 12 rows to it to determine the last payment row (the end of the print range). A formula of this type is preferable because the user does not have to keep track of the print range. If no formula can be derived, however, a visual check and manual input of this row will serve the same purpose.

When you invoke the \p macro, it performs the following operations:

1. The last payment row (formula) is converted to a label and entered into a cell in the macro itself. The cursor is then returned to A1.

2. Any borders are cleared.

3. The title and beginning inputs are printed.

4. Column headings are set as borders.

5. The used portion in the body of the model is printed (range being determined by last payment row label).

6. Borders are cleared.

7. Totals are printed, and the paper is advanced to the top of the page.

With the \p macro, the whole printing process can be accomplished with only one two-keystroke combination instead of more than 65 keystrokes, and printing can be accomplished by even an inexperienced 1-2-3 user.

Macro for Printing Form Letters

Although Symphony lets you print form letters from data bases and create address files for printing labels, 1-2-3 cannot perform such tasks through the program's normal functions and commands. But you can make 1-2-3 macros for printing form letters and creating address labels. The macro in this section will read addresses from a data base and print each address in a form letter.

From a data base of customer names and addresses, like the one shown in figure 6.20, the macro will print a letter to each customer (see fig. 6.21) that includes the customer's name and address and the customer's name in the letter's salutation.

To use a macro for printing this form letter, you need to create three different areas on your worksheet: (1) the data base containing the names and addresses to be read into the form letter, (2) the form letter, and (3) the macro. When you set up the worksheet for printing form letters, be sure to put the data base, form letter, and macro in locations where they won't interfere with each other.

Consider putting the data base in a place where you can easily add names and addresses whenever you want. For example, you can locate the data base in columns A through I and the form letter in column K. (Remember that text is entered as a long label into the cells of a single column.) The macro can begin in AA1. (See fig. 6.22 for a diagram of the worksheet.)

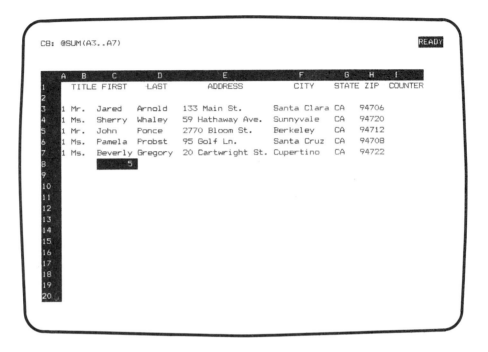

Fig. 6.20.

No matter where you decide to locate the data base, form letter, and macro, you'll need to follow certain specifications for the macro to run properly.

Making a macro that will print form letters requires the following steps:

1. Setting up the data base for names and addresses in the form necessary for running the macro

2. Creating the form letter you want printed with different names and salutations

3. Entering the macro

4. Assigning range names

Creating the Data Base

Your first step is to create the data base containing the names and addresses you want printed in each form letter. In figure 6.20 the data base begins at A1 and ends at I8. When creating the data base, you

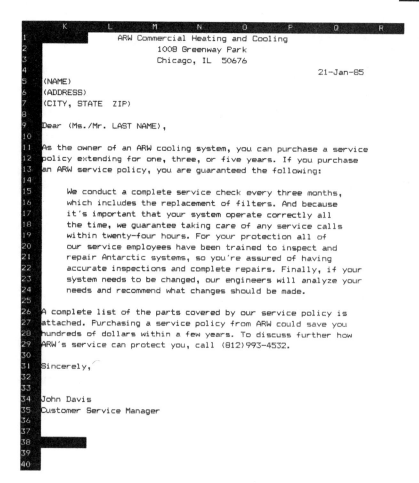

K1:   ARW Commercial Heating and Cooling   READY

```
            K        L        M        N        O        P        Q        R
1                          ARW Commercial Heating and Cooling
2                                 1008 Greenway Park
3                                 Chicago, IL  50676
4                                                         21-Jan-85
5     (NAME)
6     (ADDRESS)
7     (CITY, STATE  ZIP)
8
9     Dear (Ms./Mr. LAST NAME),
10
11    As the owner of an ARW cooling system, you can purchase a service
12    policy extending for one, three, or five years. If you purchase
13    an ARW service policy, you are guaranteed the following:
14
15         We conduct a complete service check every three months,
16         which includes the replacement of filters. And because
17         it's important that your system operate correctly all
18         the time, we guarantee taking care of any service calls
19         within twenty-four hours. For your protection all of
20         our service employees have been trained to inspect and
21         repair Antarctic systems, so you're assured of having
22         accurate inspections and complete repairs. Finally, if your
23         system needs to be changed, our engineers will analyze your
24         needs and recommend what changes should be made.
25
26    A complete list of the parts covered by our service policy is
27    attached. Purchasing a service policy from ARW could save you
28    hundreds of dollars within a few years. To discuss further how
29    ARW's service can protect you, call (812)993-4532.
30
31    Sincerely,
32
33
34    John Davis
35    Customer Service Manager
36
37
38
39
40
```

Fig. 6.21.

should set it up exactly like the one in figure 6.20. If you already have a data base of names and addresses and you want to send form letters to some customers listed in your data base, you can easily extract records from the original data base and make a smaller one for printing form letters.

Although figure 6.20 shows the usual headings for a data base containing customer names and addresses, three extra columns of data are included: (1) a column of ones (1's), (2) a column with the title for

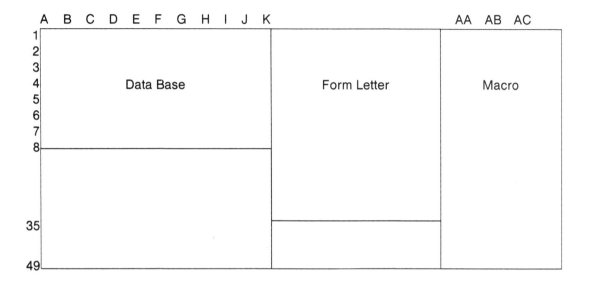

Fig. 6.22.

each customer, and (3) an empty last column labeled COUNT. The ones (1's) in column A and the COUNT column keep track of the number of letters that have been printed, and the title column is used for copying the appropriate title into each letter.

For every name and address in your data base, be sure to enter a 1 in the column to the left of the TITLE column. You should also enter headings as they appear in figure 6.20 and include an empty row between the headings and the records entered below the headings. (If you use the /Worksheet Insert Row command to add a row between the headings and the names and addresses, make sure that the command doesn't affect any other data in the worksheet.)

After you enter the appropriate headings, you then enter the names and addresses to be printed in the form letter. You should place all names and addresses in the order in which you want the letters to be printed. For example, you may want to print letters in ZIP Code order. The /Data Sort command makes this task fairly easy, particularly when your data base contains a large number of names and addresses. After you have created your data base, you should adjust column widths so that all information is displayed on screen.

197

In addition to entering the headings and the data, you also need to enter a formula for keeping count of the number of records in the data base. In the sample data base in figure 6.20, the formula @SUM(A3..A7) has been entered into C8.

Creating the Form Letter

After you have entered into the data base the headings, names and addresses you want printed, and special labels and formulas, your next step is to type in the form letter. As previously suggested, a good location for the form letter is column K. Although 1-2-3 does not have word-processing capabilities, you can produce a professional-looking form letter by following these tips:

1. Set the column width to the same setting as for the right margin. If your right margin is 65, for example, set /Worksheet Column-Width at 65.

2. Use label prefixes to center (^) or right-justify (") text.

3. Use an indent macro (see Chapter 3) whenever you want to indent a section of text. The middle section of the form letter in figure 6.21, for instance, is indented five spaces. If you use an indent macro, you won't need to press the space bar for every line of text you want indented.

Although your form letter can be as long or short as you want, you should be careful about the spacing in two places: (1) between the lines in the inside address of the letter, and (2) between the inside address and the salutation. In the sample form letter, the lines containing name, address, city, state, and ZIP Code are single-spaced, with one blank line between the inside address and the salutation. To check for correct spacing, you should type a description of what data belongs on each line of the form letter, as shown in figure 6.21.

Creating the Macro

Once you have completed the data base and form letter, your next step is to enter the macro as it appears in figure 6.23. Let's analyze the parts of this macro.

You should be aware of two important conditions before analyzing the parts of the macro. First, the macro depends on a number of range names—those within the data base, the form letter, and the macro itself. Second, the macro, as originally entered, contains a number of empty cells that serve two purposes. Some cells in the macro are

AA1: `'\p`

```
      AA              AB                    AC     AD     AE     AF
1   '\p  {GOTO}SUR_DB~                 Move cursor to beginning of data base
2        {END}{DOWN}                   Move cursor to top record
3        /c~TITLE~                     Copy title to cells in macro
4        /c~TITLE2~{RIGHT}
5        /c~FIRST NAME~{RIGHT}         Copy first name to macro
6        /c~LAST NAME~                 Copy last name to macro
7        /c~LAST2~{RIGHT}
8        /c~ADDRESS~{RIGHT}            Copy address to macro
9        /c~CITY~{RIGHT}               Copy city to macro
10-      /c~STATE~{RIGHT}              Copy state to macro
11       {EDIT}{HOME}'~                Convert to label
12       /c~ZIP~{RIGHT}               Copy ZIP to macro
13       1~                            Enter record number
14       {GOTO}ADDRESS~{EDIT}{HOME}'~  Convert to label
15       {GOTO}HEADING~                Go to first line of address
16                                     Enter title
17                                     Space
18                                     Enter first name
19                                     Space
20                                     Enter last name
21       {DOWN}                        Move cursor down
22                                     Enter address
23       {DOWN}                        Move cursor down
24                                     Enter city
25       ,                             Add comma after city
26                                     Enter state
27                                     Space
28       '                             Enter ZIP
29       ~                             Enter city, state, and ZIP
30       {DOWN}                        Move cursor to salutation
31       {DOWN}                            in letter
32       Dear                          Enter Dear
33                                     Space
34                                     Enter title
35                                     Space
36                                     Enter last name
37       ,~                            Enter comma
38       /pprLETTER~agpq               Print letter and advance page
39       /xiCOUNT=@SUM(COUNTER)~/xg\e~End macro
40       {GOTO}SUR_DB~                 Move cursor to data base
41       {END}{DOWN}                   Move cursor to next record
42       /re{END}{RIGHT}~              Erase old record
43       /xg\p~                        Loop back to begin again
44
45  \e   /reCOUNTER COL~               Erase counter column
46       /xq                           Quit
47
```

Fig. 6.23.

empty so that names and addresses can be copied to them, and other cells provide spacing between items as they are copied into the letter. When you set up the macro, you need to make sure that all cells used for spacing do in fact have a label prefix (') with the appropriate number of spaces entered. Forgetting to add a label prefix in these cells will stop the macro.

Five general operations are performed by the macro shown in figure 6.23. First, the macro begins by copying data from the data base to cells in the macro itself (lines AB1..AB12). Title, name, and address data are all pulled into the macro. Second, the macro enters a 1 in the COUNT column (line AB13) to keep a count of the record currently being processed.

Third, the macro pulls the title, name, and address data from the macro lines and enters that data into the appropriate cells in the form letter (lines AB14..AB37). Fourth, the macro then prints the form letters with name and address information (line AB38). Finally, the macro checks the number of records to determine whether to continue or quit execution (lines AB39..AB46). If more than one record is still left in the data base, the macro continues. When only one record remains, the correct number of form letters has been printed, and the macro quits execution.

As already suggested, your most important concern when you make the macro is to make sure the correct cells are left blank. And when you leave certain cells blank, you must remember to distinguish between cells used to receive data being copied into the macro, and cells used to enter the appropriate spacing into the form letter. AB16, for example, enters the space between an individual's title and name. For the macro to include this space, you must type the label prefix ('), press the space bar once, and press ENTER at cell AB16. For the macro to enter two spaces between the state and ZIP Code, you must type the label prefix ('), press the space bar twice, and press ENTER at cell AB26.

Assigning Range Names

The final step, which is one of the most important steps for getting the macro to work properly, is to assign range names. Because the macro depends on a number of range names from the data base, the form letter, and the macro itself, you need to make sure that all range names have been assigned.

If you glance again at the macro in figure 6.23, you will notice a number of range names that duplicate the headings in the data base: TITLE, FIRST NAME, LAST NAME, ADDRESS, CITY, STATE, and ZIP. These range names are assigned to cells in the macro to which data is copied from the data base. And whenever the same data is used twice in the macro, the second cell contains a name like TITLE2 and LAST2. For example, both title and last name are copied into the letter twice— once in the inside address and once in the salutation.

Also in the macro is a second type of range name for keeping count of the number of records that have been processed: COUNT, COUNTER, and COUNTER COL. Other types of range names include those used for moving the cursor to the right cell in the data base (SUR_DB) and in the form letter (HEADING); a range name used for the print range of the letter (LETTER); and range names used for naming the macro lines (\p and \e). A complete list of range names with their cell references includes the following:

ADDRESS	AB22
CITY	AB24
COUNT	C8
COUNTER	I3..I8
COUNTER COL	I3..I7
FIRST NAME	AB18
HEADING	K5
LAST NAME	AB20
LAST2	AB36
LETTER	K1..K35
STATE	AB26
TITLE	AB16
TITLE2	AB34
SUR_DB	B1
ZIP	AB28
\p	AB1
\e	AB45

The macro for printing form letters can be adapted in various ways to fit the kind of data base or form letter you are using. If, for example, your data base contains company names in addition to addresses, you need to add only three extra lines into the macro: (1) a line to copy the company name into the macro, (2) a line where the company name can be copied, and (3) a line to move the cursor down one cell. (See fig. 6.24.)

AB8: '/c~COMPANY~{RIGHT}   READY

	AA	AB	AC	AD	AE	AF
1	\p	{GOTO}SUR_DB~	Move cursor to beginning of data base			
2		{END}{DOWN}	Move cursor to top record			
3		/c~TITLE~	Copy title to cells in macro			
4		/c~TITLE2~{RIGHT}				
5		/c~FIRST NAME~{RIGHT}	Copy first name to macro			
6		/c~LAST NAME~	Copy last name to macro			
7		/c~LAST2~{RIGHT}				
8		/c~COMPANY~{RIGHT}	Copy company name to macro			
9		/c~ADDRESS~{RIGHT}	Copy address to macro			
10		/c~CITY~{RIGHT}	Copy city to macro			
11		/c~STATE~{RIGHT}	Copy state to macro			
12		{EDIT}{HOME}'~	Convert to label			
13		/c~ZIP~{RIGHT}	Copy ZIP to macro			
14		1~	Enter record number			
15		{GOTO}ADDRESS~{EDIT}{HOME}'~	Convert to label			
16		{GOTO}HEADING~	Go to first line of address			
17			Enter title			
18			Space			
19			Enter first name			
20			Space			
21			Enter last name			
22		{DOWN}	Move cursor down			
23			Enter company name			
24		{DOWN}	Move cursor down			
25			Enter address			
26		{DOWN}	Move cursor down			
27			Enter city			
28		,	Add comma after city			
29			Enter state			
30			Space			
31		'	Enter ZIP			
32		~	Enter city, state, and ZIP			
33		{DOWN}	Move cursor to salutation			
34		{DOWN}	in letter			
35		Dear	Enter Dear			
36			Enter title			
37		TOTAL	Space			
38			Enter last name			
39			Enter comma			
40		,~	Print letter and advance page			
41		/pprLETTER~agpq	End macro			
42		/xiCOUNT=@SUM(COUNTER)~/xg\e~	Move cursor to data base			
43		{GOTO}SUR_DB~	Move cursor to next record			
44		{END}{DOWN}	Erase old record			
45		/re{END}{RIGHT}~	Loop back to begin again			
46		/xg\p~				
47			Erase counter column			
48	\e	/reCOUNTER COL~	Quit			
49		/xq				
50						
51						
52						
53						
54						
55						
56						
57						

Fig. 6.24.

If you want to use 1-2-3 for simple word-processing and data-merge tasks, macros can provide these capabilities, as illustrated by the macro for printing form letters.

Macro for Printing Labels

A simple variation of the macro for printing form letters will create and print an address list. This section describes how to set up a data base and a macro for printing address labels.

Suppose that you have a data base of customer names and addresses (see fig. 6.25) and that you want to print address labels for each entry. The macro in figure 6.29 will create an address label column, keep count of the number of records in the data base, and print each name and address on a label.

To use this macro, you must do the following:

1. Set up worksheet areas for both the data base and the list of names and addresses created from the data base.

2. Create the data base in the form shown in figure 6.25.

3. Create the macro.

4. Assign range names to ranges in the data base, the address labels column, and the macro.

To run the macro, you need three areas on the worksheet: (1) the data base from which the address label list will be created, (2) an area where the label list can be stored, and (3) the macro.

As for the macro for creating form letters, you should begin by determining where on the worksheet you want to locate the data base, the address list, and the macro so that they won't interfere with one another as you continue to use the macro. Keep in mind that you may want to locate the data base where room will be available to add new names and addresses.

In addition to locating the data base, you need to determine where on your worksheet the address list should be created. When the macro runs, it will create a list within one column. If your list is fairly long, you will want to make sure that you have enough rows to accommodate all entries. Suppose, for example, that your data base consists of 200 records and that you want to print address labels each with the following three lines: (1) name; (2) street address; and (3) city, state, and ZIP Code. Such a list will require a column extending, say, from

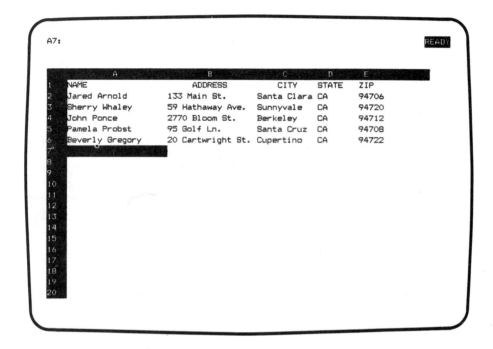

Fig. 6.25.

A1 to A1200. This amount of space is enough for storing each entry and leaving three rows between entries.

Notice in figure 6.26 the locations of the data base, address list area, and macro. First, column A is reserved for the address list that the macro will create. Second, the data base from which the list is created is located in B1..H8. Third, the macro is entered in AA1..AB38.

When you create the data base, you should set it up like the one in figure 6.27. Although this data base contains headings for name, address, city, state, and ZIP Code, three extra columns of data are included: (1) a column of ones (1's), (2) a column listing the appropriate title for each name, and (3) an empty last column labeled COUNT. The ones (1's) in column A and the COUNT column keep track of the number of records that have been copied to the address list, and the title column is used for copying the appropriate title before each name.

Like the macro for creating form letters, this macro requires that you enter a 1 in the column to the left of the TITLE column. When you set up your data base, be sure to include all headings as they appear in figure 6.27, with an empty row between the headings and the records.

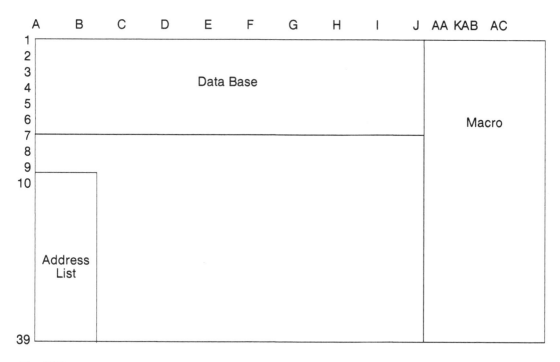

Fig. 6.26.

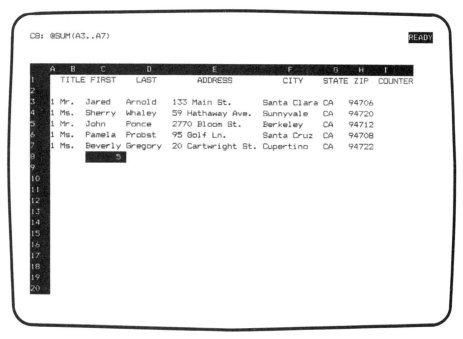

Fig. 6.27.

If you use the /Worksheet Insert Row command, be sure that you add a row between the headings and the names and addresses. This command may affect your macro and prevent it from running.

Once you have set up the correct data base headings, you should enter the names and addresses you want printed on the address labels. You won't be able to sort the address label list after it is created; therefore, you should sort your data base in the order you want names and addresses printed. If, for example, you want to list the data in alphabetical or ZIP Code order, use the /Data Sort command. One other step in creating the data base is to adjust column widths so that all information is displayed on screen.

For the macro to keep count of the number of records in your data base, you need to enter a formula in the cell directly below the last entry in the FIRST column. For example, the data base in figure 6.27 contains the formula @SUM(A3..A7), which has been entered into cell C8.

Setting up the area where names and addresses will be listed is an easy task. A couple of important operations, however, will ensure that the macro works correctly. First, you should begin the address label list column with a heading and divider line, as shown in figure 6.28.

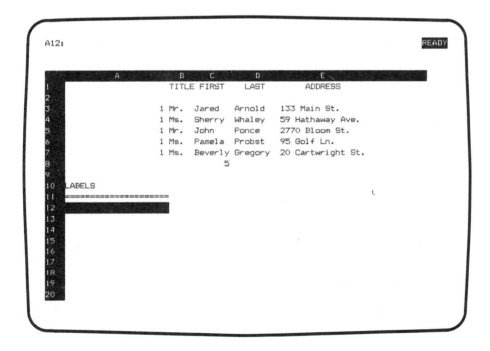

Fig. 6.28.

In addition to heading the column, you need to create two range names. First, the cell where you have entered the column heading should be named ENTRY. Second, you need to assign a name to the print range for the labels. If, say, you are printing 25 labels, each containing three lines and with three lines separating each label, your print range will be A12..A162. For the data base in figure 6.27, the name MAIL was assigned to A12..A42.

After creating and assigning range names to the address label column, your next task is to make the macro as it appears in figure 6.29.

AA1: '\p   READY

	AA	AB	AC	AD	AE	AF
1	\p	{GOTO}SUR_DB~	Move cursor to beginning of data base			
2		{END}{DOWN}	Move cursor to top record			
3		/c~TITLE~{RIGHT}	Copy title to cells in macro			
4		/c~FIRST NAME~{RIGHT}	Copy first name to macro			
5		/c~LAST NAME~{RIGHT}	Copy last name to macro			
6		/c~ADDRESS~{RIGHT}	Copy address to macro			
7		/c~CITY~{RIGHT}	Copy city to macro			
8		/c~STATE~{RIGHT}	Copy state to macro			
9		{EDIT}{HOME}'~	Convert to label			
10		/c~ZIP~{RIGHT}1~	Copy ZIP to macro and enter number			
11		{GOTO}ADDRESS~{EDIT}{HOME}'~	Convert to label			
12		{GOTO}ENTRY~	Go to first line of list			
13		/rndENTRY~	Delete ENTRY			
14		{END}{DOWN}	Move cursor down			
15		{DOWN}{DOWN}{DOWN}				
16			Enter title			
17			Space			
18			Enter first name			
19			Space			
20			Enter last name			
21		{DOWN}	Move cursor down			
22			Enter address			
23		{DOWN}	Move cursor down			
24			Enter city			
25		,	Add comma after city			
26		CA	Enter state			
27			Space			
28			Enter ZIP			
29		~~	Enter city, state, and ZIP			
30		/rncENTRY~{END}{UP}~				
31		/xiCOUNT=@SUM(COUNTER)~/xg\e~				
32		{GOTO}SUR_DB~				
33		{END}{DOWN}{LEFT}				
34		/re{END}{RIGHT}~				
35		/xg\p~				
36						
37						
38	\e	/pprMAIL~agpq				
39		/reCOUNTER COL~				
40						

Fig. 6.29.

Like the macro for printing form letters, this macro contains a number of empty cells. The macro copies names and addresses into some of the empty cells. Other empty cells are used to provide the spacing between lines of data containing names and addresses as this data is copied to the address label list area. When you enter the macro, you must be sure that each cell to be used for leaving spaces betweeen items contains a label prefix (') followed by the appropriate number of spaces. If you forget to add the label prefix in each of these cells, the macro will stop.

If you make the macro shown in figure 6.29 and you have problems running it, check to make certain that you have left the correct cells blank. The documentation in figure 6.29 will help you determine which cells should be left empty for copying data and which cells should be left empty for providing spaces in the label list. The space between name and title, for instance, is created by entering a label prefix (') and a space in cell AB17. Cell AB27 contains a label prefix (') and two spaces so that two spaces will be entered between the state and the ZIP Code in the address list.

Again, like the macro for printing form letters, this macro includes a number of range names. You must make sure, therefore, that all names have been assigned. The range names used for cells in the macro itself are these:

TITLE	AB16
FIRST NAME	AB18
LAST NAME	AB20
ADDRESS	AB22
CITY	AB24
STATE	AB26
ZIP	AB28

The range names used in the data base include the following:

SUR_DB	B1
COUNT	C8
COUNTER	I3..I8
COUNTER COL	I3..I8

As previously indicated, you will also need to assign two other range names: (1) a name for the heading for the address label list column (A10 in the example in figure 6.28), and (2) a name for the range for printing address labels (A14..A44 in fig. 6.30).

```
         Mr. Jared Arnold
         133 Main St.
         Santa Clara, CA 95051


         Ms. Sherry Whaley
         59 Hathaway Ave.
         Sunnyvale, CA 94086


         Dr. Christopher Ponce
         2270 Bloom St.
         Berkeley, CA 92005


         Ms. Pamela Probst
         95 Golf Ln.
         Santa Cruz, CA 92005


         Ms. Beverly Gregory
         20 Cartwright St.
         Cupertino, CA 95014
```

Fig. 6.30.

When you run the macro, it copies names and addresses into the label list, keeps count of the records, and finally prints the label list. Several macro operations take place. Lines AB1..AB9 copy data (title, name, and address) from the data base to the cells in the macro. Line AB10 enters a 1 in the COUNT column to keep a count of the record currently being processed. Lines AB12..AB29 enter the title, name, and address data from the macro lines into the appropriate cells in the address label list column. If more than one record is still left in the data base, the macro continues. When only one record remains, all addresses have been entered into the list, and the macro moves to the print operation. Finally, the macro prints the address labels (line AB37).

After the macro has copied names and addresses to the label list column, the list will appear as it does in figure 6.31. You can then save the list and add more entries to it later.

Conclusion

1-2-3 macros can greatly simplify the task of printing worksheets, especially when you want to print multiple copies of a worksheet or print worksheets from different files. Macros can also expand 1-2-3's print capabilities. In this chapter, you've seen how these versatile print macros can help with printing not only complicated worksheets, but also range names, form letters, and labels. Print macros eliminate the need to enter print settings whenever you want to print a report, particularly when you want to print multiple copies of one report or print many different reports.

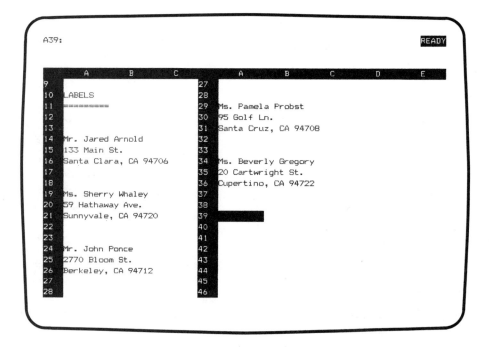

Fig. 6.31.

7

Macros for Graphics

Although 1-2-3's graphics capability is not as powerful and sophisticated as that of some dedicated graphics programs, it is an outstanding feature of the program, particularly when 1-2-3's graphics are used for business applications. And because of 1-2-3's integration of graphics and worksheet commands, making graphs is really a simple task. Nevertheless, selecting 1-2-3's graph commands and entering ranges can require many steps. Macros can reduce the number of menu selections required and even the amount of data you enter. In fact, you can customize your macros so that the whole process of making graphs from worksheet data is done automatically.

In this chapter are macros that simplify the making of graphs. Some of the macros are generic and therefore can be used for many types of worksheet data. Other macros are customized for specific spreadsheets and data bases.

The chapter also shows you how to increase 1-2-3's macro capability. One macro, for example, automatically makes multiple graphs from different worksheets. Another macro creates logarithmic plots. The capability of making such plots is now offered in Symphony but not in 1-2-3. Included in the chapter are the following macros:

1. Macros for simple graphs

    A. Macro for making a pie chart

    B. Macro for making a line graph

    C. Macro for making a bar graph

    D. Menu macro for making graphs

2. Graphics slide show macro

3. Macro for making multiple graphs

4. Macro for making logarithmic plots

5. Macro for producing both label and value titles in pie charts

6. Macro for printing graphs with ProKey macros

Macros for Simple Graphs

In 1-2-3, automating the process of creating graphs is simple with the help of a basic macro. Presented here is a series of macros that can be used for making pie charts and line and bar graphs. If you know that you will be making graphs frequently from a spreadsheet or data base, you can use macros, and you won't have to enter graph commands for each different graph created from the spreadsheet or data base.

Macro for Making a Pie Chart

Suppose you want to make a macro that produces a generic pie chart. You can save the macro in your macro library file and then insert the macro into many different worksheets whenever you need it. If you make pie charts often, the macro in figure 7.1 can be used for many types of worksheet data.

As indicated in the documentation, this macro automates the selection of all commands needed to produce a pie chart. When you press Altg to invoke the macro, it begins by selecting the type of graph (a pie chart in this case). The second line of the macro selects the data range and pauses for you to enter the range from your data base or spreadsheet. The third line selects the x-axis setting so that you can enter the range for pie slice labels. The fourth line selects the /Options Titles First command so that you can enter a heading. And, finally, the last line displays the chart.

A major advantage of this kind of graph macro is that it can be used for many different data ranges, labels, or titles. If, however, you want to automate completely the process for producing a pie chart from the data in figure 7.2, you can easily adapt the generic macro in figure 7.1 so that all data is entered for you through the macro.

The macro in figure 7.3 completely automates the making of a pie chart. When run, this macro will produce a chart like the one shown in figure 7.4.

Fig. 7.1.

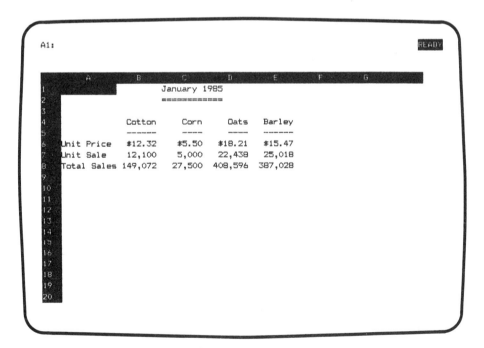

Fig. 7.2.

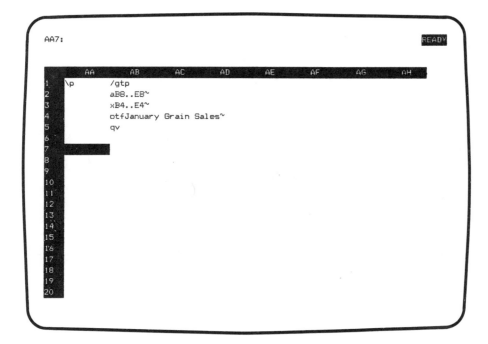

Fig. 7.3.

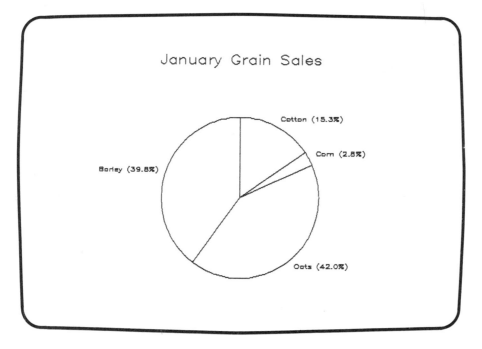

Fig. 7.4.

Macro for Making a Line Graph

In addition to creating a generic macro for making pie charts, you can make macros that simplify the creation of line or bar graphs. Let's look at the macro in figure 7.5.

Like the macro for producing pie charts, this macro contains the settings required to produce a simple line graph. If you want to use this macro to make a line graph from the data for "Working Capital" in figure 7.6, you simply invoke the macro and enter each of the settings when you are prompted.

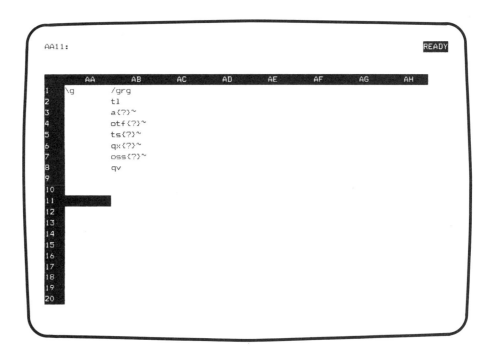

Fig. 7.5.

After you press Altg, the macro begins by clearing all previous settings. Line 2 selects the type of graph (in this case, line). The third line pauses for you to enter the data range for the graph. To select the data in "Working Capital," you enter D7..D12.

Line 4 pauses for you to enter the first line of your title. For the Working Capital graph, you may enter, for example, the company name, GHERKINS, INC. The fifth line of the macro lets you enter a second line to your title. If you don't need a second line, you simply press EN-

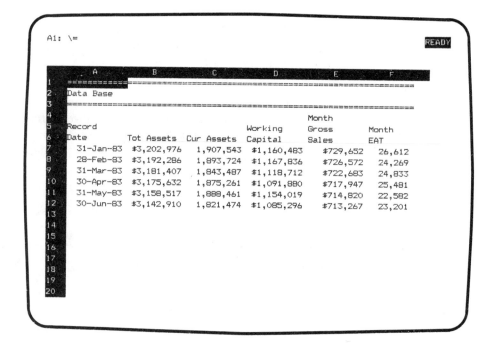

A1: \=   READY

```
        A          B           C            D            E          F
1  ============================================================================
2  Data Base
3  ============================================================================
4                                              Month
5  Record                          Working     Gross        Month
6  Date       Tot Assets  Cur Assets  Capital     Sales        EAT
7    31-Jan-83  $3,202,976  1,907,543  $1,160,483   $729,652     26,612
8    28-Feb-83  $3,192,286  1,893,724  $1,167,836   $726,572     24,269
9    31-Mar-83  $3,181,407  1,843,487  $1,118,712   $722,683     24,833
10   30-Apr-83  $3,175,632  1,875,261  $1,091,880   $717,947     25,481
11   31-May-83  $3,158,517  1,888,461  $1,154,019   $714,820     22,582
12   30-Jun-83  $3,142,910  1,821,474  $1,085,296   $713,267     23,201
13
14
15
16
17
18
19
20
```

Fig. 7.6.

TER when the prompt "Titles Second" appears. For this graph, you may want to enter *Working Capital* as the second line title.

Line 6 of the macro prompts you for a range for x-axis and line 7 lets you change x-axis scaling if necessary. Because the x-axis range contains six different dates in the data base in figure 7.6, you will need to adjust scaling to 2. The last line of the macro displays the line graph. (See fig. 7.7.)

To customize the line graph macro so that all settings for the Working Capital graph are included, you can make the changes shown in the macro in figure 7.8.

This macro completely automates the process of making the graph illustrated in figure 7.7. Keeping a macro library of graphics macros enables you to copy them into many of your worksheets, customize the macros for the data on a particular worksheet, and save them along with the data.

Macro for Making a Bar Graph

One other useful addition to your library of graphics macros is a macro for producing simple bar graphs. Like the macro for making line

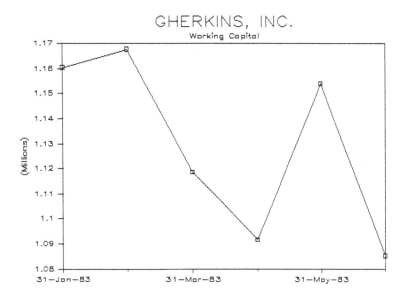

Fig. 7.7.

```
AA1:  '\g                                                    READY

        AA        AB         AC       AD       AE       AF       AG       AH
1    \g           /grg
2                 tl
3                 aD7..D12~
4                 otfGHERKINS, INC.~
5                 tsWorking Capital~
6                 qxA7..A12~
7                 oss2~
8                 qv
9
10
11
12
13
14
15
16
17
18
19
20
```

Fig. 7.8.

graphs, the bar graph macro in figure 7.9 is generic and therefore can be used with many kinds of worksheets. The macro can also be customized for specific data whenever you copy the macro into a worksheet.

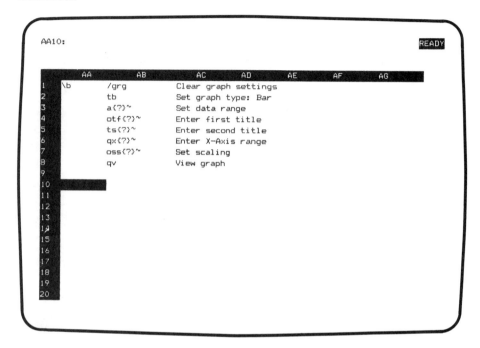

AA10:   READY

	AA	AB	AC	AD	AE	AF	AG
1	\b	/grg	Clear graph settings				
2		tb	Set graph type: Bar				
3		a{?}~	Set data range				
4		otf{?}~	Enter first title				
5		ts{?}~	Enter second title				
6		qx{?}~	Enter X-Axis range				
7		oss{?}~	Set scaling				
8		qv	View graph				

Fig. 7.9.

Like the macro for line graphs, the macro for bar graphs contains prompts for entering the following: (1) the data range, (2) the first line of the title (**Titles First**), (3) the second line of the title (**Titles Second**), (4) the x-axis range, and (5) the scaling factor.

To customize the bar graph macro, you should copy it to your worksheet by using /**File Combine Copy** and then edit each macro line to fit the specific spreadsheet or data base. If, for example, you decide to customize the macro so that it will create a bar graph from the "Working Capital" data (see fig. 7.6), you can make the changes shown in the macro in figure 7.10. After the macro is run, the result is the bar graph illustrated in figure 7.11.

Menu Macro for Making Graphs

Like many other macros in this library, those that produce graphs can be linked together by using the /xm command. This command lets you

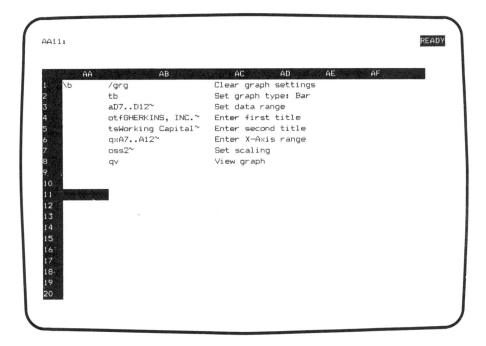

Fig. 7.10.

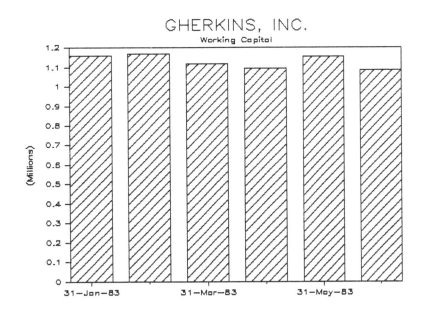

Fig. 7.11.

combine within one menu system your most frequently used graphics macros. You can then copy the menu macro into any worksheet and have two or more graphics options. For example, you can easily create a menu containing the macros for simple graphs: a macro for making a pie chart, another macro for making a line graph, and a third macro for making a bar graph.

The menu macro in figure 7.12 uses the /xm command, which provides you with a choice of creating from your worksheet data either a pie chart, a line graph, or a bar graph. When you invoke the macro by pressing Altm, the menu will appear as in figure 7.12. When you move the cursor to the type of graph you want to make, the macro will then prompt you to enter data for ranges and titles. This type of menu macro lets you easily view data in different forms.

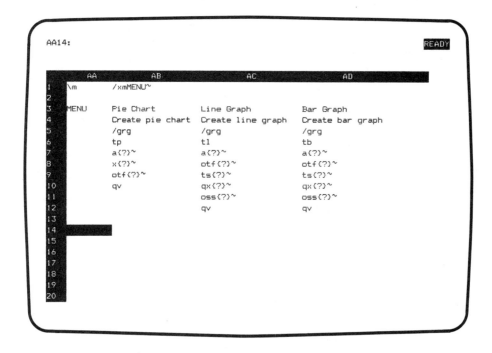

Fig. 7.12.

Keep in mind that you can adapt any of these graphics macros so that they will provide the options you need. If, say, you frequently change y-axis scaling and you want to incorporate a command line for changing the scaling, you just add the following lines to your macro:

```
gosyml{?}~
u{?}
```

To change the line graph macro so that it includes this scaling option, you add the same two lines before the final line of the macro, as shown in figure 7.13.

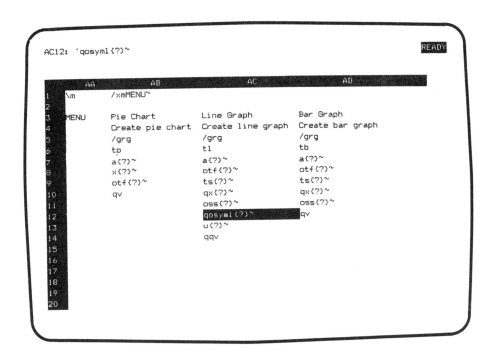

Fig. 7.13.

Graphics Slide Show Macro

One of the advantages of 1-2-3's graphics capability is that you can easily create presentational graphics. And if you are using graphics to present data for other people to view on screen, the /Graph Name Use command allows you to save graph settings and to display a graph by selecting the name you have assigned to the graph.

The macro in figure 7.14 uses /Graph Name Use to present a graphics slide show. With this macro, you can display four graphs by first pressing Altf and then pressing the space bar whenever you want to display a new graph.

To use this macro, you must enter all settings for each graph and then name each one by using /Graph Name Create. Also notice that the macro displays a graph, returns briefly to a blank worksheet, and then displays the next screen with a new graph.

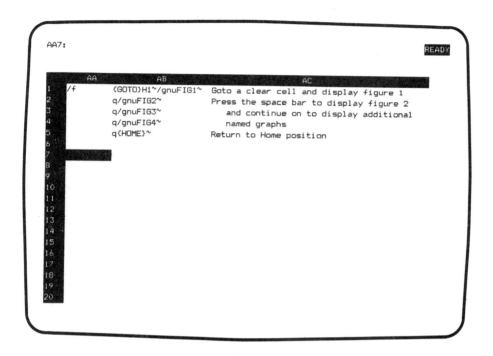

Fig. 7.14.

Macro for Making Multiple Graphs

You can use a macro to produce graphs automatically, using data brought in from separate worksheets. If you do a lot of graphing, such a macro can help automate your graph production.

Let's look at a specific application. Suppose, for example, that you have created 20 different worksheets containing data for various divisions of your company. As indicated in figure 7.15, data for each division fills nine columns (A1..I31), and each division is stored on a separate worksheet file.

The macro for creating multiple graphs, shown in figure 7.16, should be stored on another worksheet. Saving this macro in your macro library file is an excellent way to ensure that your original macro won't be changed accidentally by other worksheet data. Then when you are ready to create graphs for any separate worksheet, you can easily copy the macro into the existing worksheet by using the /File Combine Copy command.

In examining this macro, you will see that it can include different graph settings for different worksheets. Settings common to all graphs

```
A1: 'Growth Factors                                                    READY

          A         B         C         D         E         F         G
1  Growth Factors
2            ---------  Measure 1  ---------  ---------  Measure 2  ---------
3   Period    Current    Yr Ago    %Chg    Current    Yr Ago     %Chg
4        1  3,919,189  3,867,644    1.33%   10.27%     9.30%    10.43%
5        2  3,847,832  3,971,000   -3.10%    9.83%     9.08%     8.26%
6        3  4,319,651  4,032,002    7.13%    9.72%     8.99%     8.12%
7        4  4,414,621  4,229,048    4.39%    9.86%     9.25%     6.59%
8        5  4,175,232  4,144,434    0.74%    9.77%     9.23%     5.85%
9        6  4,301,499  4,322,041   -0.48%    9.88%     9.26%     6.70%
10       7  4,725,107  4,589,139    2.96%    9.93%     9.55%     3.98%
11       8  4,749,361  4,574,026    3.83%    9.88%     9.53%     3.67%
12       9  4,748,812  4,520,334    5.05%    9.92%     9.50%     4.42%
13      10  4,558,076  4,145,969    9.94%    9.96%     9.66%     3.11%
14      11  4,555,896  4,073,339   11.85%   10.11%     9.83%     2.85%
15      12  4,350,069  3,986,951    9.11%   10.31%     9.93%     3.83%
16      13  4,379,664  3,886,828   12.68%   10.91%    10.54%     3.51%
17       1  4,237,372  3,919,189    8.12%   10.57%    10.27%     2.92%
18       2  4,472,391  3,847,832   16.23%   10.29%     9.83%     4.68%
19       3  4,913,169  4,319,651   13.74%   10.32%     9.72%     6.17%
20
```

Fig. 7.15.

are included in the body of the main macro, and a counter redirects the macro to read individual graph specifications.

Here's how the macro works. First, each loop of the macro creates a new graph. This particular macro is set up to loop twice; however, you can modify the macro so that it will loop any number of times. When the macro begins to run, the first line (AA1) sets recalculation to manual, which allows the counter to work. Each time through the loop, when the worksheet is recalculated, the counter is incremented by 1. (See line 13 of the macro in fig. 7.16.)

Line 2 of the macro creates a counter called COUNTER. The original value of COUNTER is 0 because the cell is blank. Line 3 places the counter formula in X1 and gives COUNTER a value of 1 the first time through. The fourth line resets the graph settings, clearing all settings for new specifications. Line 5 assigns the name CONTINUE to cell AA4, thus making AA4 the starting point for the graph-creating loop. In other words, the macro loops back to AA4 after entering the settings for each graph.

Lines 6 and 7 set parameters common to all the graphs to be created (two graphs in this example). The common parameters are type, format, X range (scaled to skip a factor of 2), x-axis titles, and color.

```
Z1:  '\g                                                             READY
```

```
        Z           AA                          AB
1   \g     /wgrm                      Set recalculation to manual
2          /rncCOUNTER~X1~            Create COUNTER at cell X1
3          {GOTO}X1~+COUNTER+1~       Place formula in X1
4          /grgg                      Reset graph settings
5          /rncCONTINUE~AA4~          Name AA4 CONTINUE
6          /gtlxB6..B31~oss2~         Set graph type, X range, and skip
7          txFOUR WEEK PERIODS~fglqcqq Set x-axis title, graph to lines,
8          /xiCOUNTER=1~/xcSPEC1~     If COUNTER = 1, call SPEC1
9          /xiCOUNTER=2~/xcSPEC2~     If COUNTER = 2, call SPEC2
10         /gv{?}~                    View named graph
11         /xiCOUNTER=1~/xcSPEC3~     If COUNTER = 1, call SPEC3
12         /xiCOUNTER=2~/xcSPEC4~     If COUNTER = 2, call SPEC4
13         {CALC}                     Recalc worksheet and bump COUNTER
14         /xiCOUNTER<=2~/xgCONTINUE~ Loop back to CONTINUE if COUNTER =
15         /wgra                      Set recalc back to auto
16         /xq                        Quit
17
18  SPEC1  /gaC6..C31~otf\A1~ts\A2~   Set A range and 1st and 2nd graph
19         tyMeasure 1~syff2~qqq/xr~  Set y-axis title, format y-axis sc
20
21  SPEC2  /gaC6..C31~otyMeasure 2~   Set A range and y-axis title
22         syff2~qqq/xr~              Format y-axis scale (F2) and ENTER
23
24  SPEC3  /gs{?}1~q/xr~              Save graph 1 specs and ENTER
25
26  SPEC4  /gs{?}2~q/xr~              Save graph 2 specs and ENTER
27
28
29
30
31
32
33
34
35
36
37
38
39
```

Fig. 7.16.

Lines 8 and 9 test the number of the graph being created (equal to the number of times through the loop), and the macro is directed to the specifications starting in SPEC1 or SPEC2. The command /xcSPEC1 causes the macro to begin reading at the cell named SPEC1 and to continue reading until the macro encounters a /xr command. At this point, control returns to the main part of the macro (AA1..AA16). The macro returns to AA1..AA16 at the line following the /xc command (either line 11 or 14).

Notice that the /gv{?} command in line 10 displays the graph on screen. The {?} allows you to leave the graph on screen for as long as you want. When you press ENTER, the macro continues by saving the graph settings for the graph just displayed. If you want to change the graph, you press Ctrl Break to stop the macro from executing.

Whenever the macro saves settings for a graph that has been created, the macro will pause for you to enter a graph file name. The last two lines of the macro let you enter a file name for each graph. Remember that if you modify the macro so that it makes more than two graphs (the number of graphs created by this sample macro), you will need to add commands for saving the additional graphs.

Once the macro has saved the settings for a graph, processing continues at line 13 in the main part of the macro. This line recalculates the worksheet, incrementing the value stored in the cell named COUNTER. Line 14 tests the value of COUNTER. If the value is less than or equal to 2, the macro loops back to CONTINUE (cell AA4). If COUNTER is greater than 2, the macro continues to line 15, where the worksheet is reset to automatic recalculation. Finally, line 16 ends the processing.

The macro for making multiple graphs is especially handy when you want to compare data from different worksheets. To use the macro this way, you must first combine separate worksheets into one worksheet and then copy your macro into that same worksheet.

This process entails several steps. First, you retrieve the original worksheet if it has enough space for combining into the worksheet both the second worksheet and the macro. If you do not have enough space on the original worksheet, you should begin with a blank worksheet and combine both the worksheets and the macro into the blank worksheet.

Next, you copy the second worksheet into the existing one by using the /File Combine Copy command. Finally, you copy the macro into the worksheet, preferably in a convenient location for pulling in data for producing the graphs. When you run the macro, it will easily make graphs like the one shown in figure 7.17.

Macro for Making Logarithmic Plots

Unlike Symphony, 1-2-3 does not provide an option for logarithmic scaling. Graphing data on a logarithmic scale, however, can be useful for comparing numbers that vary greatly in magnitude. With linear

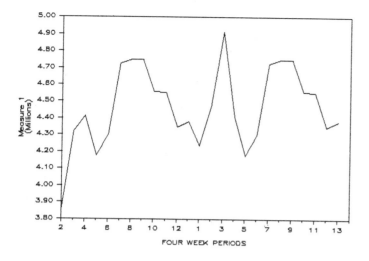

Fig. 7.17.

scaling, very large numbers in a range can dwarf their smaller companion numbers.

Figure 7.18 illustrates the problem of scaling large numbers. Because of the relatively high sales figures for December ($35,000,000), the smaller figures for July through September ($250 to $35,000) cannot be seen. With this linearly scaled graph, distances on the y-axis correspond to the numbers in the graph range. Thus, equal spacing exists between 0, 10 million, and 20 million on the y-axis.

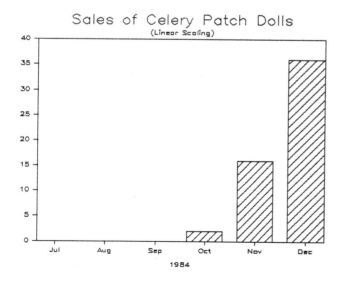

Fig. 7.18.

In contrast, the graph in figure 7.19, which presents the same sales data, is logarithmically scaled. With logarithmic scaling, distances on the y-axis correspond to the logarithm of the numbers in the graph range. Each tick mark along the y-axis of a logarithmically scaled graph corresponds to a power of 10. Thus, the scaling of larger numbers is compressed. For example, on the y-axis the distance between 10 and 100 is the same as that between 1,000,000 and 10,000,000.

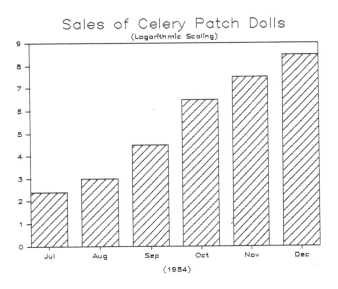

Fig. 7.19.

In 1-2-3, you can use the macro shown in figure 7.20 to generate logarithmically scaled graphs.

To invoke the macro, you press Altl. Next, you are prompted to specify a range. It can be a column or row of up to 25 data points to be graphed on a logarithmic scale. Because the macro copies this range, any cell references must have absolute cell addresses. When the macro is finished, the logarithmically scaled graph appears. To see the same graph again, you press the {GRAPH} key, F10.

If the data changes, you recalculate the graph by again invoking the macro. All the graph parameters can be modified except the A through F data ranges and the y-axis title. Because of the logarithmic scaling, the y-axis title is always set by the macro to (Powers of Ten). By adjusting the other graph parameters, you can select line or bar graphs, first and second graph titles, an x-axis title, and other options.

When evaluating logarithmically scaled graphs, you must remember that even though data values may appear in close proximity on the

A19: @LOG(B19)

`READY`

	A	B	C	D	E	F	G
1		ERR	ERR				
2	ERR				ERR	ERR	ERR
3	ERR	\1		/rncLOG DATA~{?}~	Get the range for the graph		
4	ERR			/reLOG COL~	Erase work area column		
5	ERR			/reLOG ROW~	Erase work area row		
6	ERR			/graqq	Reset graph's A range		
7	ERR			/goty{ESC}	Get ready to enter a title		
8	ERR			(Powers of Ten)~qq	Enter special y-axis title		
9	ERR			{GOTO}LOG DATA~	Go to the range to be graphe		
10	ERR			{DOWN}	Move down the column		
11	ERR			/c~LOG STORE~	Store the cell's contents		
12	ERR			654321~	Put a test flag in the cell		
13	ERR			/cLOG DATA~LOG~	Copy graph data to work area		
14	ERR			{GOTO}LOG R/C~	Go to the row/column indicat		
15	ERR			1~	Initially assume it's a row		
16	ERR			/xiLOG COL FLAG=654321~0~	Change if it's a column (0)		
17	ERR			{GOTO}LOG DATA~	Go to the range to be graphe		
18	ERR			{DOWN}	Move down the column		
19	ERR			/cLOG STORE~~	Restore the cell's contents		
20	ERR			/cLOG DATA~LOG~	Copy graph data to work area		
21	ERR			{GOTO}LOG~	Put cursor at work area base		
22	ERR			/xiLOG R/C=0~/xgLOG PCOL~	Branch to row or col process		
23	ERR		LOG PROW	{UP}	Move up to log scaled data		
24	ERR			/gA.	Get ready to enter graph row		
25	ERR			{END}{RIGHT}{RIGHT}	Move to the end of the row +		
26	ERR			{DOWN}{END}{LEFT}{UP}	Move back to the end of data		
27				~q	Graph row is defined		
28				/xgLOG JOIN~	Skip over column process		
29							
30			LOG PCOL	{LEFT}	Move left to log scaled data		
31				/gA.	Get ready to enter graph col		
32				{END}{DOWN}{DOWN}	Move to bottom of the col +		
33				{RIGHT}{END}{UP}{LEFT}	Move back to the end of data		
34				~q	Graph column is defined		
35			LOG JOIN	{HOME}	Put the cursor at Home		
36				{GRAPH}	Display the graph		
37							
38				------- VARIABLES -------			
39							
40			LOG STORE		LOG STORE		------- VA
41			LOG R/C	1	LOG R/C		
42							

Fig. 7.20.

graph, the figures actually vary by a factor of ten or more. Logarithmic graphs can therefore be deceiving, but if used properly, they can be of great benefit.

Here's what happens in the macro for making logarithmic plots. First, the macro copies to a work area the row or column to be graphed. The cells in the work area have corresponding cells that take the logarithm of each data point. Then these logarithmic functions are graphed. As is true of all macros, the best way to understand this sequence is to run through the macro manually while you use 1-2-3's STEP mode. A step-by-step analysis of the macro's execution is included here.

First, lines 3 through 8 initialize the macro. The data range is specified by the user, work areas are erased, the graph's A range is reset, and the y-axis title is set to the label (Powers of Ten). Notice the trick in line 7. This line erases whatever may have been previously entered as the y-axis title. Because you do not know whether a title was stored earlier, the extra space assures you that the {ESC} will always have something to erase and, therefore, will never move you back to the previous menu.

Second, lines 9 through 19 determine whether a row or column has been specified. Essentially, the sequence works by placing a flag in the data column. The data is copied to the work area, and if the flag shows up, the macro reads the data as occupying a column. Otherwise, the macro reads the data as occupying a row. The variable LOG R/C is set to 0 if the data occupies a column and to 1 if the data is in a row.

Third, lines 20 through 22 copy a fresh set of data to the work area. If the data is in a column, processing is transferred to LOG PCOL; otherwise, processing continues with LOG PROW.

Fourth, lines 23 through 28 are used for processing a row. The graph's A range is specified as the logarithmic form of the row that has been copied into the macro. (This range is the one specified in line 1.)

Fifth, lines 25 and 26 ensure that all data points in the range will be graphed, even if blank cells are mixed in. The processing then omits the sequence that processes a column and next moves down to LOG JOIN in line 35.

Sixth, lines 30 through 34 are used when the macro is processing a column. The graph's A range, which is found in column A, is specified as the logarithmic transform of the column copied into the macro.

Finally, lines 35 through 37 terminate the macro. The cursor is returned to Home, the graph is displayed, and the macro processing ends.

A number of important formulas are included in the macro. The cells in row 1 (columns B through Z) contain the @LOG functions for the cells immediately below these columns, in row 2. For example, cell B1 contains the formula @LOG(B2). The cells in rows 2 through 26 of column A contain the @LOG functions for the cells to the right, in column B. For example, cell A2 contains the formula @LOG(B2). All the @LOG functions appear as ERR in figure 7.20 because data has not yet been entered into the worksheet.

Besides checking to make sure that the correct formulas have been entered, you will need to be certain that all range names have been created before you run the macro. The labels in column C of figure 7.20 are range names for the cells to the right. These labels include the following:

> \l
> LOG PROW
> LOG PCOL
> LOG JOIN
> LOG STORE
> LOG R/C

You can use the /Range Name Labels Right command to define these ranges. Other range names to define are these:

LOG	B2
LOG COL	B2..B26
LOG COL FLAG	B3
LOG ROW	B2..Z2

Although no "perfect" solution exists for graphing widely divergent numbers, logarithmic scaling can help. The one danger is that logarithmic graphs can be easily misinterpreted. Whenever you use a logarithmic graph, therefore, you should always include a note of caution to the users. Providing a simple explanation of your reason for using logarithmic scaling is also a good idea.

Macro for Producing Both Label and Value Titles in Pie Charts

A limitation of 1-2-3's pie chart is that you can include only one set of labels on the chart with the X range option. You can make the pie chart with labels only, as shown in figure 7.4, or you can include the actual values represented by each pie slice. You cannot, however, have both labels and values displayed on the chart at the same time.

If you want to illustrate a pie chart with both labels and values, you can, however, make a macro that will display both. Suppose, for example, that you want to make a pie chart from the sales data in figure 7.21. You also want to show beside each pie slice the city and the sales totals.

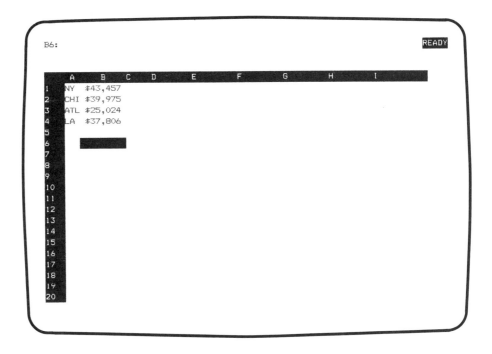

Fig. 7.21.

Here's how you can use the macro in figure 7.22 to make such a pie chart. The first step is to make sure that the label range and value range are in consecutive columns, as shown in figure 7.21. If the label and value ranges are not in consecutive columns, you should copy them into a blank area of the worksheet. Next, you make the macro as it appears in figure 7.22. Finally, you assign names to the X and A data ranges. In the macro the name LABELS has been assigned to the X range, and VALUES has been assigned to the A range.

To use the macro, you must position the cursor on the cell containing the first label of your labels column. For use with the city and sales data in figure 7.21, you place the cursor at A1. Next, you invoke the macro.

```
AA1:  '\l                                                              READY

        AA          AB          AC          AD          AE      AF      AG
1   \l          /pfTEMP~r                Create a print file (Replace)
2               ca                       Clear all print settings
3               r.{END}{DOWN}{RIGHT}~    Enter range to write to disk
4               o                        Select options
5               ml0~                     Set left margin at 0
6               mt0~                     Set top margin at 0
7               mb0~                     Set bottom margin at 0
8               ou                       Select Other Unformatted
9               q                        Select Quit
10              gq                       Save file and quit
11              {RIGHT}{RIGHT}           Move cursor two columns
12              /fitTEMP~                Import labels from disk
13              /grg                     Reset graph settings
14              tp                       Set graph type: pie
15              xLABELS~                 Enter X data range (Named LABELS)
16              aVALUES~                 Enter A data range (Named VALUES)
17              otfMETRO SALES~          Enter first line title
18              qv                       Select quit and view chart
19
20
```

Fig. 7.22.

The macro performs two general operations. First, it creates a single column of labels in the column directly to the right of the original values column. The macro uses the /Print File command to write the two columns to the disk. Then the /File Import Text command is used to read them back into the column to the right of the original values column. (See fig. 7.23.) This procedure combines both the original labels and values columns into one.

After producing the new labels column, the macro creates a pie chart from the data. (See lines 13-18 of the macro.) Notice that the A range for the pie chart consists of the column of values (B1..B4), whereas the X range consists of the new labels column (C1..C4). After the macro is run, it produces the pie chart as illustrated in figure 7.24. Depending on the position of the chart's labels, your screen may not display the complete title, but the chart will be printed with complete labels. In this example, each printed label includes the city, sales totals, and percent of total sales.

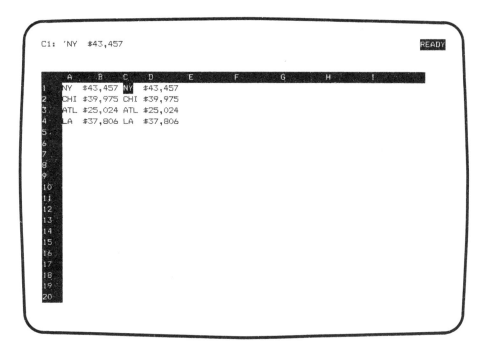

Fig. 7.23.

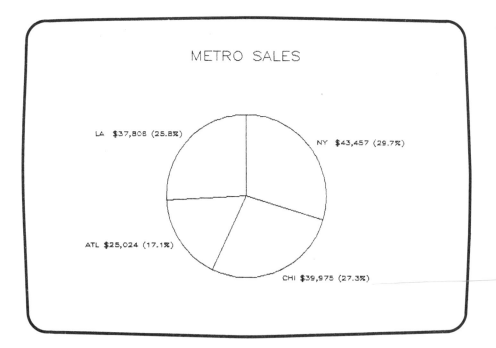

Fig. 7.24.

Making and Printing Graphs with ProKey Macros

1-2-3's integration capability makes moving among spreadsheet, data base, and graphics applications a very simple task. Unfortunately, the task of printing graphs is not so easy. Because the Printgraph program is separate from the main 1-2-3 program, you must switch disks whenever you have created a graph file and want to print it immediately.

If you want to use a 1-2-3 macro to automate the process for printing graphs, you can only automate half the operation. For example, you can make the macro shown in figure 7.25, which will select and save all graph settings.

```
A1: '\s   /grg              Reset graph settings                    READY

        A         B        C        D        E        F        G        H
1   \s    /grg                      Reset graph settings
2         t1                        Select graph type: line
3         aRANGE~                   Enter A data range
4         xRANGEB~                  Enter X data range
5         otfGHERKINS, INC~         Enter first title
6         tsWorking Capital~        Enter second title
7         sGRAPH1~                  Save graph settings
8         q                         Quit
9         /qy                       Quit main program and return
10                                     to Access System
11
12
13
14
15
16
17
18
19
20
```

Fig. 7.25.

This macro does everything required to produce a graph file, but the work of printing the graph must be done manually. To print the graph, you must access the Printgraph program (which means switching disks if you have a system for two disk drives). After accessing the Printgraph program, you must then enter all the settings for printing.

A 1-2-3 macro, such as the one in figure 7.25, will take you only halfway through the process of creating a graph file and printing it—that is, unless you use an add-in macro program such as ProKey from Rose-Soft. ProKey allows you to make macros that, unlike 1-2-3 macros, are not limited to a single worksheet file. Because ProKey runs in the "background," you can use the program for operations that require moving from one worksheet file to another or moving from one disk to another, as in the case of using 1-2-3's Printgraph program.

Using ProKey isn't much more difficult than using 1-2-3 macros. In fact, making macros with ProKey can be easier because ProKey, like Lotus Symphony, can record keystrokes automatically. This capability allows you to make macros interactively. In other words, you don't need to type in the complete macro lines as you do when developing 1-2-3 macros.

Consider making a macro to automate as much as possible the process of creating a line graph and then printing it. To show the differences between a 1-2-3 macro and a ProKey macro, let's use the example of making a line graph to display the "Working Capital" data shown in figure 7.26.

You will recall that the simple 1-2-3 macro for making a line graph of "Working Capital" data consists of the following:

\g	/grg	Reset graph settings
	tl	Select graph type: line
	aD7..D12~	Enter data range
	otfGHERKINS, INC.~	Enter first title
	tsWorking Capital~	Enter second title
	qxA7..A12~	Enter x-axis range
	oss2~	Set skip factor at 2
	qv	View graph

In a ProKey macro the same series of operations appears as displayed in figure 7.27.

A few differences distinguish the ProKey macro from the 1-2-3 macro. First, the ProKey macro is marked with both a beginning and an ending command—<begdef> and <enddef>, respectively. Second, instead of the tilde (~) to designate ENTER, ProKey uses <enter>. Third, ProKey macro lines follow a special rule: commands continue across the screen until an <enter> occurs, which tells ProKey to begin a new macro line.

With ProKey, you can enhance the power and flexibility of 1-2-3's macro capability. You can create, for instance, the simple graph macro shown in figure 7.8 by having ProKey record the keystrokes for you.

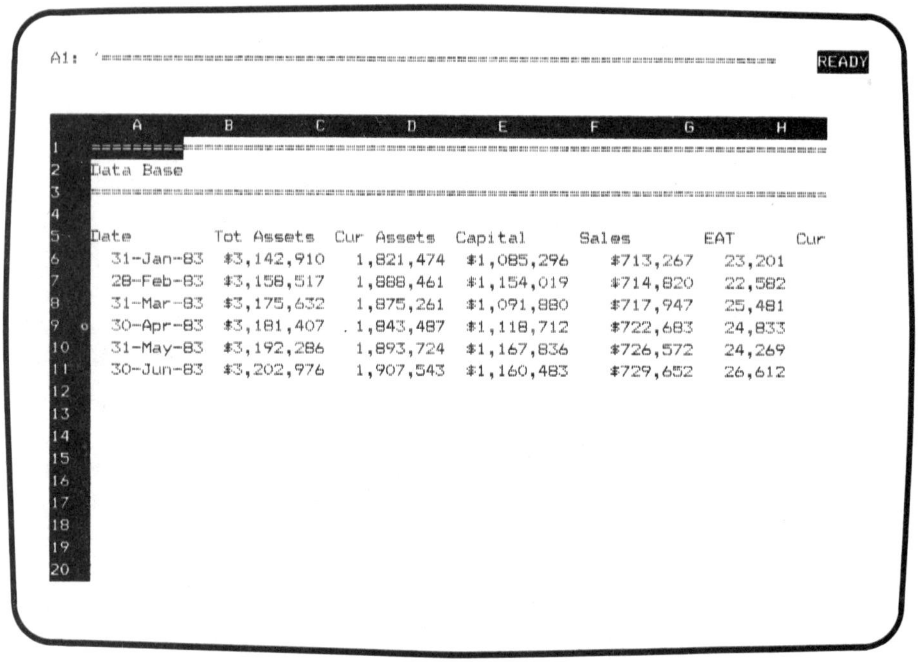

A1: '==

Date	Tot Assets	Cur Assets	Capital	Sales	EAT	Cur
31-Jan-83	$3,142,910	1,821,474	$1,085,296	$713,267	23,201	
28-Feb-83	$3,158,517	1,888,461	$1,154,019	$714,820	22,582	
31-Mar-83	$3,175,632	1,875,261	$1,091,880	$717,947	25,481	
30-Apr-83	$3,181,407	1,843,487	$1,118,712	$722,683	24,833	
31-May-83	$3,192,286	1,893,724	$1,167,836	$726,572	24,269	
30-Jun-83	$3,202,976	1,907,543	$1,160,483	$729,652	26,612	

Fig. 7.26.

You can also use time delays at key points in the macro. Look again at the macros for making the Working Capital graph. Both macros will create and display the graph for you and end with the graph in view. But because each macro ends at this point, you must press {ESC} to return to the Graph menu. If you want the macro to display the graph for a specified time and then return you to READY mode, ProKey lets you do both tasks under macro control.

When you use ProKey's time delay command, you can modify the macro shown in figure 7.27 so that your graph remains displayed for as long as you want before the macro returns to READY mode. The variation in figure 7.28 will display the graph for 1 minute.

In this ProKey version, line 6 contains the additional command for displaying the graph. The line begins by selecting the View com-

```
<begdef><ctrls>/grgtlad7..d12<enter>
otfGHERKINS, INC.<enter>
tsWorking Capital<enter>
qxa7..a12<enter>
oss2<enter>
qv<enddef>
```

Fig. 7.27.

```
<begdef><ctrls>/grgtlxa7..a12<enter>
ad7..d12<enter>
otfGHERKINS, INC.<enter>
TSWorking Capital<enter>
ss2<enter>
qv<cmd>D1:00<enter>
<esc>q<enddef>
```
Fig. 7.28.

mand from 1-2-3's menu. The second part of line 6—
<cmd>D1:00<enter>—tells ProKey to delay the macro for 1 minute
before continuing execution of the next command. After the delay,
the macro returns to 1-2-3's Graph menu and, finally, to the READY
mode.

With ProKey, can you make a single macro to automate the whole process of creating and printing the Working Capital graph? The answer
is yes. The ProKey macro in figure 7.29 will do the job.

```
<begdef><ctrls>/grgtlxa7..a12<enter>
ad7..d12<enter>
otfGHERKINS, INC.<enter>
TSWorking Capital<enter>
ss2<enter>
sGRAPH1<enter>
q/qy<ffld>..<ffld><enter>
ofl<enter>
sfqqagq<enddef>
```
Fig. 7.29.

You invoke the macro by pressing Ctrls (the Ctrl key and the *s* key).
The first five lines of the macro contain commands and settings for
making the graph, and the sixth line saves all settings in a graph file.
Line 7 moves 1-2-3 from the Graph menu to the Access System. At this
point, the macro stops to give you a chance to switch the 1-2-3 System
disk with 1-2-3's PrintGraph program (if you have a system with two
disk drives). Once you have switched disks, you must select two commands for the macro to resume control: (1) P to load the PrintGraph
program, and (2) S for the macro to enter print settings.

You can also modify this macro to include whatever Graph and
PrintGraph options and settings you want. The macro in figure 7.30,
for example, contains settings for both font and graph size. If you want
the graph to be displayed briefly on screen before saving the graph to
a file, you can add the /Graph View command and a delay, before you
have all the settings saved, as shown in figure 7.30.

If you decide that you want to change graph settings before they are
saved to a file, you must press Ctrl Esc to stop the macro. Afterward,
you can either redefine the macro or replace the original macro with
another one. Or you can simply edit the macro by changing or adding
new settings.

```
<begdef><ctrls>/grgtlxa7..a12<enter>
ad7..d12<enter>
otfGHERKINS, INC.<enter>
TSWorking Capital<enter>
ss2<enter>
qv<cmd>D1:00<enter>
<esc>sGRAPH1<enter>
q/qy<ffld>..<ffld><enter>
of1<enter>
sfqqagq<enddef>
```

Fig. 7.30.

In addition to helping you make macros for operations that require moving from 1-2-3's System program to other programs, ProKey macros offer other advantages. For example, many types of macro names can be used as alternatives to Alt followed by an alphanumeric character. Function keys can also be reassigned. When you use ProKey, you will soon discover other ways in which the program can enhance your 1-2-3 macros.

Conclusion

Combining the macro capabilities of 1-2-3 and ProKey can give you enormous power and flexibility for graphics applications. First, 1-2-3 macros can automate the process of making any type of graph, including line graphs, bar graphs, and pie charts. Second, you can extend 1-2-3's graphics capabilities by using such macros as the one for making logarithmic plots. Third, if you use ProKey, you can include time delays in your macros or develop macros for both making and printing 1-2-3 graphs.

8

Macros for Special Applications

Chapters 3 through 7 contain macros that generally are not limited by special applications but can be used for many kinds of spreadsheet, data base, and graphics tasks. Although a few of the macros are intended for use only with specific applications, most of the macros in this book can be added unchanged to your macro library.

For a complete understanding of the real power of 1-2-3 macros, you will want to consider in this chapter some of the macros for use with specific applications. You may be able to use a number of the macros and accompanying models with little or no modification. But even if you can't transfer these macros and models directly to your use of 1-2-3, you will discover ways to program 1-2-3 for your specific needs. The chapter shows, for example, how macros can help you use 1-2-3 as a word processor. A little imagination and the tools provided by 1-2-3's macro language are all you need to get the most out of 1-2-3.

Included in the chapter are the following macros for special applications:

1. Macro for creating customized help screens

2. Reminder macro

3. Macros for building amortization tables

4. Macro for comparing data from different worksheet files

5. Macro for managing client files

6. Macros for use with a 1-2-3 ledger

7. Macros for use with an integrated financial planning model

8. Macro for projecting water consumption

9. Macros for using 1-2-3 as a word processor

Macro for Creating Customized Help Screens

This macro lets you create special help screens that provide directions for using macros, running models, or updating worksheets and data bases. The macro is particularly useful if you make models that are used by other people. Help screens can aid beginning users by supplying special directions or reminders to complete certain steps.

Suppose, for example, that you are using the macro for printing address labels, described in Chapter 6. Often you have other users enter names and addresses, create a label list, and print out labels. To help these users, particularly the novices, you can make a macro that will automatically present a help screen at the beginning of a 1-2-3 session and a help screen for reference while the address label macro is running.

A macro that automatically retrieves a help screen at the beginning of a 1-2-3 session is shown in figure 8.1. If you assign the name

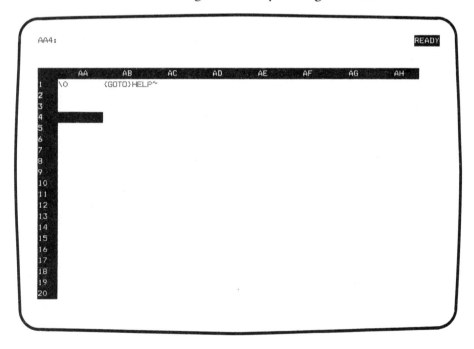

Fig. 8.1.

AUTO123.WKS to the file containing this macro, it will be retrieved as soon as the program is loaded.

Figure 8.2 contains an example of a help screen for users who are creating and printing address labels.

If you want the help screen to remain displayed while the user makes and prints the labels, you can use the macro in figure 8.3. This macro will move the cursor to the data base and split the screen so that the help screen remains in view, as shown in figure 8.4.

Reminder Macro

You can easily create a macro that will remind you of important dates. Let's assume that you have developed the project plan in figure 8.5. Suppose also that you want to be reminded of the date for placing an order for supplies.

The macro shown in figure 8.6 will remind you to order supplies. This macro works by comparing @TODAY's date with the date in the START column of the project plan. Whenever @TODAY's date is the same as the date in cell D4, the cursor moves to the project plan to

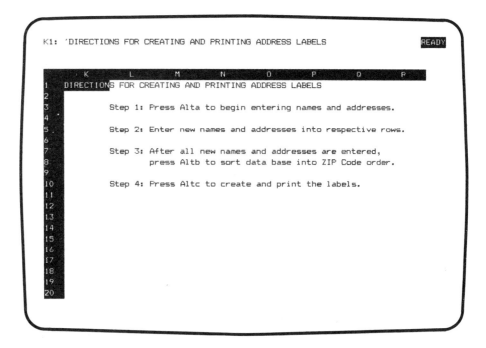

Fig. 8.2.

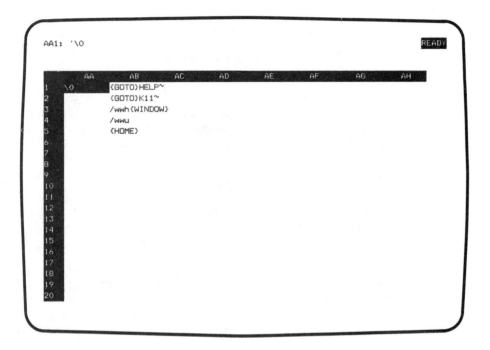

Fig. 8.3.

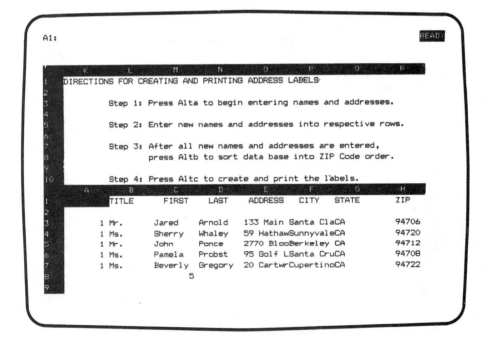

Fig. 8.4.

```
A1:  'Project: Catalog Reprint                                    READY

        A         B           C        D        E           F
1   Project: Catalog Reprint
2   ==============================
3
4   Task #    Description   Start    Days     End         Slack
5   -----------------------------------------------------------------
6         1   Cover Design   05-Oct      7   12-Oct
7         2   Supplies Order 12-Oct      7   19-Oct +SUPPLIES_DATE-E6
8         3   New Photos     19-Oct      6   25-Oct
9         4   Copy Edit      25-Oct      1   26-Oct +C9-E8
10
11            MESSAGE =>
12
13
14
15
16  Important Range Names: C7  = SUPPLIES_DATE
17                         C11 = PROJECT
18
19
20
```

Fig. 8.5.

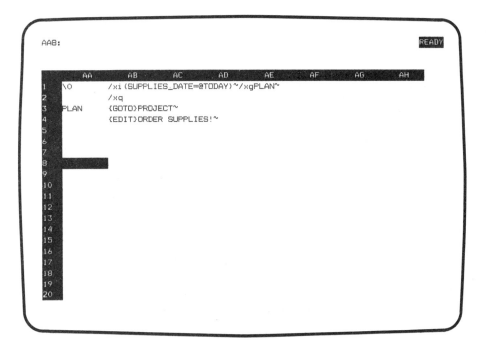

```
AA8:                                                             READY

        AA         AB        AC       AD       AE       AF       AG       AH
1   \0         /xi(SUPPLIES_DATE=@TODAY)~/xgPLAN~
2              /xq
3   PLAN       {GOTO}PROJECT~
4              {EDIT}ORDER SUPPLIES!~
5
6
7
8
9
10
11
12
13
14
15
16
17
18
19
20
```

Fig. 8.6.

remind you to place your order. Otherwise, the macro presents a menu so that you can retrieve an existing file or begin a clean worksheet.

Macros for Building Amortization Tables

If you want to enter into a worksheet an amortization table with 360 monthly payments, a macro will have to do the @COUNT function 359 times and issue the /c command 359 times. Of course, such a macro is incredibly slow. The macros described in this section, however, solve the problem of slowness and are especially beneficial for building long amortization tables.

The macro in figure 8.7 is a simplified version of the fast counter macro. To use the macro, you must enter a formula into cell B45 and also enter into cell B43 the number of rows you want the formula copied to. Then when you invoke the macro, the formula is copied to the specified number of cells below the starting point (cell B46).

When you set up the macro, remember to assign the following range names:

FORMULA	B45
STARTCOPY	B46
ROWS DESIRED	B43
COUNTER	B38

After you press Altc to invoke the macro, it performs the following operations. The first line of the macro disables global protection. In the next two lines, the macro moves to STARTCOPY and places zeros in that cell and in the cell directly below STARTCOPY. (Because a portion of the worksheet will be erased in the next step, the zeros give the macro something to erase if no previous entries have been made.) In lines 4 and 5 the macro begins at STARTCOPY and erases any entries below it.

In lines 6 and 7 the macro goes to the cell named COUNTER and enters the value into the cell named ROWS DESIRED + 44. The number 44 is simply one less than the row number where the formula to be copied resides. Line 8 converts the number in COUNTER to a label. In line 9 the range to which the formula is to be copied is set up. First, the start of the range is entered, followed by the end of the range, which corresponds to the value in COUNTER. Finally, the cursor is po-

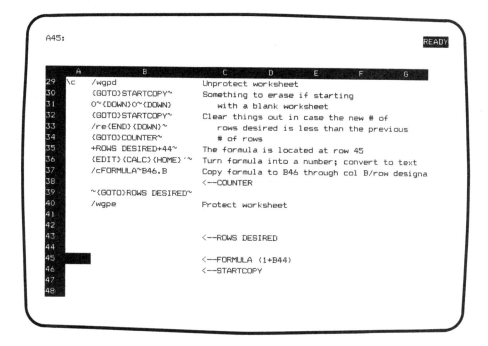

A45:   READY

```
      A        B                    C       D       E       F       G
29  \c    /wgpd                  Unprotect worksheet
30        {GOTO}STARTCOPY~       Something to erase if starting
31        O~{DOWN}O~{DOWN}          with a blank worksheet
32        {GOTO}STARTCOPY~       Clear things out in case the new # of
33        /re{END}{DOWN}~          rows desired is less than the previous
34        {GOTO}COUNTER~           # of rows
35        +ROWS DESIRED+44~       The formula is located at row 45
36        {EDIT}{CALC}{HOME}'~   Turn formula into a number; convert to text
37        /cFORMULA~B46.B        Copy formula to B46 through col B/row designa
38                                <--COUNTER
39        ~{GOTO}ROWS DESIRED~
40        /wgpe                  Protect worksheet
41
42
43                                <--ROWS DESIRED
44
45                                <--FORMULA (1+B44)
46                                <--STARTCOPY
47
48
```

Fig. 8.7.

sitioned at the cell called ROWS DESIRED, and global protection is enabled.

Now that you have some understanding of how the macro works, figure 8.8 shows the results when values are entered and the macro is invoked.

Notice that the formula chosen for the example in figure 8.8 is rather simple (1+B44), and the number entered for ROWS DESIRED is only 5. Other formulas and values for ROWS DESIRED can easily be entered to test the power and speed of the macro.

Now let's see how the macro works with an amortization table. Figure 8.9 contains the macro, and figure 8.10 contains the associated amortization table for the example. Note that the amortization table variables have not yet been selected.

The ranges to be named in the worksheet are the following:

STARTCOPY	A18
COUNTER	H12
ROWS DESIRED	B7
FORMULA	A17..F17

245

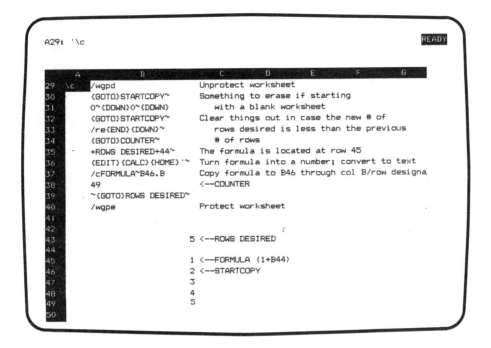

```
A29: '\c                                                    READY

        A        B             C        D        E     F        G
29  \c    /wgpd               Unprotect worksheet
30        {GOTO}STARTCOPY~    Something to erase if starting
31        0~{DOWN}0~{DOWN}       with a blank worksheet
32        {GOTO}STARTCOPY~    Clear things out in case the new # of
33        /re{END}{DOWN}~       rows desired is less than the previous
34        {GOTO}COUNTER~         # of rows
35        +ROWS DESIRED+44~   The formula is located at row 45
36        {EDIT}{CALC}{HOME}'~ Turn formula into a number; convert to text
37        /cFORMULA~B46.B     Copy formula to B46 through col B/row designa
38        49                  <--COUNTER
39        ~{GOTO}ROWS DESIRED~
40        /wgpe               Protect worksheet
41
42
43                       5 <--ROWS DESIRED
44
45                       1 <--FORMULA (1+B44)
46                       2 <--STARTCOPY
47                       3
48                       4
49                       5
50
```

Fig. 8.8.

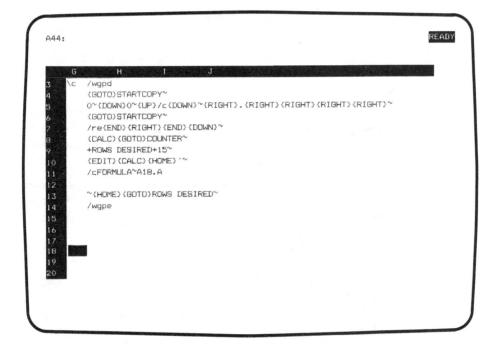

```
A44:                                                        READY

        G        H        I        J
3   \c    /wgpd
4         {GOTO}STARTCOPY~
5         0~{DOWN}0~{UP}/c{DOWN}~{RIGHT}.{RIGHT}{RIGHT}{RIGHT}{RIGHT}~
6         {GOTO}STARTCOPY~
7         /re{END}{RIGHT}{END}{DOWN}~
8         {CALC}{GOTO}COUNTER~
9         +ROWS DESIRED+15~
10        {EDIT}{CALC}{HOME}'~
11        /cFORMULA~A18.A
12
13        ~{HOME}{GOTO}ROWS DESIRED~
14        /wgpe
15
16
17
18
19
20
```

Fig. 8.9.

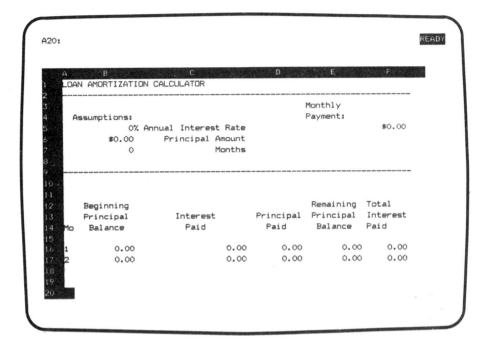

Fig. 8.10.

The names in the loan amortization table are these:

INTEREST	B5
PRINCIPAL	B6
MONTHS	B7
PAYMENT	F5

And the following formulas are part of the loan amortization table:

F5: @IF(PRINCIPAL=0,0,@PMT(PRINCIPAL,INTEREST/12/100,MONTHS))

A16: @IF((E375<0.005),1,(A375+1))

B16: +PRINCIPAL

C16: (($INTEREST/(100*12))*B16)

D16: @IF((C16<0.005),0,($PAYMENT-C16))

E16: (B16-D16)

F16: @IF($C16<=0,0,$F15)+$C16

A17: 1+A16

The primary difference between the macro for the amortization table in figure 8.9 and the original counter macro in figure 8.8 is found in the number of formulas being copied down the worksheet. Otherwise, the lists of macro commands are nearly the same.

Figure 8.11 shows a portion of the amortization table after the variables have been selected and the fast counter macro has been invoked. Using a rather sizable number of periods (360 months), the macro created an amortization table in about 20 seconds. If you need to build variable-length tables quickly, the fast counter macro is obviously beneficial.

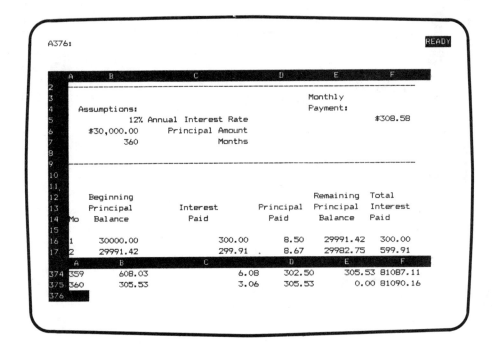

Fig. 8.11.

Macro for Comparing Data from Different Worksheet Files

As previous chapters have illustrated, macros can save time and eliminate mistakes by automating long processes, such as combining worksheets, copying and moving ranges, and building graphs. Another advantage of using macros is that 1-2-3 novices can experience the power of 1-2-3 without having to understand all the 1-2-3 commands.

/File Combine Copy is a 1-2-3 command that may be a little tricky for the inexperienced user to understand because of the difference between file names and range names. When used for combining worksheets, the /File Combine command provides a convenient way to analyze sets of data that are managed in separate software packages. The model described in this section allows an experienced user to make a self-modifying macro that helps beginning users get the full benefit of the /File Combine command even though they may not fully understand the difference between range and file names.

The model consists of five worksheets. The first four worksheets—JAN83, JUL83, JAN84, and JUL84—show the percentage of growth or decline between the two periods. (See fig. 8.12.) The fifth worksheet—STOCKS.WKS—is the receiving worksheet that combines named ranges from four data worksheets.

Special ranges in each of the worksheets include the following:

PRICE	A1..A7
PE_RATIO	B1..B7
VOLUME	C1..C7

By using the macro shown in figure 8.13 and just making menu selections, you can compare price per share, P/E ratio, or sales volume at four different times. In figures 8.13 and 8.14 the worksheet STOCKS.WKS is shown as it appears before execution of the \s macro. The first figure (fig. 8.13) contains the main body of the \s macro. The second figure (fig. 8.14) shows the menus that are called from \s.

```
        *JAN83.WKS*                              *JAN84.WKS*
          A        B         C                     A        B         C
    1   PRICE   PE_RATIO  VOLUME             1   PRICE   PE_RATIO  VOLUME
    2   JAN 83   JAN 83    JAN 83            2   JAN 84   JAN 84    JAN 84
    3    40.75        8       541            3   42.375       12       505
    4    29.5        17        48            4   31.25        15        41
    5    11.125      11        40            5   10.125       12        36
    6    24.25       13       627            6   28           14       594
    7    14.75       10      4278            7   15.75        10      3642

        *JUL83.WKS*                              *JUL84.WKS*
          A        B         C                     A        B         C
    1   PRICE   PE_RATIO  VOLUME             1   PRICE   PE_RATIO  VOLUME
    2   JUL 83   JUL 83    JUL 83            2   JUL 84   JUL 84    JUL 84
    3    32          10       362            3   46           15       522
    4    28.125      17        59            4   30           16        44
    5     8.75       13        36            5   11.625       12        38
    6    21.375       9       541            6   27.125       15       600
    7    14.5        10      3160            7   16           12      4463
```

Fig. 8.12.

In addition to entering the main body of the macro into the worksheet (shown in figure 8.13), you also need to enter three formulas: (1) in A11 you enter @SUM(A5..A9), (2) in B11 you enter @SUM(B5..B9), and (3) in B13 you enter (B11-A11/A11).

When you invoke the \s macro from STOCKS.WKS, a menu of items to compare (price, P/E ratio, or volume) is displayed, beginning in cell

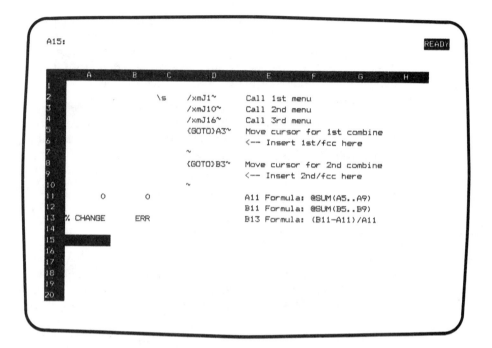

Fig. 8.13.

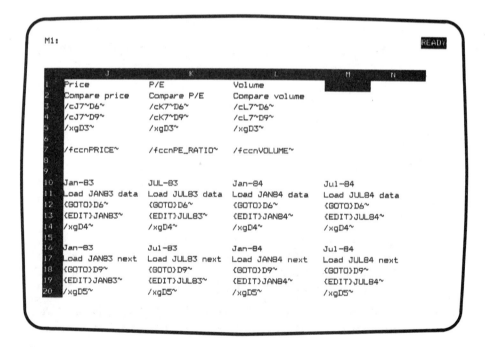

Fig. 8.14.

J1. (See fig. 8.14.) When you select the item you wish to compare, a /fccnNAMED RANGE˜ string is copied to cells D6 and D9. (See cells J3..L4 in fig. 8.14.) For example, if you select volume as the comparison value, the string /fccnVOLUME˜ will be copied to cells D6 and D9.

Beginning at cell J10 (see fig. 8.14), the macro presents a second menu and asks you to select the first period in the comparison. (Jan-83 is selected in the example.) After this selection is made, a third menu is called (beginning at cell J16 in fig. 8.14) so that you can select a second period to serve as the other half of the comparison. (Jan-84 is selected in the example.) Depending on the two time periods selected, the macro edits cells D6 and D9 so that they contain the appropriate file names.

Finally, the macro executes the newly created macro statements and combines the selected named range from the appropriate data files into STOCKS.WKS. In the current example, VOLUME is the named range, and JAN83.WKS and JAN84.WKS are the selected worksheets. The results appear in figure 8.15.

This model is not limited to stock comparisons. It can easily be modified to handle much larger sets of data, and the menu options can be

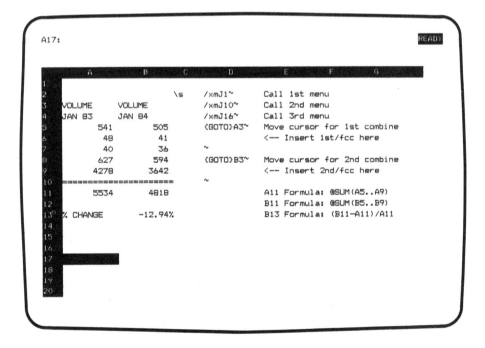

Fig. 8.15.

tailored to suit your application. By simply entering some statistical analysis formulas, you can let the user select and combine data, then see the relationship between sets of data (in numbers or graphs) without the user's having to know range and file names.

Macro for Managing Client Files

Is it possible to retrieve and save 1-2-3 files on the basis of logical conditions within a worksheet? The macro described here provides an answer.

Suppose you have a series of client files. You can manage these files through the following procedure. First, you use integer file names for the client files—for example, 1.WKS for the first client, 2.WKS for the second client, and so on. Second, you make the macro shown in figure 8.16.

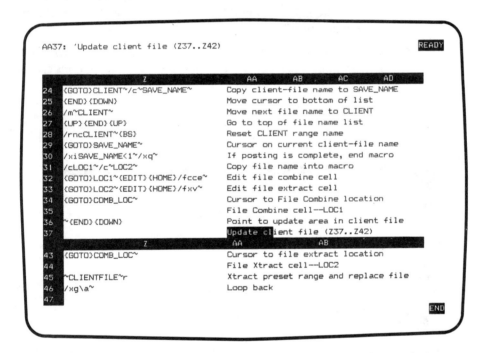

Fig. 8.16.

This self-editing macro combines and extracts the client files on the basis of a listing of files that need posting. The list of client files is produced by the /Data Query Unique command and is stored in a column with one integer per cell. For an example, see cells AA1 through AA5 in figure 8.17.

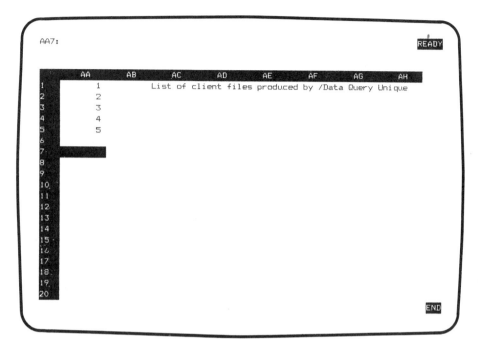

Fig. 8.17.

The macro shown in figure 8.16 combines each client file into the spreadsheet at COMB_LOC (cell AC1 in this case), updates the file name listing to reflect client files already posted, and updates the client file by posting new charges. Then the macro extracts the updated client file, replaces it under its old integer file name, and loops back for the next client file (if one exists).

The first line of the macro copies the client-file name (CLIENT) to a temporary cell (SAVE_NAME). In the next line, the macro moves the cursor first to the bottom of the client list (in this example, cell AA5). Next, the macro moves the file name at the bottom of the list to the top. In line 4 the cursor is positioned at the top of the list where (in line 5) the macro resets the range named CLIENT.

In line 6 the macro moves the cursor to the temporary cell, SAVE_NAME. Line 7 tests whether posting is completed. If posting is done, the value in SAVE_NAME is less than 1. (Actually, the value in SAVE_NAME equals zero because it is blank.) If posting is not completed, line 8 causes the macro to copy the file name into the macro at two different locations (LOC1 and LOC2). The next line edits the value in LOC1, inserting a /File Combine Copy Entire command in that cell. Similarly, line 10 inserts a /File Xtract Values command before the value in LOC2.

253

The remaining macro statements are used to read in a customer file from disk, modify the file, and write it back out. First, line 11 positions the cursor for the /fcc statement that is dynamically created in line 12. Next, line 13 moves the cursor to the bottom of the client file (in this case, the position for adding or deleting customer records). Lines 14 through 19 (not shown here) include statements that update the client file. Line 20 moves the cursor to cell COMB_LOC for the /fxv statement in line 21 (another macro-created command). Next, line 22 invokes the final portion of the /fxv statement and names the range CLIENTFILE (a preset range that includes the newly updated client file records) as the range to be extracted. Then the macro loops back to the start.

So that the macro runs properly, don't forget to assign the following range names:

\a	Z24
SAVE_NAME	AB1
LOC1	Z35
LOC2	Z44
COMB_LOC	AC1
CLIENT	AA1
CLIENTFILE	AC1..AF10

Macros for Use with a 1-2-3 Ledger

This section presents a 1-2-3 model that can help you manage a ledger. You will be "walked" through the steps necessary in constructing a simplified version of this model, which is an advanced 1-2-3 macro application. Besides macros, several data base functions and commands are used, including @DSUM formulas and the /Data Query, /Data Table, and /Data Sort commands. The end result is a 1-2-3 application that will post over 1,800 transactions to over 100 account numbers, with just one two-keystroke combination. And that's on a computer with only 256K of memory.

Specifically, here's what the model does. It enables you to enter checks quickly into a data base and provides an even faster way to summarize them by account number. The model is particularly useful when you have several hundred transactions but only a few dozen transaction numbers. Using together the ledger model, macros, and data base functions and commands will greatly simplify your ledger tasks.

To create the model, you use the /Data Query Unique, /Data Table 1, and /Data Sort commands, along with a single @DSUM formula.

In its simplified version, the ledger application has three main components, as illustrated in figure 8.18.

The two macro routines that run with the model are \a and \s. The first, \a, is used to speed up data entry, and the second, \s, summarizes the transactions by account number. Before making the macros, you'll need to set up a small data base.

Fig. 8.18.

The Data Base

You must set up the data base in order to test the macro routines. For the macros to work correctly, you must set up your worksheet exactly as instructed. The data base is quite simple and contains only three fields: date, account number, and amount. (See fig. 8.19.)

You begin by setting up the title section as shown in figure 8.19. You enter the repeating label (\=) in cells B79 through E79 and in B81 through E81. Then you enter the label "Transaction Data Base," in cell C80. You'll need to adjust the widths of columns A, B, C, and D to 7, 14, 12, and 12, respectively, using the /Worksheet Column-Width Set command. Finally, you enter the field names "Date," "Account#," and "Amount" in cells B83, C83, and D83, respectively.

The Data Entry Macro: \a

To speed up the entry of transactions, you should set up the macro just as it appears in figure 8.20. You begin by entering the previously mentioned labels in cells B5 through B10. Then you assign the range name \a to cell B5 by using the /Range Name Create command or /Range Name Labels command.

Now you're ready to try out the \a macro. To add a transaction, you just move the cell pointer to the Date column, and press Alta. Here's how the macro works. In the first line the macro begins by entering an @DATE formula and pauses for the user to type in the month and day (such as 4,1 for the first transaction in fig. 8.19), followed by EN-

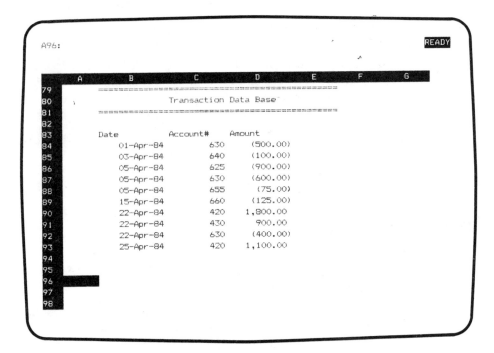

Fig. 8.19.

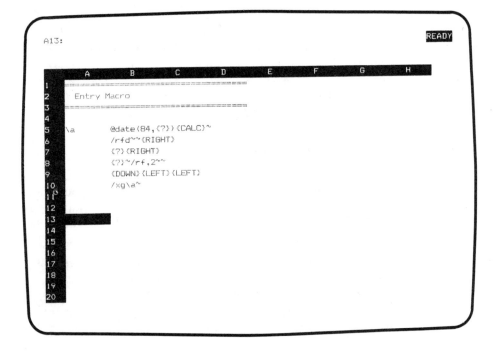

Fig. 8.20.

TER. The macro then completes the @DATE formula, converts it to a number with {CALC}, and enters that number into the cell.

Before moving on to the Account# column, the macro (in line 2) changes the cell to Date format. Line 3 simply waits for the user to press the ENTER key and moves to the right one cell. The fourth line again waits for the user to press ENTER, then formats the cell as Comma (,) with two decimal places. In line 5 the macro positions the cell pointer for entering the next transaction. Finally, the last line causes the macro to loop back to the beginning, and the macro is repeated. Ctrl Break can be used at any time to break out of the loop.

The Summary Macro: \s

The summary macro in figure 8.21 will make the posting of the transactions in the data base as easy as pressing Alts. Notice that this macro contains four subroutines: NAME, ACCT#S, CALC, and SORT.

In addition to the subroutines, two other named ranges—CRIT and INPUT—are indicated in column A. CRIT and INPUT are used by the CALC subroutine to calculate the balances for each account. (This process will be discussed later in the chapter.) First, you must build the main macro and then build each subroutine called by the main macro.

The Main Macro

You begin by entering the macro as it appears in figure 8.22 and assigning the range name \s to the macro.

All these macro routines can be lumped into a single continuous macro. But it is a good programming habit to divide large macros into smaller, manageable units and then link them with subroutine calls. This approach makes macros easier to debug—and much easier to explain.

The \s macro works in the following way. The first line sets recalculation to manual, which speeds up the execution of the macro subroutines. Line 2 calls a macro subroutine that reassigns to the data base a range name which includes any new transactions that have been added. The third line calls a macro subroutine that uses the /Data Query Unique command to create a list of the different account numbers used in the data base. This list becomes, in effect, the new chart of accounts.

A12: '\s   READY

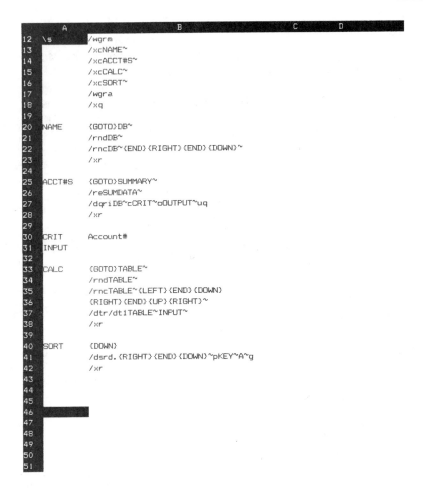

```
     A                B                      C          D
12  \s               /wgrm
13                   /xcNAME~
14                   /xcACCT#S~
15                   /xcCALC~
16                   /xcSORT~
17                   /wgra
18                   /xq
19
20  NAME             {GOTO}DB~
21                   /rndDB~
22                   /rncDB~{END}{RIGHT}{END}{DOWN}~
23                   /xr
24
25  ACCT#S           {GOTO}SUMMARY~
26                   /reSUMDATA~
27                   /dqriDB~cCRIT~oOUTPUT~uq
28                   /xr
29
30  CRIT             Account#
31  INPUT
32
33  CALC             {GOTO}TABLE~
34                   /rndTABLE~
35                   /rncTABLE~{LEFT}{END}{DOWN}
36                   {RIGHT}{END}{UP}{RIGHT}~
37                   /dtr/dt1TABLE~INPUT~
38                   /xr
39
40  SORT             {DOWN}
41                   /dsrd.{RIGHT}{END}{DOWN}~pKEY~A~g
42                   /xr
43
44
45
46
47
48
49
50
51
```

Fig. 8.21.

In line 4 the macro calls a subroutine that uses a single @DSUM formula to do a /Data Table 1 analysis of this list of account numbers. The end result is that each account balance appears to the right of its account number. The fifth line calls a subroutine that sorts by account number and in ascending order the list of account numbers and balances. Automatic recalculation is turned back on in line 6. Finally, the macro terminates execution with the last line.

Now that you've seen how the \s macro works, you are ready to build the individual subroutines.

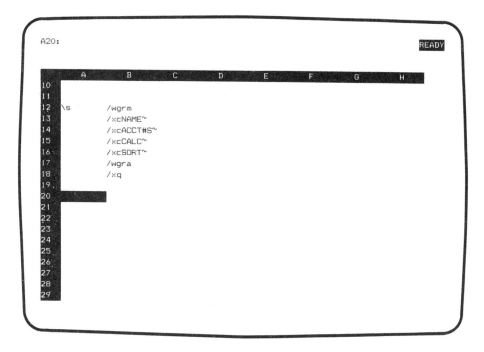

Fig. 8.22.

The NAME Subroutine

The NAME subroutine consists of four macro lines, as shown in figure 8.23.

After entering the subroutine, remember to assign NAME to it. Also, before this subroutine will work, you must assign a range name to the data base. In the subroutine in figure 8.23, DB is the range name assigned to the data base. You must assign a range name to the data base only once in order to get the macro working, but not each time you summarize.

Here's how the NAME subroutine works. In line 1 the macro moves the cell pointer to the top of the data base, and in line 2 the range name DB is deleted. In the third line the macro then uses {END} to re-create the range name so that it includes all new transactions. Note, however, that if a blank line is left in the data base, the routine will not work.

The remaining subroutines deal primarily with the Summary Area of the ledger application, as shown in figure 8.24. Before building these subroutines, you will need to set up the Summary Area exactly as it appears in figure 8.24, including the divider line and all labels.

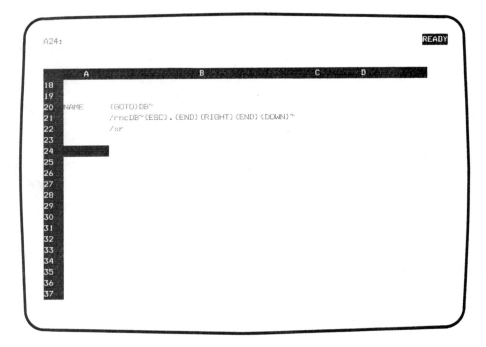

Fig. 8.23.

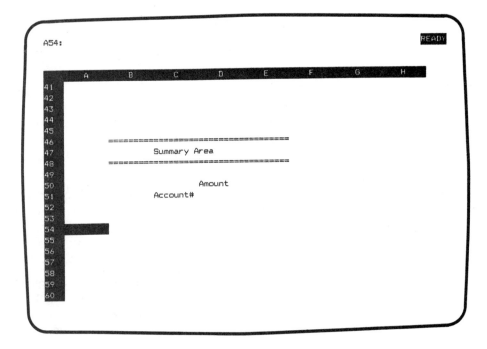

Fig. 8.24.

The ACCT#S Subroutine

This subroutine uses the /**Data Query Unique** command to create a list of the different account numbers used in the data base. The nice thing about this subroutine is that it eliminates the need to maintain a chart of accounts within the application. To build the ACCT#S subroutine, you must enter the labels as shown, set up a Criterion range for /**Data Query Unique**, and then create a few range names. You begin by entering the macro lines shown in figure 8.25.

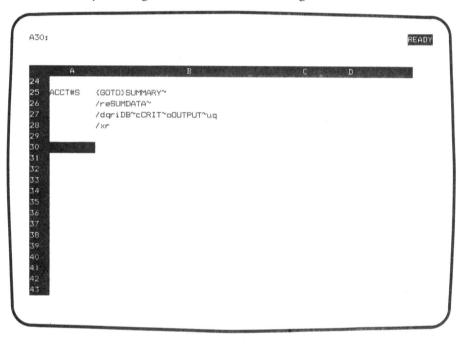

Fig. 8.25.

Three other steps are necessary for the subroutine to work. First, you need to assign the name ACCT#S to the subroutine. Second, you must set up the Criterion range. This range consists of the label "Account#" in cell B30. Finally, the name CRIT must be assigned to the cell containing "Account#." The Criterion range will also be used by the data table analysis routine that follows. The Account# field is used because of this subsequent analysis routine.

You will also need to create the following range names in order for this macro to work:

SUMMARY	A46
OUTPUT	C51..C78
SUMDATA	C52..D78

Note that the technique of using range names in macros instead of using specific cell references is strictly adhered to in this application. (A listing of all range names is included in Table 8.1 at the end of this section.)

Here's how the ACCT#S subroutine works. In line 1 the macro moves the cell pointer to the top of the Summary Area. Line 2 erases all data from the Summary Area to make room for the new list of account numbers and balances.

In line 3 the macro begins by clearing the data query settings and then sets up the Input, Criterion, and Output ranges for the /Data Query Unique command. The Input range is assigned as the DB range originally created in the NAME subroutine. The Criterion range is the range CRIT—the name assigned to the cell containing the "Account#" label (cell B30) and the blank cell directly below B30 (cell B31). Finally, OUTPUT is the name assigned to the area where you want the list of account numbers to appear.

The CALC Subroutine

The CALC subroutine is important for calculating the balance for each acount number in the list of account numbers. In fact, this subroutine is the heart of the entire application and is centered on a single @DSUM formula.

To set up the CALC subroutine, you should follow these steps:

1. Enter @DSUM formula.

2. Set up the data table macro.

3. Create range names used by the macro.

The @DSUM formula you need to enter in cell D51 is

```
@DSUM(DB, 2, CRIT)
```

which tells 1-2-3 to add up the numbers in the amount column for all data base entries that meet the criteria. You may recall from the previous section that you assigned the name CRIT to the range B30..B31.

With cell B31 blank, the @DSUM formula will give you the total amount for all transactions in the data base. By plugging the different account numbers into cell B31, this @DSUM formula will provide these totals for each account.

After having set up the @DSUM formula, you're ready to enter the CALC subroutine. As indicated in figure 8.26, this subroutine uses

1-2-3's /**D**ata **T**able 1 command. The command will take a list of entries, plug them one at a time into a designated cell, recalculate a formula that depends on the designated cell, and place the result of the calculation just to the right of the entries in the list.

To set up the CALC subroutine, you enter the lines as indicated in figure 8.26.

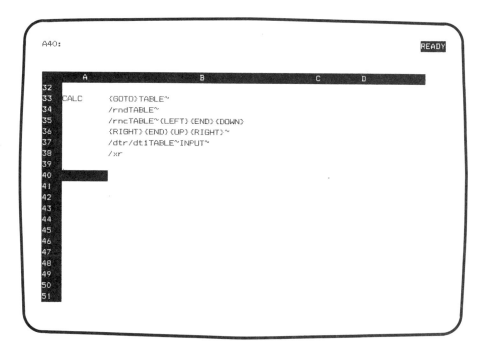

```
A40:                                                              READY

       A                          B                    C          D
32
33 CALC        {GOTO}TABLE~
34             /rndTABLE~
35             /rncTABLE~{LEFT}{END}{DOWN}
36             {RIGHT}{END}{UP}{RIGHT}~
37             /dtr/dt1TABLE~INPUT~
38             /xr
39
40
41
42
43
44
45
46
47
48
49
50
51
```

Fig. 8.26.

Three range names are important in this subroutine. The name CALC should be assigned to the subroutine. The remaining two range names are necessary to do a data table analysis from within the macro. The first name is TABLE, which should be assigned to the range C51..D58. This is the answer that the macro will give to the first question asked by 1-2-3's /**D**ata **T**able 1 command (Enter Table Range:). The final name is INPUT, which must be assigned to the cell in the Criterion range B30..B31 (CRIT). This range is the location to which 1-2-3's /**D**ata **T**able command will copy each account number in the list.

When executed, the CALC subroutine operates in the following way. The first line moves the cell pointer to the top of the Data Table range. The second line deletes the range name TABLE. In lines 3 and 4, the name TABLE is re-created to include the entire list of account numbers created by the latest /**D**ata **Q**uery **U**nique command, as issued in

ACCT#S. The direction keys find the bottom of the list by going around it and coming up from the bottom. This technique is useful because users occasionally omit the account number from entries. Thus, a blank space is created in the list of account numbers.

The fifth line of the subroutine clears the data table settings (/dtr) to speed up processing and then executes the /Data Table 1 command that computes the totals for each account number. Here's exactly what happens. The /Data Table 1 command takes each account number in the first column of the table range (TABLE) and plugs the number into the cell INPUT. The @DSUM formula at the top of the TABLE range calculates the total amounts for all transactions that match the account number currently in the cell called INPUT. As each account number in TABLE is plugged into INPUT, the @DSUM formula is recalculated, and the result is placed in the column to the right of the account numbers in the range TABLE.

The SORT Subroutine

Once you have the totals for all account numbers, the final step is to sort the list by account number. This is the job of the SORT subroutine. (Note: You may want to save your work to disk again if you haven't done so recently.)

Now you are coming down the home stretch. You begin to build the SORT routine by entering the lines as they appear in figure 8.27. Two range names are needed here. You first assign the name SORT to the subroutine. Then you assign the name KEY to any cell in column C.

When executed, the SORT subroutine completes the following process. The first line moves the cell pointer to the top of the range to be sorted. The next line begins by clearing the data sort settings (/dsr). Then the macro defines the Data-Range by anchoring the cell pointer at the current cell, moving right one cell, and then doing an {END}{DOWN} to reach the bottom of the list. The primary key is specified by using the named range KEY, which was set up earlier. Finally, the sort is executed.

Testing the Macro

If you've set up the data base and the Summary Area and you've built all the macros, you are now ready to test the application. First, however, you may want to double-check your range names. Table 8.1 serves as a handy reference for this purpose.

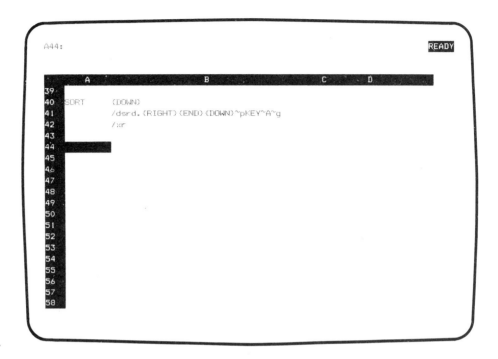

Fig. 8.27.

ACCT#S	B25
CALC	B33
CRIT	B30..B31
DB	B83..D93
INPUT	B31
KEY	C51
NAME	B20
OUTPUT	C51..C78
SORT	B41
SUMDATA	C52..D78
SUMMARY	A46
TABLE	C51..D58
\a	B5
\s	B12

Table 8.1. The 1-2-3 Ledger Range Names

If your range names are correct, you can give the macro a try by pressing Alt s. The resulting Summary Area should correspond to that in figure 8.28. If they don't match, make sure that the field name (Account#) in the Criterion range is entered exactly as it appears in both the data base and the Summary Area.

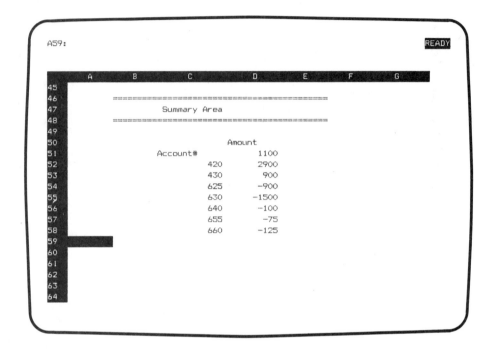

Fig. 8.28.

Macros for Use with an Integrated Financial Planning Model

The larger the 1-2-3 models you create, the harder they will be to manage. And the larger the models, the more difficult becomes printing, making graphs, or just moving around the worksheet. A series of macros, however, can make the management of a large model much easier.

Let's consider, for example, an integrated financial model. Suppose you have created a large model for your company, which contains three major divisions and a corporate headquarters. Because you need to prepare a detailed profit and loss forecast for each division, you must combine the consolidated company income statement with certain key assumptions to produce projected cash flow statements, balance sheets, and ratio analyses. The resulting financial planning model for your company might look like the model presented in figure 8.29.

	Consolid.	Chicago	LA	Atlanta	Corporate
Assumptions	RPT1	RPTB1	RPTS1	RPTT1	RPTCR1
I/S	RPT2	RPTB2	RPTS2	RPTT2	RPTCR2
I/S Summary	RPT3	RPTB3	RPTS3	RPTT3	
COGS Analysis	RPT4	RPTB4	RPTS4	RPTT4	
Cash Flow	RPT5				
Balance Sheet	RPT6				
Ratio Analysis	RPT7				

Fig. 8.29.

Description of the Model

Notice from the model that all 21 reports are included in a single worksheet file. For each division, key variables—such as sales forecasts, gross profit margin percentages by product category, capital budgets, and inventory purchases—are entered in the Assumptions section. This information is combined with operating expense data to produce a detailed Income Statement supported by an Analysis of Cost of Sales. The Income Statement summaries are high-level income statements with several vital ratios added to them.

The Income Statements (RPTB2, RPTS2, RPTT2, and RPTCR2) of each division are added to form the Consolidated Income Statement (RPT2). Beginning balance sheet figures are combined with important cash flow assumptions-such as timing of collections, interest charged on short-term borrowings, and minimum acceptable cash balance—to produce the Projected Cash Flow, Balance Sheet, and Ratio Analysis worksheets.

Macros Used in the Model

As previously mentioned, key macros for such a large model as the financial planning model would include those for printing, creating

267

graphs, and moving around the worksheet. All three kinds of macros can be combined by using a menu macro (/xm).

In the menu, you can include macros for jumping around the worksheet to each of the 21 reports. And you can store in a print macro the print settings for each of the 21 reports, thus enabling you to print reports for a single division or a whole company. Finally, you can set up a graph menu that offers a set of graphs for viewing. (See fig. 8.30 for the complete menu macro. A discussion of the parts of the macro is provided later in the section.)

For the standard macro that jumps around the worksheet, the macro lines will have the following format:

A20: Assumptions
A21: Goto Assumptions screen and lock titles
A22: {GOTO}RPTB1~
A23: {RIGHT}{RIGHT}{DOWN}{DOWN}{DOWN}/wtb

The macros for all other Jump options are easily created by copying the macros in A22 and A23 and modifying one character (the B in RPTB1). The macro in cell A23 for locking the titles is used for all routines. Titles are cleared immediately after the user selects the Jump option and before the program brings up the main Jump menu.

The same named ranges are used in the print macros. Again, using a standard print macro and modifying it can save considerable time. The following is a set of macros used to print the consolidated reports:

A30: Consolidated
A31: Print all Consolidated reports
A32: /xlALIGN PAPER AND PRESS ENTER ~HOLD~
A33: /ppcrrRPT1~agpq
A34: /ppcrrRPT2~agpq
A35: /ppcrrRPT3~agpq
A36: /ppcrrRPT4~agpq
A37: /ppcrrRPT5~agpq
A38: /ppcrrRPT6~agpq
A39: /ppcrrRPT7~agpq

The macro in cell A33 is set up and copied to cells A34..A39. Then a single character is modified in each cell to complete each macro. The same procedure is used for setting up the print options for the other divisions.

The /xl command is used to remind you to align the printer paper. HOLD is a named range assigned to some out-of-the way cell. You'll

A27:   READY

```
          A          B           C            D            E
12  /xmMENU~
13
14  JUMP       PRINT       GRAPH        QUIT
15  Jump Macro Print Macro Graph Macro Return to READY mode
16  /xgJUMP~    /xgPRINT~   /xgGRAPH~    /xq~
17
18
19
20  Assumptions
21  Goto Assumptions screen and lock titles                    Jump Macro
22  {GOTO}RPTB1~
23  {RIGHT}{RIGHT}{DOWN}{DOWN}{DOWN}/wtb
24
25
26
27
28
29
30  Consolidated
31  Print all consolidated reports                             Print Macro
32  /xlALIGN PAPER AND PRESS ENTER: ~HOLD~
33  /ppcrrRPT1~agpq
34  /ppcrrRPT2~agpq
35  /ppcrrRPT3~agpq
36  /ppcrrRPT4~agpq
37  /ppcrrRPT5~agpq
38  /ppcrrRPT6~agpq
39  /ppcrrRPT7~agpq
40
41
42
43
44
45  Net Income                                                 Graph Macro
46  Display bar graph of after-tax net income
47  /gnuNET_INCOME~q
48  /xmGRAPHMENU~
49
50
51
```

Fig. 8.30.

also notice that the print range is cleared before each new range is specified. Thus, macro execution is faster because 1-2-3 insists on highlighting the old range before letting you specify the new one. Clearing the print range saves you a screen flash or two and some macro execution time.

Graph macros are produced by using the same technique for making jump and print macros. The standard graph macro appears as follows:

    A45:   Net_Income
    A46:   Display bar graph of after-tax net income
    A47:   /gnuNET_INCOME~q
    A48:   /xmGRAPHMENU~

The financial planning model described here is an excellent tool for determining the financial impact that a decision made at a detailed level will have on the whole company. And, of course, macros make using such a model much easier.

Macro for Projecting Water Consumption

With a little imagination, you can find hundreds of ways to use 1-2-3 macros for saving time in creating, changing, and printing worksheets and graphs. But probably the greatest satisfaction comes when you design a macro that helps solve a problem—either on the job or at home. Here's a 1-2-3 macro that illustrates a unique application: projecting home water consumption.

This macro was developed by a 1-2-3 user who was concerned about the high water bills he was receiving. He decided to create a 1-2-3 model to help determine the reasons for his high costs. The macro was used to track water consumption and project monthly water bills.

Using the macro-driven model, you can graph either the actual water consumed or the projected consumption, depending on the menu item you select. Figure 8.31 shows the first screen that appears when you use /**File Retrieve** to retrieve the model. The figure also shows the macro menu that appears automatically when the model is loaded.

The following formulas must be included in the model:

```
B6:  (F2) @MAX(E5..E105)-@MIN(E5..E105)
B7:  @MAX(F5..F105)-@MIN(F5-F105)
B8:  (C2) +B4*B7
B12: (F2) +B7/B6
B13: (C2) +B12*B4
B17: (F2) +B12*30
B18: (C2) +B13*30
```

The Date.Time field in figure 8.31 illustrates the method for showing dates and times in 1-2-3. The day of the month appears to the left of the decimal point, and the time appears to the right. The time is given in percentages of the day. For example, the Date.Time number used for the 20th day of the month at 12:00 noon is 20.50. Because the water bill arrives on the 18th day of the month, the numbering on the graph axis begins with 18 and continues throughout the year. The macros used in the model appear in figure 8.32.

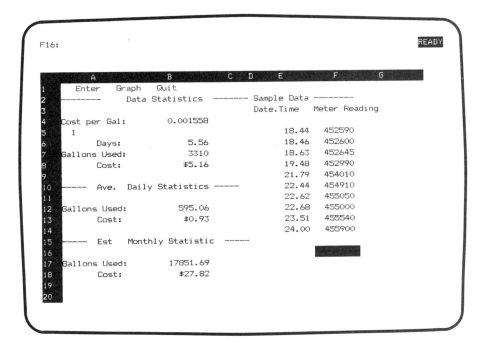

Fig. 8.31.

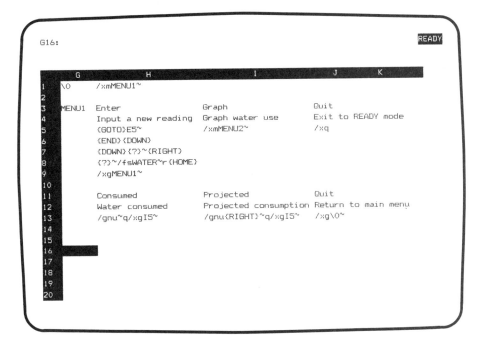

Fig. 8.32.

When you choose Enter from the main menu, the macro requests that you enter a new date and meter reading. Then the macro does a /File Save. If you choose Graph, the macro branches to a second menu (called MENU2) and asks you to select whether you want to graph the projected water consumption or the actual water consumed. Depending on the menu item you choose, the macro selects the PROJECTED or CONSUMED named graph settings. Figure 8.33 shows a graph of the projected consumption, and figure 8.34 shows a graph of the actual water consumed, using the data from figure 8.31.

The X and A ranges for the graph of projected consumption include the following:

> X range: E5..E105
> A range: F5..F105

The X and A ranges for the graph of actual water consumed include the following:

> X range: F5..F107
> A range: E5..E107

Normally, when 1-2-3 draws a line graph where there are blank cells between data items in the graph range, the line is broken up. However, as you can see in figure 8.34, the line is continuous. Figure 8.35 shows the data points at the bottom of the graph's X and A ranges. Notice that the final data items for the X and A ranges (cell E107 and F107) are the same as the maximum data items in the ranges E5...E105 and F5...F107, respectively. By including these data items at the end of the graph ranges, you can get 1-2-3 to draw a continuous line.

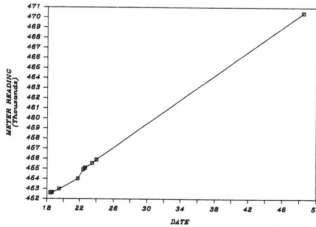

Projected Water Consumption

Fig. 8.33.

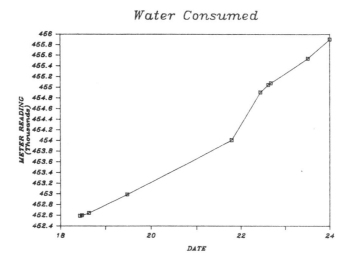

Fig. 8.34.

The @MIN and @MAX formulas for the cells in figure 8.35 include the following:

E106: @MIN(E5..E105)+30
F106: @MIN(F5..F105)+B17
E107: @MAX(E5..E105)
F107: @MAX(F5..F105)

Macros for Using 1-2-3 as a Word Processor

Although 1-2-3 is not meant to be used as a word processor for creating long blocks of text, some people have used the program for producing short letters, memos, and sections of discussion for reports. When 1-2-3 is used this way, you can eliminate the need to switch disks and move to a new program. But using the program this way is also awkward, particularly when you must justify paragraphs or indent text. A few simple macros can provide some of these capabilities.

The two macros presented in figures 8.36 and 8.37 enable you to justify paragraphs and indent sections to an even width (that is, as even as possible in 1-2-3). With these macros, you won't have to justify each of your text lines manually—which is a big help to those who are accustomed to the convenience of word wrap in stand-alone word-processing packages.

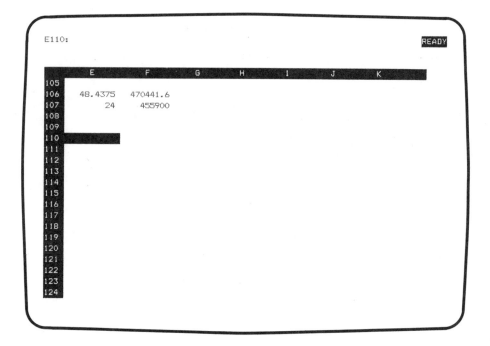

Fig. 8.35.

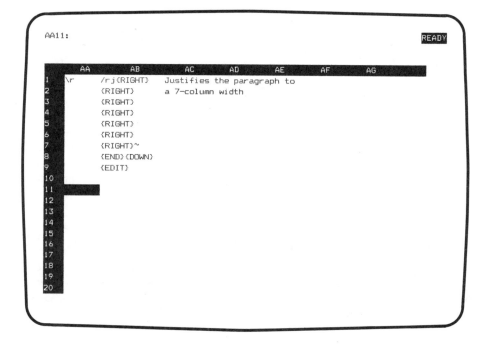

Fig. 8.36.

To use either of these macros, you begin by placing the cursor in the column where you want the text to begin, for example, column A. You then type in the text for the paragraph or indented section and continue typing until you have reached the limit for the characters that can be entered (240 characters and spaces in all). (See fig. 8.38.)

1-2-3 will beep when you have reached the limit. Your next step is to press ENTER to enter the label into the cell. Finally, you press Altr (or Alts, depending on the justification you want). The macro will justify all text, move the cursor down to the last line of text, and move to EDIT mode so that you can continue right where you stopped entering text. (See fig. 8.39.)

Conclusion

If you want to automate operations when using 1-2-3 as a word processor, you can. If you want to automate a 1-2-3 ledger, the task is easy. And if you want to simplify cursor movement or print and create graphs for a complex financial planning model, you can use a number of techniques presented in this chapter. 1-2-3 macros provide the capability for achieving these various goals. This final chapter has shown some of the unique ways macros can be applied to sophisticated models. The capability is there. And with the tips and guidelines presented throughout this book, you can significantly increase your use of 1-2-3 macros.

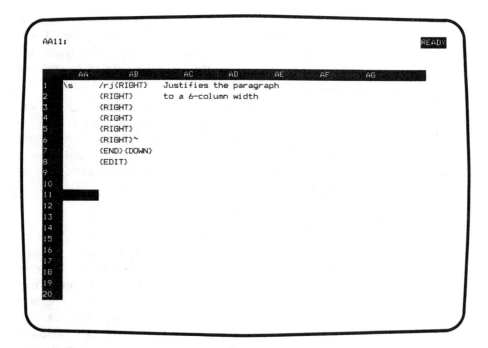

Fig. 8.37.

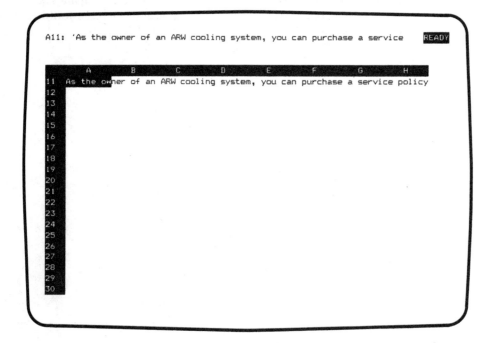

Fig. 8.38.

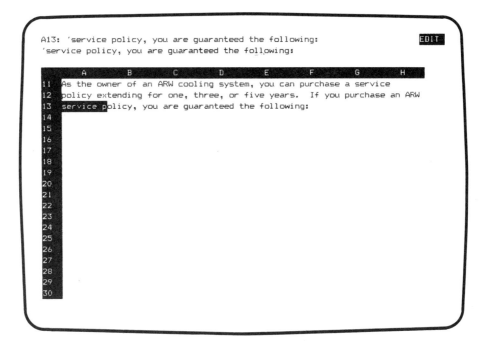

Fig. 8.39.

Index

More Computer Knowledge from Que

LOTUS SOFTWARE TITLES	1-2-3 for Business	$16.95
	1-2-3 Financial Macros	19.95
	1-2-3 Macro Library	19.95
	1-2-3 Tips, Tricks, and Traps	16.95
	Using 1-2-3	17.95
	Using 1-2-3 Workbook and Disk	29.95
	Using Jazz	19.95
	Using Symphony	19.95
	Symphony: Advanced Topics	19.95
	Symphony's Macros and the Command Language	18.95
	Symphony Tips, Tricks, and Traps	19.95
WORD-PROCESSING TITLES	Improve Your Writing with Word Processing	12.95
	Using DisplayWrite	16.95
	Using Microsoft Word	16.95
	Using MultiMate	16.95
	Using the PFS Family: FILE, WRITE, GRAPH, REPORT	14.95
	Using WordPerfect	16.95
	Using WordStar 2000	17.95
IBM TITLES	IBM PC Expansion & Software Guide	21.95
	IBM's Personal Computer, 2nd Edition	17.95
	Networking IBM PCs: A Practical Guide	18.95
	PC DOS User's Guide	16.95
	PC DOS Workbook	14.95
	Real Managers Use Personal Computers!	14.95
APPLICATIONS SOFTWARE TITLES	dBase III Advanced Programming	19.95
	dBase III Handbook	17.95
	Multiplan Models for Business	15.95
	Spreadsheet Software: From VisiCalc to 1-2-3	15.95
	SuperCalc SuperModels for Business	16.95
	Using AppleWorks	16.95
	Using Enable	17.95
	Using Dollars and Sense	14.95
	VisiCalc Models for Business	16.95
COMPUTER SYSTEMS TITLES	MS-DOS User's Guide	16.95
	The HP Touchscreen	19.95
	The HP 110 Portable: Power to Go!	16.95
	Using NetWare	24.95
PROGRAMMING AND TECHNICAL TITLES	Advanced C: Techniques and Applications	19.95
	Common C Functions	17.95
	C Programmer's Library	19.95
	C Programming Guide, 2nd Edition	19.95
	CP/M Programmer's Encyclopedia	19.95
	CP/M Software Finder	14.95
	C Self-Study Guide	16.95
	Turbo Pascal for BASIC Programmers	14.95
	Understanding UNIX: A Conceptual Guide	19.95
	Understanding XENIX: A Conceptual Guide	19.95

Que Order Line: **1-800-428-5331**

All prices subject to change without notice.

LEARN MORE ABOUT LOTUS SOFTWARE
WITH THESE OUTSTANDING BOOKS FROM QUE

1-2-3 for Business

by Leith Anderson and Douglas Cobb

Step-by-step instructions show you how to build fourteen practical business applications, using all the features of 1-2-3. The book includes models for Fixed Asset Management, Ratio Analysis, and Project Management.

Using 1-2-3 Workbook and Disk

by David Ewing

Using 1-2-3 Workbook and Disk guides the user through building a 1-2-3 model, explaining how to use all the commands necessary to create a practical, comprehensive 1-2-3 application. The workbook also includes a bound-in disk that contains the workbook model at various stages of development.

1-2-3 Tips, Tricks, and Traps

by Dick Andersen and Douglas Cobb

A must for 1-2-3 users. This book explains 1-2-3's little-known features and offers advice in problem areas. Tips include shortcuts for creating macros, producing graphs, and using Data Tables. Traps help with special problems that may arise when using 1-2-3.

Using Symphony

by Geoffrey LeBlond and David Ewing

This book explains all the basic concepts you will need to use Symphony effectively and explores the program's advanced capabilities in detail. If you decide to move up from 1-2-3 to Symphony, this book will help you master Symphony quickly and take advantage of its powerful features.

Item	Title	Price	Quantity	Extension
34	1-2-3 for Business	$16.95		
127	1-2-3 Tips, Tricks, and Traps	$16.95		
39	Using 1-2-3	$17.95		
142	Using 1-2-3 Workbook and Disk	$29.95		
141	Using Symphony	$19.95		

Book Subtotal	
Shipping & Handling ($1.50 per item)	
Indiana Residents Add 5% Sales Tax	
GRAND TOTAL	

Method of Payment:

☐ Check ☐ VISA ☐ MasterCard ☐ American Express

Card Number _____ Exp. Date _____

Cardholder Name _____

Ship to_____

Address _____

City _____ State _____ ZIP _____

All prices subject to change without notice.   123ML-858

Get your FREE issue of . . .

Absolute Reference
THE JOURNAL FOR 1-2-3™ AND *Symphony™* USERS

Join thousands of business and professional people who have made *Absolute Reference: The Journal for 1-2-3 and Symphony Users* their first choice for vital 1-2-3 and Symphony knowledge. If you would like to see a sample copy, we will send one to you **FREE**—just for requesting it before December 31, 1985.

If after reviewing the sample, you don't want a subscription, simply write *cancel* on your invoice and mail it back. But keep the sample copy—it's our gift to you.

However, after you discover the helpful macros, models, tips, and applications *Absolute Reference* has to offer, you won't want to miss one information-packed issue. To receive one full year of issues loaded with 1-2-3 and Symphony knowledge, simply send your payment with the invoice after you receive your free issue. You'll get 13 information-packed issues but pay for only 12. Your first issue is absolutely free.

Fill out this card and return it today or call toll free:
1-800-227-7999, Ext. 500

---(FOLD HERE)---

☐ **YES.** I want *Absolute Reference* at the regular price.
☐ One year
☐ Two years

Within the U.S.
☐ 12 issues—$60
☐ 24 issues—$105

Outside the U.S.
☐ 12 issues—$80
☐ 24 issues—$135
Payable by International Money Orders drawn on U.S. banks only.

☐ **SEND MY FIRST ISSUE FREE.** Then bill me for 12 issues. If after reviewing the sample, I decide that I do not want *Absolute Reference*, I can discontinue my subscription by writing *cancel* on the invoice and owe nothing. I understand that if I subscribe, I will be receiving 13 issues for the price of 12.

Method of Payment: Check ☐ VISA ☐ MasterCard ☐ AMEX ☐ Bill me ☐

Card Number _____ Expiration Date _____

Cardholder Name_____

Ship to _____

Address _____

City_____ State_____ ZIP _____

Mail to: Que Publishing, Inc. • 7999 Knue Road • Indianapolis, IN 46250

All prices subject to change without notice.

123ML-858

FOLD HERE

——————————————————

——————————————————

——————————————————

——————————————————

THE JOURNAL FOR 1-2-3™ AND SYMPHONY™ USERS

Que Corporation
7999 Knue Road
Indianapolis, IN 46250

MAKE IT EASY ON YOURSELF.
1-2-3 MACROS ON DISK

Available on disk, these 1-2-3 Macro models are ready to use. You will be able to apply macros immediately, create sophisticated models controlled by 1-2-3 macros, and modify macros for your own special needs.

Avoid the delay and inconvenience of manual entry, while you ensure that each macro line is accurate. Models are available in IBM PC format on request. To order, fill out this card and return it to Que Corporation, along with your payment, or call Que at: **1-800-428-5331**

Please send _____ copy(ies) of 1-2-3 Macro Library models on IBM PC format disk ($79.90 each).

Subtotal	_____
Shipping & Handling ($2.50 per item)	_____
Indiana Residents Add 5% Sales Tax	_____
TOTAL	_____

Check ☐   VISA ☐   MasterCard ☐   AMEX ☐

Card Number _____ Expiration Date _____

Cardholder Name _____

Ship to _____

Address _____

City _____ State _____ ZIP _____

If you can't wait, call **1-800-428-5331** and order TODAY.

FOLD HERE

- -

_____

_____

_____

_____

7999 Knue Road
Indianapolis, IN 46250